Combat Nurse

By the same author

Front Line City – Cologne
Yorkshire at War
York Blitz
Operation Millennium: Bomber Harris's
Raid on Cologne, May 1942
Women Who Went to War: 1938–46
Forces Sweethearts: Service Romances in World War I
Heroines of World War II
Showbiz Goes to War
Front-line Nurse

COMBAT NURSE

ERIC TAYLOR

ROBERT HALE · LONDON

ISBN 0 7090 6212 5

Robert Hale Limited
Clerkenwell House
Clerkenwell Green
London EC1R 0HT

2 4 6 8 10 9 7 5 3 1

Typeset in North Wales by
Derek Doyle & Associates, Mold
Printed in Great Britain by
St Edmundsbury Press, Bury St Edmunds, Suffolk
and bound by
WBC Book Manufacturers Limited, Bridgend

Contents

Perhaps, on certain days,
the talk will be of the past,
And we shall remember dimly,
Places and names, and the feel of war
But not accurately, and not for long;
We shall be sentimental
In retrospect.

H.V.S. Page, 'Prospectus'
from the collection *Poems from Italy*

Illustrations

Credits

Marjorie Mathews: 1. Lorna Kite: 2, 21. Yvonne Jeffrey: 3. Sheila Bambridge: 4. Freda Reid: 5, 6. Agatha Tinne: 7, 31. Vera Dunnett: 8, 9, 23, 24, 25, 37, 50. Betty Halliday: 10, 11, 33. Anne Cockburn: 12. Helen Long: 13. Ann Radloff: 38. Pat Stephens: 39. Iris Ogilvie: 42, 46.

Maps

Acknowledgements

This book could not have been written without the invaluable help, advice and encouragement of former Matrons-in-Chief of the Queen Alexandra's Royal Naval Nursing Service (QARNNS) and the Director of Army Nursing Services and Matron-in-Chief, Queen Alexandra's Royal Army Nursing Corps (QARANC). I am therefore deeply indebted to Miss Pat Gould, CBE, RRC, Captain Claire Taylor, RRC, and Captain Julia Massey, RRC, for providing opportunities for research in the archives at the Institute of Naval Medicine, Gosport. They generously made available to me an assembly of documents and recollections relating to the activities of QARNNS nurses as well as helping me to contact QARNNS nurses who served in Second World War combat zones. With equal gratitude and for similar reasons, I should like to acknowledge the support and help extended to me by Brigadier J.M. Arigho, Major Ethel McCombe and Major Diane Wilson at the QARANC Headquarters and Museum at Aldershot.

With the passage of time, the Public Record Office has been able to yield up even more of its secrets and I am once again grateful for the patience and help of its staff. I owe special thanks also to the staff of the Imperial War Museum Archives Department for finding and allowing me to read the unpublished recollections of Second World War nurses, in particular those of Ann Reeves, Helen Luker, Josephine Pearce and E. Leigh Hunt. I owe special thanks to Judith M. Perkins and Victoria Ball for granting permission to use material from Helen Luker's memories. I have received considerable assistance also from the staff of the British Newspaper Library at Colindale.

It has been my great good fortune to have had the generous help of so many nurses who responded to my appeal for their wartime

11

recollections. In particular I was most grateful for comprehensive accounts of their years of military nursing service from Lorna Bradey (now Kite) who, sadly, died just before this book was published, Winifred Barnfather (now Reid), Vera Bryan (now Dunnett) and Betty Lawrence (now Halliday). Their experiences weave a thread of continuity throughout the book.

For accounts of the great contribution made by members of the Voluntary Aid Detachment I owe much to Helen Long, who generously allowed me to draw upon her book, *Change into Uniform*, published by Terence Dalton, and also to Joyce Drury's book of VAD anecdotes, *We Were There*, published by the Jupiter Press. I must also mention here how much I valued having as a reference book, Kathleen Harland's *History of Queen Alexandra's Royal Naval Nursing Service*, published by the Royal Naval Medical Service.

For many invaluable reports and stories I received from service personnel and nurses tending combat casualties I want especially to thank: Ann Reeves, Yvonne Jeffrey, Sheila Bambridge, Margaret Harris, Marjorie Mathews, Agatha Tinne, Anne Cockburn, Hazel Thomas, David Oates, E. Parslow, Ruth Patterson, Bernard Hallas, Stanley Mitchell, Michelle Higgs, Mary Johnston, Hazel Bickerdyke, Lillian Calderly, Iris Wilkinson, Muriel Castledine, June Eaton, Mabel Halewood, J. Barr Beveridge, Mary Pinkney, John Macpherson, David Macpherson, Eileen Haynes, Diana Wells, R.D. Williams, H. Jennings, Pat Stephens, Betty Alexander, Helen Stranger, Enid Ware, R.D. Williams, Hazel Thomas, K.M. Wrixton, Sonia Courtney, Frank Palmer, Len Upton, Doris Kingsford and Pamela Barker. If, by oversight, I have omitted anyone's name, I apologize.

For additional information on the sinking of merchant vessels and troopships I am most grateful to Captain David Parsons, MNI, General Secretary of the Merchant Navy Welfare Board.

Finally I owe an immense debt to my wife, Sheila, who has accompanied me on so many journeys in the course of research and in meeting wartime members of the Navy and Army nursing services. Throughout, as usual, she has been a constructive and wise enquirer and critic.

Without the generous help of all these people the book would not have been so comprehensive, especially with regard to the treatment and medication given to those wartime casualties. To everyone I express my sincere gratitude. The responsibility for any shortcomings or errors is, of course, my own.

1 Where Do We Go from Here?

I find it difficult to believe now that we took the heavy bombing raids as though they were just part of life to be expected then. We were young and just got on with our duties.

Sister Margaret Harris (née West) QARNNS

As far back as she could remember, Vera Bryan had always wanted to be a nurse. As a child she played doctors and nurses with the youngest of her four brothers. Dolls in shoe boxes lined up were patients in a ward and the brother's Meccano set was used as a telephone.

When she was a little older she was even more definite. She pictured herself in the smart uniform of Queen Alexandra's Royal Nursing Service. Her father had served in the Royal Marines and her sister lived close to the Royal Naval Hospital Haslar, at Gosport, a huge hospital built by French prisoners of war during the Napoleonic Wars. Frequently Vera spent weekends with her. Many a time on these visits she saw nurses of the QARNNS coming out of that imposing hospital and imagined herself also stepping out proudly in that uniform one day.

There was a time later, when I was doing my nursing training at King's College Hospital, I'd visit my brother in Haslar Hospital. He was suffering from brucellosis. He got it, they said, when serving in Malta when he was in the Royal Navy. It all happened very suddenly. He was looking the picture of good health one week, ruddy cheeked, and the next he was in bed with a high fever, dreadful headaches and a terrible cough.

The nurses were always very friendly to me on my visits and that too, I suppose, fixed the idea more firmly in my mind that as soon as I finished my nursing training, I'd join the QARNNS and do my bit for the country now that war was coming.

My mother and father were anxious and had hoped I'd be working in a civilian hospital near our home, but when they saw my mind was made up they gave their blessing. They were like that. I loved them. Fortunately, perhaps, I didn't know then just how little time I would have with them. Otherwise ... well ...

There was then a spirited patriotism about the country that motivated both men and women to join one of the services. Many nurses were similarly moved, like Yvonne Jeffrey, who had just qualified from University College Hospital and now readily admits that it was in a fit of patriotic fervour that she joined the Queen Alexandra's Imperial Military Nursing Service (QAIMNS). Lorna Kite (then Bradey) also remembers the strong patriotic feelings that spurred her into volunteering.

I felt ready for military service as soon as I finished my general nurse's training at King's Hospital, London. I'd qualified despite the scepticism expressed by my father when I first mentioned my nursing ambitions.

Unknown to me then, my father told my mother that I'd never stomach the hard work and bossing about that student nurses had to face. He thought because I'd been brought up as a rather spoilt child of a rich diplomat stationed in India, with all the perks of the old Raj available, I'd soon come running back to the comfort of home.

I got really angry when my mother told me what he had said and I was determined to prove him wrong. As it happened I took to the new life like a duck takes to water, though it was far from easy. How tired we used to be as students! We had to wear black cashmere stockings and tightly laced-up shoes, and at the end of the day those stockings often stuck to blisters on my swollen feet. Every night, copying up lecture notes and learning them took hours. No time or energy then for dancing. Though we saw the staff nurses going out, we were always far too tired. The dreaded cry next morning of 'six o'clock, Nurse' seemed to come moments after our heads touched the pillow. If you were even half a minute late on the ward it was a mark against you. But at last I achieved the coveted blue belt. I felt a very important person. And one day, I thought, I'd even wear black silk stockings like the staff nurse and sisters.

That day when she could wear a smarter uniform came sooner than she expected. She saw the opportunity coming, and grabbed it.

I was sure there would be war and I was going to have a hand in it. The Military Nursing Service was just what I needed. And patriotically I suppose, I felt they needed me.

I could hardly wait to get into that smart uniform too: a grey dress, with impeccably starched white apron, cuffs and collars, topped with a scarlet cape of fine velour bearing on the left breast the distinctive Queen Alexandra Silver Cross mounted on a navy, red and white ribbon.

Most impressive of all, I thought, was the 'veil' as the white cap was called, made of fine white cotton folded to form a deep 'V' at the back with the embroidered red cross. For special 'dress' occasions we had a veil of voile.

You couldn't help feeling proud to be a nurse in that outfit. I felt I'd achieved something.

If anyone ever asked Freda Barnfather, later Reid, why she became a nurse she neatly side-stepped the question. Somehow there had been an inevitability to it all which could not be put into words, though nursing had never been in any plans her parents had for her.

Somewhere, at some time, the idea of becoming a nurse had captured her imagination. She could no longer remember how it happened but she was sure that by the time she was eight her imagination had already been fired and the fire would not go out. When she grew up she was definitely going to be a nurse. Her teachers at school in the North-east encouraged her.

She was a stubborn girl, and when her mind was made up she stuck out for what she wanted.

As soon as she was eighteen, Freda applied for a course at the East London Hospital. One of her first jobs after she qualified was at the Royal Naval Hospital Haslar. She and five of her colleagues found employment as civilian nurses and soon got into the Navy way of nursing. They learnt to call floors 'the deck' and walls 'the bulkhead'. Rooms were 'cabins' and kitchens 'galleys'. Patients never went to the lavatory but to the 'heads'.

The daily routine of nurses' chores was just as arduous as in civilian hospitals but one in Navy style. Beds were pulled out each morning, wet tea-leaves sprinkled liberally over the highly polished deck so that they could remove the fluff from under the beds when it was swept with a soft brush.

That done, the deck would then be bumpered with long-handled polishers weighted down to achieve a high gloss. Fortunately, this bumpering was a job for which the 'walking wounded' often volunteered. This allowed the highly qualified nurses time for tending the black iron coal stoves, clearing the locker tops, polishing brasswork and generally bringing the ward up to the standard required by the Matron before the rounds.

Corporal of Marines Bernard Hallas, who later served on HMS *Warspite* for most of the war, remembers visiting some of his men in one of Haslar's highly polished wards. They were in 'Rose Cottage', a pseudonym for the venereal diseases ward. 'No one of the family visiting would have known why the men were there because on days when they visited men had arms or legs put in bandages so no one felt ashamed.'

Freda Barnfather was well into the Navy way when war broke out – even into the Sunday lunchtime ritual of taking cider with cheese and biscuits after the main course of the meal. The civilian nurses felt part of the scene and accepted by the Matron and senior sisters. Freda and her colleagues therefore thought their jobs would be secure now there was a war on.

They were not. Suddenly they were sacked; the Admiralty could not have civilians in military establishments in wartime. 'After the first surprise, I didn't care much. I was already a member of the Territorial Army Nursing Service – the TANS – and knew I should soon be getting orders from them.'

A month later her mobilisation papers arrived, instructing her to report to No. 7 Casualty Clearing Station at Tidworth, the first of many postings.

One surprise after another awaited her.

A surprise was in store for Vera Bryan too when she applied to join the QARNNS. 'To my surprise and annoyance I got a letter saying their establishment was full. It just didn't make sense to me. With everyone making preparations for war I was sure there'd be a need for more nurses everywhere.'

The Naval Nursing Service, however, was a step ahead of Vera. Plans had already been made for the contingencies of war. It had been estimated that 180 nursing sisters would be required. At the declaration of war 85 were already available and 168 were on the Reserve. Thus, with a total of 253, there was a surplus of 73 over the estimated requirement.

Vera Bryan wasted no time moping over her disappointment. She went straight away and joined the Army Nursing Service. Had she waited a little while she would have found a rapidly expanding Naval Nursing Service keen to accept nurses with her qualifications. For Haslar and other naval hospitals in the south of England, priority was given to increasing the wartime establishment of nurses in order to cope with the estimated rush of casualties from air raids. A new reserve branch of the regular QARNNS was created, into which fully trained nurses could enlist. Plans were made for it to expand as the war went on and, in fact, by 1945 the establishment had grown ten-fold to 1,129 fully qualified nursing sisters.

Furthermore, in the expansion scheme, the Voluntary Aid Detachments (VADs) were mobilized so that training and employment was provided not only in nursing posts but also as dispensers, clerks and cooks. Fortunately the Naval Nursing Service had looked ahead and given training to VADs in naval hospitals. Consequently, during the first few months of the war these volunteers were quickly fitted into the naval hospitals.

Lillian Calderly – 'Skips' as she was affectionately called after she became Commandant and skipper of her own VAD 'ship' – had started training as a VAD in 1923 and went regularly to her eight-day camp. By 1939 she had spent training time with four naval hospitals.

'I'm one of those people who when I take something on I like to do it properly,' she said in her forthright Bolton manner. 'I was given more responsibility than other VADs because I was older than most of them.' And now at 96 has outlived most of her younger contemporaries in the VAD. She recalls so well the details of those wartime patients she 'specialled'. It was the burns casualties she remembers most vividly.

The Royal Marines Infirmary at Deal was a small one and there were some sailors brought in from a ship that had been bombed. One of the bombs had caused ammunition to explode and the flash had burnt all the front of their bodies, legs, arms, chests and faces. They were brought in at night and we just went from one to the next bathing them night and day. Many could not see because their eyelids were so badly burnt and shrivelled so that their eyes would not open. Another lad had taken the full blast of steam from an exploding boiler. He was scalded and red as a boiled lobster. They all had to sit up in bed and we came round and bathed them with saline, and applied acriflavine.

One of the big problems with burns, sometimes not so easily recognized at first, was the effect upon the air passages. Searing flames, blasts of high-pressure steam and hot gases could injure the upper air passages so that they too poured out fluid and froth, so we had to be ever watchful.

But we had to be careful also not to concentrate entirely on the burns themselves. We had to control shock. If we didn't they died quickly. Dangerous shock symptoms came first with the pain due to so many sensitive nerve endings being exposed. Then came a second phase of shock caused by the loss of body fluids seeping from the burnt surfaces of the body. This fluid came from the vascular system, plasma was lost from the circulation and it had to be replaced as soon as possible.

All VADs were expected to get on with whatever situation arose. And there were some horrible ones. Many VADs had some previous experiences either through courses run by the Navy or by the Red Cross. Nevertheless they found caring for wartime casualties more harrowing than they could ever have imagined.

One can understand the feelings of horror, for example, when 18-year-old Joy Felks, who, as a Red Cross nurse with a little experience at the North Middlesex Hospital, was suddenly called upon to treat air-raid casualties from Edmonton Fire Brigade. They were in agony with terrible phosphorus burns on their hands and faces. She found that when phosphorus landed upon the skin it burnt a hole in the tissue and continued to burn until put out by immersion in water.[1]

Their arms and faces were soaked in water as far as practicable, whilst Joy and her colleagues scraped the burning, ingrained phosphorus bit by bit from their wounds. 'They were so brave when their burns burst into flames once they were dry.' They had to be soaked in water and scraped again until the last red-hot piece was removed from the scorched flesh.

Phosphorus burns were particularly difficult, as Surgeon Rock Carling found when a casualty had been washed and his burns covered with bicarbonate of soda and some copper sulphate. What the nurse did not realize was that 'the wool which she used to take off the phosphorus, when thrown on the floor, immediately caught fire and set alight the linoleum.'[2]

It is difficult now to imagine how those young VADs managed to hide their emotions as they treated the Edmonton firemen. But VADs were little different from new nurses in the services. 'We were pitchforked into the job,' recalled Joyce Drury, a VAD with the Royal Navy. 'And we just made the best of it.'

Sister Margaret Harris, who served in the QARNNS, remembers so well the awful raids in the early years of the war.

I was under training at St George's in London. One day a bomb dropped right on the hospital but did not explode. Everyone was evacuated. Green Line buses converted to take patients drew up in the rubble-strewn street outside the hospital and took all our staff, patients and theatre equipment away until the bomb had been removed. It was so well organized. Everyone rolled up their sleeves and did what was needed. One night it seemed as though the whole of London was on fire.

What I remember particularly well was the night the Café de Paris dance hall was hit. Casualties came in with blood all over their long dresses and evening suits. Some had legs or arms blown off. So many to deal with all at once. First task for us all was to stop the bleeding. With profuse bleeding from a stump we used a tourniquet. Wounds were horrific. They all needed cleaning before we could dress them properly. A good soap and water wash in most cases.

A 50 kg Luftwaffe bomb had landed right in front of the band, killing its leader, Ken 'Snakehips' Johnson and thirty-two dancers. At the time, the dance floor was packed with young men and women in uniform. By the time the air-raid victims had reached hospital all nurses were involved, whether they were fully trained or not. Young Margaret West, later Harris, like the young VADs alongside her, was handling blood-soaked men and women like a veteran. As many have said since: 'We were thrown in at the deep end and it was a case of sink or swim. We swam.'

Many of the VADs in the naval hospitals in the Portsmouth and Plymouth areas had their baptism of fire early in the war. Those ports were picked as special targets for German bombers attempting to cripple the British war machine. Portsmouth, near which the Royal Naval Hospital Haslar was working at full stretch, was but a few minutes flying time from French airfields. The port had 792 air raid warnings during the first eleven months of the war, and over 65,000 of the city's houses were bomb-damaged. Some of those raids were horrendous in their intensity.

Hazel Dobson, later Gatherer, had just joined the RNH Stonehouse, Plymouth when her hostel received a direct hit and caught fire. Nurses fled from the burning building but there seemed to be fires all around so that they did not know which way to turn.

'The tar on the roads was on fire, we were surrounded by smoke which made it difficult to see.' More by good luck than good navigation Hazel and her VAD colleagues reached the Citadel on Plymouth Hoe, where soldiers took them into the safety of their underground bunker.[3]

Just two months after Helen Long joined the nursing staff of RNH Haslar as a VAD, the hospital had one of the heaviest bombing raids that Gosport and Portsmouth ever had to endure. The splendid Guildhall was gutted, both the main shopping centres and many public buildings were completely burnt out. Nurses felt particularly vulnerable, as the hospital was almost ringed by dockyards undeniably legitimate military targets.

At Haslar on one memorable evening, as soon as the alarm went, nurses took their stretcher cases down to the huge cellars below the wards. Helen recalled the speed at which this was done and the strange arrangements made for those who could not be moved. She recorded the scene in her autobiography, *Change into Uniform*.[4]

Patients in plaster with limbs strung up on weighted pulleys had to be left in their wards, with a knife at the foot of each bed to cut them down should the hospital be badly bombed.

In the midst of the crunching of bombs and the falling plaster, the lift taking patients down to the cellars stuck between floors. VAD Helen spent the rest of the raid cheerfully lighting 'fag-ends' and Woodbines, and passing them through the wire grill of the lift cage to the men inside, stuck on their stretchers like rats in a trap. 'I did a roaring trade in urine bottles, which we managed to squeeze between the bars of the lift cage.'

In the midst of all the barbarity of the wartime bombing there were inevitably moments of laughter. Sister Ann Cockburn (née Powis) of the QARNNS remembers one particular incident which happened when she was on night duty at RNH Sherborne Naval Hospital.

The hospital had a long colonnade with huts on both sides. One hut led into another. Each hut was heated by an oil stove and had twenty to thirty beds, with the usual kitchen and Sister's office. It was a happy posting for me and off duty we often cycled round the lovely Dorset countryside and met doctors and nurses of the nearby American hospital. Their nursing sisters wore khaki dresses and envied us our more colourful uniform.

Anyway, back to that memorable night. I was sitting writing reports, having done my two o'clock rounds of all the wards and signed the 'rounds' book, when the door was thrown open and a very scared VAD minus cap, burst in and blurted out: 'There's a cow in the ward, Sister! What shall I do?' The thought crossed my mind that she had been drinking.

'Where's the other VAD?' I asked.

'She's locked herself in the lavatory,' came the reply.

I rushed to that ward. It was true. There was a milking cow with long horns, the focus of all the patients' eyes now. They were waiting to see what would happen next. Most of the patients had had knee or leg operations. Not one of them could leave his bed. It was impossible for me to turn the cow round to face the exit door. I tapped it gently on its rump and drove it down the ward and into the other. Never has any great actress had such an appreciative audience. I told them all to keep quiet and you could have heard a pin drop. After driving the animal out of the wards, down the colonnade and having pushed a bar back into position in the fence I returned to the ward and settled everyone down with a mug of hot chocolate.

The Matron got a surprise when she read my report the next morning.

Life at Sherborne was never a dull routine for me. Shortly after the cow episode I was sent on a tropical medicine course at the Army School of Hygiene at Mitchett, near Salisbury. There we were lectured by specialists on what to expect and what to do in emergencies on the field of battle. How to test and make up water supplies, make fly-traps, organize latrines in the field (we inspected over a hundred different types of these!). We had to learn how to set up showers using only one pint of water per person. The most dramatic of all the demonstrations, though, was what to do with dead cattle left on the battlefield when it came to clearing the area of smells. First the cattle had to be given a burst of machine gun fire in order to release the gas which accumulates in all dead bodies, then petrol had to be poured over the carcass and set afire with a lighted match thrown onto it. After a week of this sort of work I was glad to rejoin the Navy. The Army personnel were kind and friendly but there were times when I wondered what I was doing there.

Sister Betty Lawrence of the QARNNS had similar thoughts when she was on night duty during one of the heaviest raids on Plymouth. She had started her nursing training at Mount Gould Hospital in 1935 when she was only sixteen. By the time she had completed her midwifery at the Freedom Fields City Hospital, Plymouth, she had grown into a dark-haired young woman who could have doubled as the film star Vivien Leigh. She was on call as a midwife when the air-raid siren sounded.

Bombs hit the children's ward first and we could hear the children screaming and crying. The rest of the bombs dropped down the centre of the
maternity ward. I was called to attend to a terrified mother-to-be amidst the
wreckage.

I was told to go into a side room with the woman about to give birth.
We could hear the planes and bombs dropping all around.

We just sat in the dark hugging each other. A doctor came with a torch
and we delivered the baby. I stumbled through the rubble with the newborn
baby in my arms, desperate to find a piece of string to tie the umbilical cord.
I had to use embroidery silk that belonged to one of the nurses. I was only
twenty-one at the time but I remember thinking that I would never be
young again after so much horror, misery and blood.

For years afterwards, Betty was troubled that she never knew the
name of the baby's mother. It troubled her so much that fifty years
later, during an interview with a reporter from the *Plymouth Evening
Herald*, on the anniversary of that heavy blitz, she said she would
dearly like to know what happened to the baby boy and his mother.

The article appeared in the newspaper on 26 March 1991, under
the headline, 'What ever became of the baby of the blitz?' Within
hours, that long-lost baby boy, delivered on the edge of a bomb
crater, telephoned the newspaper. He was Mr Dennis Blagdon of
Millbrook.

The one-time nurse and baby came face to face a few days later
and, surprisingly, Betty said, 'I knew him straight away. I remember
vividly his mother's terrified face as if it were yesterday and he looks
just like her. I never forgot her face as the bombs came down, killing
nurses, patients and babies.'

German bombers intensified their raids on British seaports and
dockyard towns throughout the summer and into the winter of
1941–2 hoping they would slow down the British war machine. 'We
had no air-raid shelters in the Plymouth City General Hospital I
worked in then,' recalled Betty Halliday, 'and whenever there was an
air raid we put patients under their beds and placed an enamel washing bowl over their heads.'

Men and women brought in from the raids had wounds which horrified us;
arms and legs blown off, bits of concrete embedded in their bodies, many
had ghastly facial wounds.

At that time we were rushed off our feet, not just with the blitz casualties but with another kind of wartime casualty that was increasingly worrying to health authorities then – men and women reporting sick with venereal disease.

However, the VD problems of the over-crowded City General Hospital were quickly forgotten when she was posted to the RN Stonehouse.

It was a culture shock! Four of us had to share a room and one wardrobe. But at least twice a week we managed to go out dancing. Of course we had to sign out and sign in by half past ten though we had ways and means of getting round this.

Those were great days for women. And they got even better as the war went on. The Americans and Poles loved dancing and soon taught us to jive. We were invited to dances in the Spa Ballroom at Torquay and the Church Hall in Devonport. It really was a wonderful time for girls.

It was truly romantic and exciting, rushing to get ready in time for the truck sent by the GIs at Devonport Barracks. And those sentimental wartime songs put into words (but expressed with far more feeling) the thoughts we often had – 'I'll Remember You' and 'Yours' as we smooched beneath the glittering revolving ball to 'Moonlight Serenade'.

Looking back upon those years now, nurses and women in all three services marvel at the way they lived – working so physically hard by day and yet, off duty, having the time and energy to dance the evenings away.

'One very interesting thing I remember about it all,' said Muriel Castledine, once a VAD at Devonport, 'is that there was never any problem in finding a dance band to play.'

One time we had all arrived for a dance at the Town Hall and the band had not turned up. Somebody started telephoning the nearby barracks and before long we had a seven-piece band on the stage!

I've never forgotten that feeling of excitement as we went into the hall and could hear the trumpet leading the band through a rousing quickstep to 'You Are My Sunshine', or when they played for a Paul Jones dance, where boys formed the outside ring and girls the inner one and we walked around in time to 'Here We Come Gathering Nuts in May' and stopped with a giggling collision opposite a new partner when the band broke off in mid-phrase. It was magic.

Where, I wonder, would you find so many musicians at short notice today?

Betty Lawrence, living in Spartan accommodation at RNH Stonehouse, found the Americans generous and jolly to be with.

They would always be sending drinks over to our table. One they called a 'Blockbuster' was a mixture of rum, gin, vermouth and coke! Phew! There were fourteen of us at that dance, eight doctors and six sisters. When we got back to the hospital we did a conga through the wards. The patients didn't mind at all. At least I thought they didn't but it wasn't long before a posting to another hospital came through for me.

2 A Funny Kind of War

I suppose with the resilience of youth, we withstood the horrors.

Ann Radloff (née Reeves) QAIMNS

Lorna Bradey did not have many weeks to enjoy wearing the smart uniform of the QAIMNS which she had been so eager and proud to get into. Posting orders soon had her packing and wearing an ill-fitting soldier's khaki battledress with the British Expeditionary Force in France.

'The funny thing about posting orders,' she said, 'was that they were always "most immediate". Invariably, you rushed around, arrived at the new unit like a racehorse in a lather of sweat and found that no one was expecting you.'

Her first wartime posting order was to No. 10 General Hospital in Edinburgh. She packed hurriedly, bade a tearful farewell to her family and took the first train to Edinburgh. Conscious of the 'most immediate' need to hurry, she took a taxi from the station to the hospital, dashed inside and announced herself to an elderly senior sister.

'She had not the faintest idea what to do with me. I wasn't expected. So she gave me a cup of tea and when she heard I was a theatre sister told me that when she was one in 1914, "they bombed them as they stood at the operating tables". That was a fine start for me,' recalled Lorna.

Other new nurses arrived. There was no place for them to sleep so they were billeted in private houses all over the city and reported to the new Matron and medical officers at a girls' school every morning until posting orders for France arrived.

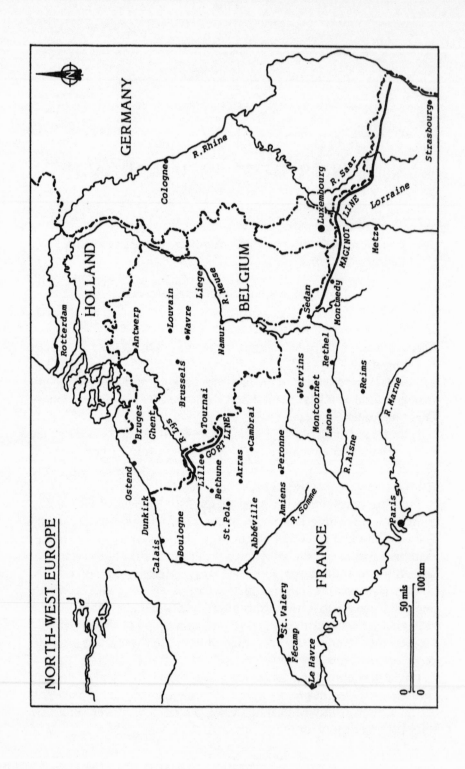

NORTH-WEST EUROPE

GERMANY

HOLLAND

BELGIUM

FRANCE

R.Rhine

Cologne

Rotterdam

Antwerp

Louvain

Wavre

Liege

R.Meuse

Namur

Brussels

Ghent

Bruges

R.Lys

Lille

Tournai

GORT LINE

Bethune

Arras

Cambrai

St.Pol

Abbéville

Peronne

Amiens

R.Somme

St.Valery

Fécamp

Le Havre

Calais

Boulogne

Dunkirk

Ostend

Vervins

Montcornet

Laon

Rethel

Reims

R.Aisne

R.Marne

Paris

Sedan

Montmedy

Luxembourg

R.Saar

Lorraine

Metz

Strasbourg

MAGINOT LINE

50 mls

100 km

0

We were given twenty-four hours' leave. After those tales about the bombing of operating theatres, I was sure I'd never return alive. I telephoned home, took the night train to London, met my mother at King's Cross Station, said hello and goodbye, and returned on the ten o'clock that morning.

We had so little time together for me to say all the silly things you said at wartime partings, but never all those you wish later you had said. We hugged and said farewell. Mother had a platform ticket ready and came with me back to the ten o'clock morning train. The grime-coated platform was crowded. The carriages were filling up quickly so I got in and squeezed into a seat by the window. Porters shouted, slammed doors, there was a billowing of steam and then slowly the train began to glide forward. On the platform children were held up to wave goodbye, women and some older men mopped their eyes. I blinked back the tears from mine.

Within seconds the train had rattled across the points of the goods yard, along the backs of drab houses of suburban London, and soon it was out in the countryside. The sun streamed through the windows and the fields, parched brown from the hottest summer anyone could remember, slid quickly past.

Newspapers kept reminding their readers that the summer of 1914 was the hottest that anyone could ever remember too. And one could not help wondering if this war was going to be as bloody.

Back in Edinburgh, Lorna and her colleagues were advised to rush to the nearest shops to buy food for a long journey and boarded the night train. With many stops they travelled through the long hours of darkness, passing through stations bearing no names and no lights, until dawn, when they were shunted off the main line for a 'brew-up'. That was the time Lorna found out that a 'brew-up' meant a mug of tea so strong that the spoon would almost stand up in it. 'What a comfort it was.'

Forty-eight hours later, tired and bad tempered, Lorna and her colleagues arrived at Cherbourg. They were in for a surprise. The port was a shambles. The quayside was a strange mixture of military and holiday traffic. Officers were arriving with a golf bag slung over one shoulder, tennis racquets sticking out of hand luggage. A red-faced man in Salvation Army uniform played popular songs on his cornet. It was all in the best musical comedy tradition. The carnage and misery of war was all to come.

Lorna, used to a well-organized life, was utterly dismayed. Fifty years later, she shook her head, still incredulous, as she recalled:

It is difficult to comprehend the utter incompetence and confusion. No one seemed to know what to do with us. We sat about for hours until finally a convoy of ambulances ferried us to our destination, a village school at Arques La Bataille. No one expected us there either. We sat waiting for the trucks carrying our personal kit and hospital equipment. At last they arrived. We started to unload. The first items were 'Pots, chamber, 8 inch, lady officers, for the use of'.

Eventually they turned that school into an efficient hospital. But, they wondered, where were the patients? Where indeed was the war? Neither side wanted to be the first to shoot. Instead they bombarded each other with leaflets. Lorna Bradey picked up one depicting an attractive French girl in frilly nightie sitting in bed alongside a pipe-smoking man wearing nothing but a monocle – the German idea of a typical British officer. The caption in French read: 'This is what the English are doing whilst you are away at the front.' The Germans were showered with millions of anti-Nazi leaflets, saying: 'Your rulers have condemned you to massacres, miseries and privations of a war they cannot ever hope to win.'

Autumn turned into the bitterly cold winter of 1940. January was said to be the coldest for forty-five years. 'My face flannel freezes to the basin every night,' wrote Lorna in a letter home.

The few patients trickling in from the front line suffering from bronchitis, pneumonia or venereal disease all said there had not been one shot fired on the Western Front and that on both sides, mammoth loudspeakers broadcast messages saying how stupid it would be for Britain and Germany to sacrifice so many men needlessly in going to war with each other. It was the 'phoney' war – eight months of inactivity. Poland had been overrun in three weeks and Hitler was sending peace feelers to British politicians who favoured an armistice right away.

Meanwhile, British soldiers, confident of what they would do to the German army, boasted, in the words of a popular song, that they were going to 'hang out their washing on the Siegfried Line' (the German western defence line). It was a boast which prompted the renegade Irishman, William Joyce, known to everyone with a wireless as 'Lord Haw Haw', to respond prophetically that 'the Englishmen's washing will be very dirty before they come anywhere near the Siegfried Line'.

Curiously, it was a medical officer serving in a casualty clearing station with the British Expeditionary Force (BEF) at that time, Captain John Macpherson, who was to have one of the last words in the William Joyce saga when he took a bullet from Haw Haw's backside in 1945 before he was taken away to London to be hanged as a traitor.

That time was still a long way ahead, however, during that phoney war in France, where complacency still reigned, as Lorna recalled:

In those early months we had no casualties. We were kept busy running as an ordinary hospital. There was lots of fun too, parties galore. We girls were in great demand, champagne flowed. Men were away from home for the first time – officers in uniform looking glamorous, all the cares of wife and home forgotten, and we young nurses were ready victims. It was the first time I heard the 'unhappy married man' story. And, dear God, how often did I hear it there!

Christmas brought little change. The Guards near to Lorna Bradey's unit were still being sent out on trench-digging duties, but they had time enough to stage a pantomime which nurses attended – Snow Knight and the Seven Giants. Naturally they made much of the dwarfs' digging song and also one of their own to the tune of the Eton boating song: 'We'll all dig together'.

'In rollicking good spirits they brought the pantomime to an end with a rousing rendering of "Kiss me goodnight sergeant major, sergeant major be a mother to me",' recalled Lorna. Before spring was over, many of that happy bunch were dead.

Posting orders were arriving again. Lorna got hers in April to No. 5 Casualty Clearing Station (CCS) the most forward field hospital with nursing sisters. There were five sisters, five medical officers and fourteen orderlies. They worked well together as a team, as Lorna recalled: 'The surgeon was a famous heart surgeon, the first man to operate on the open heart in 1938, and here he was doing minor surgery and mending fractured limbs. The War Office had not found a more appropriate posting for him. It turned out to be a tragic and fatal blunder.'

The CCS moved to Arras in April 1940, close to where the Welsh Guards were stationed. There they set up ready to receive casualties. Shortly after daybreak on 10 May, however, they got orders to move 'immediately' westwards to Fravent. A powerful German force of 136 divisions had pushed into Belgium and threatened the whole of the BEF.

One can imagine the surprise of the nurses when they received an invitation from the Welsh Guards to a concert that night, despite their orders for an 'immediate' move. Their packing finished, they sat in the front rows of an excited audience to listen to Britain's most popular variety artist of that time, Gracie Fields. 'It did seem a funny kind of war to us.'

'We set off the next day, excitement mingled with doubt and fear. No one in our unit then had any experience of real war. We were soon to get more than enough.'

It was a long day as they struggled through roads packed with refugees and harassed by Stuka dive-bombers until they arrived at Fravent chateau late the following evening. There the CCS joined a small British hospital and, as soon as they had eaten, the nurses went to bed and slept soundly.

They woke refreshed but puzzled. The corner of the hospital where they had been billeted was extraordinarily quiet. All the men of the CCS had gone – doctors, medical orderlies, ambulance drivers, the lot.

The senior sister explained the mystery of their disappearance. 'I found a short note from the CO by my bedside this morning saying: "We have been ordered forward. You are to go back." '

The nurses never saw the men again, except for one whom Lorna Kite (née Bradey) met by chance in London years later, just before D-Day. 'He told me they were all killed in the retreat to Dunkirk. And that brilliant heart surgeon? Well, during a stonking from German artillery, he took refuge with the rest of the unit in a cave. But soon he could no longer stand being closely confined. He went out for a breath of fresh air. He was killed as he took his first lungful.' He had told no one he was claustrophobic.

In that hectic week of May 1940, Lorna's unit had orders to move west again, 'immediately'. Army and Navy nurses from all units with the BEF were being told to converge upon ports in northern France. Pamela Barker, who had been in France since the autumn of 1939 and was now serving on a hospital train, was already on that route. For her, those last few weeks had been an eye-opener.

It all came as a great shock to me. Nothing I had ever seen in my brief time in Ancoats Hospital and Manchester Royal had prepared me for the awful wounds which we had to treat at the CCS and later on the hospital trains. It was pitiful.

We, as sisters, gave morphine and prepared patients for the operating theatre according to a list scribbled out. Never again have I seen surgeons work so fast, especially on open wounds, of which most were septic. Nearly all of the soldiers brought in during those days of fighting rearguard actions were dirty, their wounds inflamed and infected. Surgeons seemed to have no hesitation in opening up wounds, scrubbing them gently clean and then packing the wound with sulphonamide powder. We hadn't then got the benefit of penicillin. A similar technique was used with a through-and-through wound made by a bullet. Often the surgeon would use his knife to open up the track of the bullet by cutting through the tissue between the two openings, clean out the tube and then, after inserting a drainage tube, pack the wound with sulphonamide powder.

You couldn't be sure with all wounds just how serious they were. At first glance some just looked like a neat hole oozing blood but we soon knew that we'd have to be prepared for a more severe injury. A small shell fragment penetrating the chest, making a small hole, could take with it bits of clothing which always caused contamination and along with that there could be splinters of bone causing great pain. The wound would have to be opened and the jagged edges of the ribs cut cleanly off.

As theatre sisters we'd see it all happening to these white-faced young men and we'd hide our own apprehension beneath a veneer of jokes and bonhomie.

Nurses of the Royal Navy and Army at many of the French ports marshalled the wounded and waited to be called forward with their stretcher-borne casualties and walking wounded. Behind all the seeming chaos was careful planning of which the nurses were unaware.

All kinds of top-secret assignments were being given at short notice to the commanders of destroyers plying to and from those Channel ports. One destroyer had to escort two ships carrying gold bullion to England at short notice. The commander of another, Sam Lombard-Hobson, drew into the quayside at the Hook of Holland and there, amongst the crowds on the jetty, he spotted two elderly ladies propping their bicycles against the bollards. One of them raised her umbrella as if to hail a cab. In faultless English she asked if the captain would be kind enough to take her to England. Before the sentry could order the ladies away the captain sprang forward and said, 'Certainly Ma'am.' So it was, without any fuss at all, that Her Majesty Queen Wilhelmina of the Netherlands stepped aboard a British destroyer and sped away at 30 knots.[1]

A day or two later, at Dunkirk, the same commander, Captain Sam Lombard-Hobson forced his old destroyer, the *Whitshed*, alongside the Boulogne quay where a throng of unarmed and demoralized troops were beginning to panic as they waited to be evacuated. Through their ranks, two hospital trains laden with wounded and their nurses drew alongside the ship. All free hands on the *Whitshed* helped the Royal Army Medical Corps (RAMC) to carry the stretcher cases on board. Then, with as many wounded as the ship could carry, it moved off to make way at the quay for the next destroyer.

The next day, when Captain Lombard-Hobson brought the *Whitshed* to the same place, a very different sight met his eyes. All around the quay troops were lying about, many of them dead drunk on looted alcohol. Again, the destroyer's crew helped RAMC stretcher-bearers to load the wounded as quickly as possible. 'We gathered up as many of the stretcher cases lying about on the jetty before they were trampled to death by the drunken mob,' recalled Captain Lombard-Hobson.[2]

All this time the destroyer was under heavy machine-gun fire from the direction of the Customs House.

It was then that Captain Lombard-Hobson witnessed an incident which he and nurses accompanying the wounded on the quay would never forget. Whilst a mixed party of walking wounded and stretcher-borne casualties was forming up to embark, a single soldier broke ranks and made a dash for their gangway. 'Without a moment's hesitation, the subaltern in charge took out his revolver and shot the man through the heart. He dropped motionless onto the gangway,' recalled Lombard-Hobson.[3]

That subaltern's action probably prevented a stampede by other troops awaiting evacuation. Minutes later the destroyer, with over 700 wounded and exhausted men aboard, sailed for Dover.

Lorna Bradey was in a convoy of eight ambulances directed from Dunkirk towards Dieppe or St Nazaire. Many a time she thought they would never reach either of those distant French ports.

We were attacked almost the whole way. The Stuka dive-bombers were remorseless, the red cross meant nothing to them. They came down with other bombers and sprayed the road we were on every half-hour. We were terrified, for the pace was dead slow with refugees from a panic-stricken throng trying to cling to the sides.

We looked through the narrow slits of the ambulance side windows and saw masses of refugees and after a particularly bad Stuka attack we could see the bodies of children and older people lying in their blood. Our instinct as nurses was to rush out and help but we had orders to get to No. 10 BGH (British General Hospital) as quickly as possible to help them with the evacuation of casualties by train. We worked feverishly against time, using whatever dressing we could find. When the last casualty was aboard we closed the doors, and the train steamed away with us all for Dieppe.

When we got to the harbour it was in flames. Bombing was intense. The hospital ship *Maid of Kent* went up before our eyes. Our train was hastily moved from the siding and off we went on a journey, stopping and starting, which took almost all night. Just before dark I was talking to a nurse in the top bunk and just as she leant over to pass me a towel, a burst of machine-gun bullets spatted the woodwork where a minute previously she had been resting her head.

I never knew France was so big. We were not travelling fast but we journeyed all day and then came upon a remarkable sight. It was at La Baule, where the population was in the midst of some festivity. No one had heard of the awful situations we had just been through but the Matron of the British military hospital there was so pleased to have us join her staff.

Incredible though it seemed to us, the festival went on without further interruption. We could swim in the sea. I bought a swimsuit and espadrilles. It was such a funny kind of war.

All that ended quite suddenly when convoys of casualties rolled up to the base hospital. I had a ward of eighty to look after. But then a nice red-headed nurse came to help me. She was very conscientious and volunteered to sit by the bedside of patients coming out of the anaesthetic. She told me she had trained at one of the well-known London hospitals but there was something about the way she spoke and did her hair – plaited into two bands which finished with a kind of earphone effect over each ear – which gave me a vague feeling she was foreign, Dutch maybe. When we went off duty she would still stay on at the bedside. 'A proper Florence Nightingale,' we said to each other, 'but she seems too good to be true.'

We voiced our doubts. And how right we were. The Field Security Police must have had a tip-off and watched the all too attentive nurse. They caught her transmitting information she had gleamed from patients coming out of their anaesthetic. They tend to talk a lot then. They took her away.

Before dawn one morning we got the order to evacuate all patients. We went to the wards to get the patients ready and stood open-mouthed with amazement.

A bizarre sight met us. Nearly all the patients were drunk! Dead drunk. Someone had heard the local NAAFI was destroying its store. The troops were damned if they were going to leave the booze to the Krauts. Those who could walk brought booze in for the bedridden. The Sergeant Major dealt with the situation. He searched every bed. Bottles were taken to the sink and poured down the drain.

At last we got everybody to the boat. Stretcher cases were loaded first. We had only just started when the Stukas came dive-bombing and machine-gunning stretcher-bearers and ambulances. What really deserves mention was the way the conscientious objectors who had joined the RAMC as stretcher-bearers never flinched. They carried on loading right through the raids until they almost dropped with exhaustion. When the last casualty had been loaded we nurses were sent below to settle all patients. Even there we could hear the crump of bombs. There were so many ships in the harbour, we had to wait until dark before sailing.

Not far away was the former Cunard passenger liner *Lancastria*, converted to a troopship. We heard later it was hit by one bomb just as it left port heading for England.

On another hospital ship, the *Llandovery Castle*, which was leaving the harbour then, was Yvonne Jeffrey, who had been one of the first nurses to land in France in 1939 and had been at the hospital, L'Hermitage La Baule. 'We waved to all the troops crowding the decks of the *Lancastria* but our attention quickly turned elsewhere. Dive-bombers zoomed down to attack us. It was still light enough for our Red Cross markings to be seen but that did not deter the bombers. Bombs fell very close but fortunately not one hit us directly.'

Neither Yvonne nor Lorna knew until years later the full story of the solitary bomb which hit the *Lancastria* and the havoc it wrought. Prime Minister Churchill forbade publication of the tragedy, saying, 'The newspapers have got quite enough disaster for today.'[4] Some years afterwards, in his postwar memoirs, he wrote: 'I had intended to release the news a few days later but events crowded upon us so black and so quickly that I forgot to lift the ban, and it was some time before the knowledge of the horror became public.'

That one bomb caused the death by drowning of 3,000 men out of the 5,000 on board.

Sister Ann Reeves of the QAIMNS(R) knew quite a lot about the horrific incident; she helped to nurse some of the survivors.

She was then a student nurse at a London hospital, under the eye of a grim-visaged, tight-lipped sister whose operative words to her were mostly 'stupid' and 'hurry'. Then suddenly they were told to clear the wards. Almost immediately the survivors of Dunkirk and the *Lancastria* came in. She was appalled by the hideous sight of some of them – filthy, unshaven, tattered, verminous and sleeping as they walked.

It was then too that the dragon of a sister changed. Now she addressed me quite differently. 'Nurse I want you to dress Private Johnson's face.' First, though, I had to feed him through what was left of his mouth, either by a tube or a tea spoon, and somehow spare him the ignominy of dribbling. Most of his face was shot away. I had to remove long lengths of congealed ribbon gauze from huge cavities before packing them with clean dressings soaked in *Eusol* (Edinburgh University solution of lime). You can smell it in bleach today. Johnson could only look at me with large hurt eyes. He was still a person – a person shattered beyond recognition.

We never knew what happened to him afterwards.

We found the burns casualties from the *Lancastria* even more awesome. They made my flesh creep. Few of them could walk. Most of them had been covered in flaming oil and were indescribably, horrifically, burnt. These were the days of tannic acid treatment for burns. Sometimes even cold tea-leaves were used for agonizing burns. We also used saline.

Sister said to me, 'Nurse you will apply Bunyan bags to Corporal Campbell's arms and legs and treat the rest of his body with tannic acid. Call me if you want any help.'

Bunyan bags were enormous cellophane bags filled with a saline solution into which the whole of a charred arm or leg could be inserted so that it was surrounded by salt water.

Corporal Jock Campbell was an unrecognizable bulk of burnt flesh with a human soul. He had been enveloped in burning oil and had jumped from the *Lancastria* as a living torch. Perhaps the salt water had at first saved him but the flaming oil, thick and cohesive, had burnt right through his tissues. He was never free from pain except when mercifully drugged with morphine.

All severe burns cases suffer from dehydration which can be remedied by giving the patient a saline solution. But if, as in Corporal Campbell's case, the lips are too corroded and swollen, and the tongue too painful for fluid, then a saline solution can be given through a vein. But they could not find a vein in Jock's charred body. So Corporal Campbell died....

Lorna Bradey's ship was more fortunate than the *Lancastria*. It slipped out of the harbour under cover of darkness and by the time the nurses got up the next morning, a bright sun beamed down upon them as they steamed far out in the Atlantic.

It was like a dream. We were served a breakfast of bacon and egg by chatty, clean waiters wearing spotless white coats held in by red cummerbunds. We had quite a cruise and two days later we arrived at Southampton. The RTO (Railway Transport Officer) issued us with rail warrants and, dishevelled as we all were, we made our way homewards.

At last there I was, home. On the doorstep. I rang the bell. My mother opened the door. I've never seen a face change so suddenly. Her mouth dropped, she put a hand weakly against the door frame and slithered to the ground in a faint. Ten days earlier a telegram had informed her that I was reported missing believed killed. Seeing me on the doorstep was seeing someone returned from the dead.

I found out later that news of No. 5 CCS having been wiped out had reached the War Office and someone there presumed the nurses were with those who had been killed. But for the foresight of our commanding officer we should have been, too.

I was given £30, a pittance even then, to buy a new uniform, so I went to our outfitter, Boyd Cooper, and bought one on the never-never. It would take me years to pay it off but I didn't give that a thought then. I was eager to get my next posting.

3 The Spectre of Defeat

I think we all felt a little apprehensive. So few of us in a cold strange land, not knowing where we were going and not knowing where the enemy might be lurking. We had no choice but to put our trust in this strange man who was piloting this little boat.

Sister Freda Reid (née Barnfather) QAIMNS

While British forces and nurses were struggling to get back to the French ports as the Allied front disintegrated all around them, those in Norway were in much the same situation. Amongst the nurses there was Freda Barnfather, of No. 7 Casualty Clearing Station.

Events had moved swiftly for her after she and her colleagues had been sacked from their posts at the RNH Haslar because their civilian status barred them from wartime work at a naval hospital. Freda, already a member of the Territorial Army Nursing Service (TANS), had been posted to the military hospital at Tidworth where the Matron told them they were there just for a short time 'to learn the way the Army do things'.

Hardly had she and her new friends got settled into their cramped quarters when another posting took them to a unit mobilized hurriedly for overseas duty. Freda had read newspaper reports of British troops landing in Norway and 'storming snow-clad heights in the face of machine-gun fire'. Others in the draft had read that British coins and notes had been made legal tender in Norway. It looked as though the army was expecting to stay there a long time.

But that, she was soon to learn, was not always 'the way the Army do things'.

The next posting order came suddenly. 'Pack all your gear and be ready to move to King's Cross Station at midnight,' said a breathless senior sister to Freda and her colleagues after their tea one evening. 'It's all very hush-hush so no one is allowed out from now on. No one, not even your nearest and dearest in the family must be told of your move. Got that?'

In a high state of excitement they reached the station. The platforms were crowded, not just with soldiers surging along the platform with their kitbags, full packs and rifles, but also with wives, families and girlfriends. They stood in small groups making inconsequential talk and nervous jokes, waiting for the train, as if sad partings were not allowed. In any case, it would not be long before they would be meeting again, as the 'Forces' Sweetheart', Vera Lynn, so often crooned reassuringly to them.

The nurses felt very let down with no one to see them off. Obviously other people had not observed the 'hush-hush' order. Now Freda and her friends were learning fast. There was more than one way of doing things in the Army.

Eventually the train pulled out of the station and made its slow way north. Typically, no one knew their destination. Twice the train stopped at stations where smart green-uniformed Women's Voluntary Service helpers doled out tea, sandwiches and rock buns. Dawn broke. All station names and sign posts had long since been removed so as to be no help to German parachutists. The next day the train pulled into Gourock on the Clyde.

Troops tumbled onto the platform, fell in and marched to the docks, where a magnificent sight greeted them: the *Monarch of Bermuda*. She looked beautiful, a peacetime cruise liner converted to a trooper. Smoke streamed from her stack and she was all ready to set off, as the Commanding Officer, Colonel 'Johnnie' Walker, wrote in his War Diary, 'for an unknown destination'. It was obviously somewhere cold from the Arctic kit they had drawn, but why had they been issued with a new filter for their respirators?[1]

Everything went smoothly with embarkation. Freda Barnfather had never tasted such luxury, sharing a sumptuous cabin, a twin stateroom, with her friend from Wales, Vera Jones. The walls were of scarlet satin brocade. A life of luxury indeed – but not for long.

They landed with No. 7 CCS in deep snow at Harstad, north of Narvik, hundreds of miles beyond the Arctic Circle. The CCS was housed in a desolate collection of school buildings set on a wild and savage coast where black-grained sheets of rock rose hundreds of feet out of the sea, home to a whirling cauldron of screaming seabirds.

By this time the nurses were dressed in soldiers' Arctic kit, which was much too large for them because the Quartermaster had not indented for women's sizes.

Perhaps it was fortunate for Freda Barnfather that she was not aware then of the real confusion and chaos besetting the North West Expeditionary Force. The discomfort of the nurses in their outsize clothing was a small matter compared with the predicament of the men who had to fight and march through deep snow in outfits which were more of an encumbrance than a battle outfit, making them move 'like paralysed bears' as their General, Carton de Wiart, was later to write.[2]

Every unit had horror stories to tell about their equipment. French mountain troops had no mountain boots, few snow shoes and no snow goggles. British territorial units landed with supplies for two days instead of two weeks.

The nurses who had been taken to Harstad were desperately short of equipment. They had to improvize to turn the small primary school into an effective casualty clearing station. 'There was no water available except from the river and wells, no electric power, and we just had to manage with a makeshift operating theatre,' wrote the CO in his War Diary.[3]

Rations for staff of the CCS were 'basic'. They lived on a diet of 'hard tack' – dry biscuits, bully beef and sometimes rice. Their 'bathroom' boasted a long row of metal bowls bolted to a stone slab opposite an equally long row of toilet pedestals, low ones fit for six-year-old schoolchildren. The nearest approach to a warm wash came when someone managed to heat a tin bowl of water on the oil-burning Beatrice stove issued as part of their camp kit.

In temperatures below zero they went to bed on narrow wooden bunks, wearing thick woollen pyjamas, woollen sweaters, a woolly cap, bedsocks and gloves. They struggled into Arctic-issue sleeping bags under as many army blankets as they could find. Even then a good night's sleep was rare. German planes bombed shipping in the fjord alongside their buildings, and guns from Royal Navy destroyers cracked with such force that the school windows rattled as if they were about to shatter.

During the first few days, the nurses did not venture out far. Even in the long hours of daylight emanating from a low pale, lemon-grey sun, going out in snow goggles, which were obligatory, was hazardous. Blizzards blew up without warning, causing a complete and frightening 'white-out' so that finding the way back to base could be very difficult indeed.

Rumours abounded, often contradictory. They were going to move. They were to plan for a long stay. No one knew what was happening. No wonder – arguments between senior commanders over tactics raged frequently. While the Commander-in-Chief, Admiral Lord Cork wanted an assault landing force to take Narvik, General Mackesy could see no sense in risking one. He wrote: 'It is not a justifiable operation of war for a numerically inferior force, scarcely able to move owing to the snow, to attack an enemy who enjoys all the advantages of the defensive. The operation becomes sheer bloody murder.'[4]

The nurses got ready to receive heavy casualties. They made up dressings and packed drums for sterilization.

Determined to prove a landing could be made, Lord Cork conducted a personal reconnaissance, and went ashore with a section of Royal Marines. These men, hardened through battle schools, were soon above their knees in soft snow. The smaller-statured admiral was up to his waist and had to be hoisted out, losing his monocle[5] in the process.

Such were the tales – a mixture of tragedy and farce – which drifted down to the lesser fry awaiting their next directives. As usual, these came to the nurses with a sense of urgency and marked 'immediate'. By this time they were not surprised at the lack of time to get ready but they were not prepared for the unusual transport provided. Freda remembers well that strange and frightening move.

We set off at midnight. We were ushered onto a small fishing boat which putt-putted noisily along the fjord. The journey was somewhat eerie. Dead of night and still, the water dark and oily as it flowed between black, forbidding mountains. It was cold enough to shock and numb to death anyone in it within minutes. Daylight had scarcely gone because we were so far north and the only visible movement was the faint swish of water at the prow as the little boat arrowed her way forward.

No one aboard told us where we were going. No one knew where the enemy might be lurking. We just had to trust the strange Norwegian piloting the little fishing boat.

Eventually we sailed through a grey early-morning mist into the quaint harbour of Taarstadt where we were to set up the casualty clearing facilities for the coming clash with the enemy. Now it really was imminent and expected.

To minimize the risks from enemy shelling and aerial bombing, our unit spread itself between five small buildings. One housed the operating theatre, the few beds we had were set up in the next building for the seriously wounded. In the others, stretchers were laid in rows, on trestles or on the floor.

I was on duty that first night from eight until eight when the first wounded from the battle were brought in. The surgical specialist worked from early morning till midnight every day, operating or putting fractures into plaster.

A big problem faced them straight away. How could they communicate with the 194 wounded soldiers they admitted? They came from the Second Polish Army, the French Chasseurs Alpins, the French Foreign Legion, the Norwegian army – and from the German army too.[6]

Urgent messages requesting interpreters were sent to Supreme Headquarters in Paris. 'They sent a man who spoke excellent Finnish but not a word of Norwegian. At Supreme Headquarters Paris no one appeared to know the difference,' wrote Colonel Passy, who was with the French force.[7]

Many of the casualties from the Narvik battle were terribly wounded, and worse still suffered from frostbite from lying in freezing snow for so long. Many died.[8]

'I had difficulty in keeping my face free from the anguish I felt as I took off the first field dressings,' Freda recalled.

Some pathetic cases were in agony with frostbite. Their feet and the lower parts of their legs were black and shrivelled, the tissue dead and oozing pus. There was no hope of saving those awful feet and sometimes even hands. Amputation as soon as possible was the only way to provide relief from excruciating pain.

Surgeons and their staff had to work quickly. Casualties were treated for shock, anti-tetanic and anti-gas gangrene serum was administered and then after the patient had been anaesthetized the edges of wounds were excised and all foreign material, debris and devitalized tissue removed from the depths of the wound. The practice in Norway then was for the wound to be packed with vaseline gauze following an application of sulphonamide powder. No penicillin was then available.

Decisions had to be made with haste. Freda had never seen anything like it before. Surgeons had little time and had to make on-the-spot decisions, often in poor light, about difficult cases. To cut off a limb or not. Some came in with limbs badly crushed by heavy equipment falling on them, others with compound fractures impairing circulation to other parts of the limb. In most such cases the limbs had to be amputated.

No one had time to think of the battle raging so close to the small CCS or of their own safety. Nurses snatching a break for a quick cup of tea and a snack could see the smoke from the artillery fire and hear the guns, while nearby in the fjord they could see crippled battleships making their way slowly towards the open sea. Freda recalled seeing the battered destroyer *Aurora* limping away and wondering if it would ever reach home port.

At night the commotion round the unit rarely abated. Noisiest of all were the naval guns firing a protective barrage as soon as any German plane dared to approach the area.

Then, quite suddenly one day, the nurses were told to pack up and get ready to move. No explanation was given. A brief entry in the War Diary recorded that 'a warning order came from the Deputy Director of Medical Services. It had to be read and burnt.'⁹

That night Freda Barnfather went on duty as theatre sister wearing her outdoor uniform, over which she wrapped her theatre gown. She had just finished attending to a small convoy of wounded when the order came: 'Go!' The nurses were rushed to the harbour to board a primitive kind of hospital carrier, upon which as many wounded as possible were packed.

Quickly, the small hospital ship took its load to Harstad and the nurses to their previous school base. Instead of deep snow, however, they saw flowers growing behind garden fences. There they were to wait for further orders. Freda was now learning that waiting and wondering was an expected part of Army life. Amazingly, it seemed in retrospect to Freda, that waiting period became a holiday. They drove to the hills where they skied, tobogganed and enjoyed themselves!

Just as suddenly, the waiting was over. They packed, again at a moment's notice, were taken down to the quayside at Harstad and embarked on the hospital ship *Aba*. This time, after twenty-four hours at sea, their destination could be safely divulged. They were going to Liverpool via the north of Scotland.

All went well on that hospital ship until, around the Faroes and the Shetland Isles, a storm hit them. Dinner was just being served when an almighty clap of thunder broke right overhead. One by one each of the nurses left the dinner table, hands clutched to mouths as they staggered across the tilting deck to lie flat out on their bunks.

Previously, Freda had always slept well on board ship, but this night, though she was desperately tired, sleep was impossible. She remembered the advice about sea-sickness given to her by an old seafaring man whilst on embarkation leave: 'Get yourself a wide belt and pull it in as tight as possible. Then take in another notch so that your guts don't roll about.' Freda had tightened her belt and it had helped a little but she could hear and feel the waves slamming viciously against the side of the ship. She gave up trying to sleep. The berth on which she lay rocked and jerked so violently that her body muscles constantly twitched to keep her balance under the blankets.

Never before had she experienced any storm like this, as the *Aba* pitched and rolled frighteningly, battling against the pounding waves. In the wards below, the wounded were in a dreadful state.

Freda raised herself on a precarious elbow and looked around the cramped quarters of the cabin, into which three other nurses had somehow been packed. In the dim blue light from the small electric bulb in the ceiling she saw them rolling uncomfortably, hoping sleep would come for a short time at least, to block out the ship's pitching and corkscrew motion.

Freda and her colleagues from the CCS were not responsible for caring for the casualties on board; the hospital ship staff were on duty in the wards. But on this trip they were having problems. Many nurses and medical orderlies were terribly sea-sick. Freda, as if she had guessed what might be happening below, was just debating whether to go to the wards to see if she could lend a hand when there was a rapid knocking and the cabin door was flung open.

The other three nurses, now awake, raised themselves and stared as a young nurse came in and grabbed a corner of the washbasin to steady herself. Her face was grey with fatigue, fright or sickness. Through the open doorway Freda saw water slopping and swirling back and forth in the narrow corridor. 'Message from the Commanding Officer. Will all nursing officers report to the wards.' With that she stumbled out of the cabin.

Freda slid off her berth and pulled on her uniform, blaspheming in a way her parents would never have believed possible.

As she got to the ward she was met by the rancid stench of vomit and urine. She looked down the rows of cots in two tiers bolted to the floor. Not one of them was empty. The side rails were raised to keep them safe. On some cots, men lay encased in plaster from neck to ankles. A thought crossed her mind which she quickly dismissed; if the ship were torpedoed these men would have little chance of survival. And what would the nurses do? But she was immediately too busy to ponder those questions.

Gradually the storm subsided and the ship's lurching and heaving settled down to a steadier motion. Eventually the patients were settled enough for Freda to take time off from the ward to go for a meal and it was just then that she noticed something odd. The vibration, so noticeable until then throughout the ship, had stopped. So much sudden silence was eerie. What had happened now?

Hours went by. British destroyers sped past the *Aba*. A ship's officer explained what was happening. A German submarine was lying somewhere ahead around Scapa Flow. That would have to be dealt with before they could go on.

Again Freda thought of the men down below, immobilized in plaster. What would they do if a torpedo hit the ship? There would be no time then to ask. She remembered the secret stories she had heard of how a German submarine had penetrated the naval defences at Scapa Flow a month after the war began, torpedoed the battleship *Royal Oak* as she lay at anchor and drowned 833 sailors. Those wounded would have no chance. She was still turning such thoughts in her head when the ship's engines started again. An officer walked briskly past them smiling. He put up his thumb. 'All OK now.'

All OK indeed. The voyage to Liverpool continued, and the further south they sailed the calmer the sea became. They steamed into the Mersey estuary with bright sunshine lighting up the Liver Building that spoke of home to Scouse mariners. It meant home also to those nurses back from the trials of a Norwegian campaign now denounced in the newspapers as 'a mad gamble', and 'a farce that became fiasco'. The verdict of history would be more severe – one of the most shameful episodes in the British conduct of the Second World War.

Fortunately for the nurses and the casualties in their care, very few people then knew just how awful the management of that campaign had been and how conflicting the orders – orders, for example, sending troops to capture the port of Narvik at the cost of terrible casualties, followed almost the next day by orders to evacuate all troops from the city.

That two-month Norwegian campaign cost Britain two thousand men dead, missing or badly wounded.

However, when the nurses fresh back from Norway opened their newspapers the next day they could see that Britain was facing a far worse situation than the one they had left. The remnants of the British Expeditionary Force were being brought back from France through Dunkirk and the few French ports still free. With the collapse of France, Britain had to fight on alone. Troops and nurses were moved from one depot to another, sometimes it seemed without reason. Freda Barnfather had three posting orders within days of each other.

A German invasion of Britain was expected hourly. Nevertheless, there were other equally vital frontiers to be defended. Italy, impressed by Germany's victories in Norway and France and believing Britain would be defeated in weeks, declared war on Britain and France. Now Mussolini's armies threatened Britain's vital waterway route to the East via the Red Sea and the Suez Canal. Italian forces were massing on the borders of British Somaliland, British East Africa and Egypt. And nurses of all three services would be needed there.

In the north of Libya, Marshal Graziani's force was ready to advance across the Egyptian border to Cairo, whilst from the south a very powerful Italian army was poised to march northwards through the Anglo-Egyptian Sudan to the Suez Canal.

Consequently, despite the threat of German invasion, Prime Minister Churchill despatched troops to the Middle East to safeguard the Suez Canal and to mount one of the most important but least-known of all the campaigns of the Second World War – the Abyssinian Campaign.[10]

It was a gamble, like Norway, but one that had to be taken. Once the Italians had invaded British and French Somaliland they could tighten their control of the southern entrance to the Red Sea. Britain had to defend her interests there. The redeployment of troops to guard all these frontiers inevitably involved the posting of nursing sisters to hospitals and CCS in those outposts.

Freda Barnfather was posted to one of them. First, though, she had to report to the holding unit in Leeds. 'An air of great excitement met me one morning when I reported for duty. Orders had been received for us all to go to London to be measured and equipped with tropical uniform. Shortly after that we entrained for the port.'

To a chorus of wolf whistles from hundreds of khaki-clad soldiers they boarded the elegant Pacific and Orient mailship the *Strathaird*, now converted into an impressive-looking troopship with a white hull and three yellow funnels.

Freda and three other nursing sisters were allocated a four-berth cabin. Unpacking was not easy. Tired from travelling they bedded down early, expecting to wake the next morning already at sea. But when they went for breakfast their colonel was waiting for them. He did not have the look of a man about to impart good news. 'Late last night I got some disappointing orders. Our movement order's been cancelled. We're to return to Leeds. Forthwith. Now, speed is the order of the moment. Pack and meet in the ship's lounge as soon as possible.'

They reported back to their unit in Leeds and were told to take Christmas leave early. The New Year had just been celebrated when orders came for them to be ready for departure at forty-eight hours' notice.

It was then, typical of wartime ironies, that Freda received a telegram from her friend Alex.

He asked me to meet him in London. He and I were penfriends when I was doing my hospital training and he was serving in the Royal Artillery in India. His sister, Olga, was training with me and asked if I would write to him as he felt lonely out there with no one keeping him in touch with England. We wrote and became fond of each other. He had come home on the *Empress of Britain*, which was torpedoed and sunk off the coast of Ireland. Alex had been one of the few lucky ones who had been picked out of the sea after some hours. He had lost everything. I longed to meet him but could not, being on stand-by. It would have to be letters again.

It was lucky that Freda did not risk going to meet Alex, because the unit moved that evening and they were at Gourock the following morning. Five months after leaving the frozen wastes of the Arctic Circle she was heading for the searing heat of the southern Sudan.

This, she realized, was 'the way the Army do things', as the imperious senior sister had said when she first joined the QAIMNS.

This time, there was a small troopship waiting for the unit at

Gourock, the *Nea Hellas*. She smelt of fish. She had been a Greek fishing vessel but was now more profitably employed as a British troopship. The cabin for Freda and her three companions was even smaller.

There was no waiting about. Surprisingly quickly the boarding was done and the ship glided into the river to take her place in the convoy. Their hazardous journey was about to begin.

4   In the Thick of It

Once in a life, when unprepared,
Death fronted us with talons bared,
And dared you venture . . . and you dared.

John Masefield, 'Epilogue'[1]

When Sister McKay volunteered for nursing duties on the Navy's hospital ship *Amarapoora*, German submarines and Atlantic raiders were sinking more ships than at any other time in the Second World War. Three times as many submarines were operating as at the beginning of the war. The Government and the Royal Navy realistically estimated that the Atlantic sinkings then gravely threatened Britain's ability to survive.

One of the first of Sister McKay's memorable voyages in HMHS *Amarapoora* was to the bleak, cold anchorage of the Home Fleet at Scapa Flow, called by the Romans *Ultima Thule* – the end of the world. Though not true geographically, this was certainly apt as an expression of what it felt like to be stationed there. On the windswept land, pounded by high tides, only a few withered, hunch-backed trees clung to the rocky earth. But life on board the hospital ship was even worse when they sailed out into the Norwegian Sea to provide support for the commando raids on vital German naval and air-force garrisons in Norway, and also for the crucial tankers and merchantmen on the Arctic Convoy run across the roof of the world to Murmansk and Archangel.

These brave men of the Royal and Merchant Navies endured ordeals below zero and faced the triple perils of surface raiders from battleships downwards, of U-boats in strength, and of bombers and torpedo bombers. More than 350 of the enemy's most powerful aircraft were used solely to intercept those ships delivering vital war cargoes – tanks, aircraft and ammunition, as well as butter, canned meat, dried eggs and lard, to the hard-pressed Russians.

The physical ordeal was severe in the extreme. To be sunk in the Arctic meant that even though men might be saved, they often lost limbs through frostbite.

The convoy's voyage was some 2,500 miles. At the height of summer it was made in almost constant daylight, apart from an hour or two of gloaming or dusk, and in the depth of winter the situation was reversed – constant night broken only by an hour or two of grey daylight. In winter there were often gales of hurricane strength lasting four or five days when the ships – to quote one captain – 'rolled like Hell'.[2]

Sometimes the convoy passed through temperatures registering from 45 to 80 degrees of frost so that ships entered harbour carrying from 50 to 150 tons of ice. It encrusted the ship's hull and icicles as thick as a man's arm hung from the rigging, while inside the ship, portholes were frozen solid and ice on the walls sparkled 'like a ballroom' as one ship's master put it.

These men, and the commando raiders, deserved all the help the Royal Navy could provide. And part of that provision was in having the professional care of Navy nurses readily available. 'The casualties from the commando raids were often terribly maimed. Worst of all were those with phosphorus burns,' recalled Sister McKay.

Commando Brigadier Durnford-Slater described how those phosphorus burns resulted from what later was to be cynically called 'friendly fire' – being bombarded by one's own aircraft or artillery. Durnford-Slater had his arms badly burnt as he leapt from the assault craft onto the beach at Vaagso in northern Norway. At that precise moment, three RAF Hampden bombers came in dangerously low and loosed their bombs. 'They flashed like a miniature atom explosion,' he recalled, 'and then some of the phosphorus came back in a great flaming sheet. Next thing I knew both my sleeves were on fire.'[3] Fortunately he was wearing gloves and managed to beat out the flames.

But worse was to follow for his troop. One of the Hampden bombers following the first was hit by anti-aircraft fire, went out of control and dropped a phosphorus bomb directly onto an incoming assault craft. Bursting phosphorus inflicted terrible burns amongst the men. The craft also burst into flames. Grenades and small arms ammunition exploded in a mad mixture of battle noises, wrote Durnford-Slater, 'faces, arms, and bodies were ablaze'.

In the unemotional language of her medical report, Sister McKay wrote: 'The sixty casualties were in a very low condition by the time they reached us. The burns involved the face, arms and upper chest and all were helpless. The majority were placed on a special care list and general shock treatment was given.'[4]

Dressing the wounds of patients, particularly those with burns, was difficult when the sea was rough. Trolleys had to be lashed to the patients' cots. 'We were lucky if we managed to keep the dressings trolley complete for each dressing,' recalled Sister McKay.

Generally, the treatment recommended then by Surgeon Lieutenant-Commander A. Ian L. Maitland, RNVR, was to observe a routine which would reduce the effects of shock, eliminate infection and prevent fluid loss. Intravenous injections of plasma or glucose helped to make up for fluid loss.[5] A diet rich in first-class protein was believed to be most beneficial as considerable weight loss occurred, even when the area burned was small. It is interesting to note too how vitamins were then considered to play an important part in wound healing. Where possible, casualties were given a daily dose of 100 mg of Vitamin C plus Vitamins A and D in the form of two dessertspoonfuls of cod-liver oil and malt.

Other extremely ill casualties came to the *Amarapoora* from the Murmansk convoys. Often those men had been transferred from ship to ship in freezing sleet.

The value of the convoys' precious cargoes to Russia was recognized on 26 May 1941 by the signing of the Anglo-Soviet Treaty – a twenty-year alliance whereby both countries agreed to give each other military and other kinds of support needed to continue the war against Germany.

Coincidentally, the day that Anglo-Soviet Treaty was signed was the day that the newly appointed Commander of the German Afrika Korps, General Rommel began a new offensive in the Western Desert. He was determined to capture Tobruk and drive on to the Egyptian border.

At the same time another hospital ship, the 5,000 ton *Vita* with eight QARNNS nurses aboard, sailed boldly into the battered harbour of Tobruk to pick up 328 wounded soldiers and 63

Australian Army nursing sisters. They were all safely delivered to Haifa. Two weeks later, the *Vita* again nosed her way carefully through 300 wrecked ships into Tobruk harbour and quickly loaded 430 army casualties. Fortunately in view of what happened a few hours later, only twenty-five of them were cot cases; the remainder were walking wounded.

At 17.26 hours that day, *Vita* had just left the mine-swept channel when a formation of German aircraft came directly in to attack the hospital ship, clearly marked on each side and on its deck with brightly painted red crosses. The first bomb lifted the stern clear of the water, others damaged the engine room, steam pipes were fractured, and both engines and the dynamo were put out of action. Five wards were wrecked and numbers 3 and 4 holds were flooded. The ship took a serious list to port and the captain decided to evacuate all patients and staff.

They were taken off by the Australian warship *Waterhen*. Within a short time *Vita* seemed about to founder and the captain gave the order to abandon ship, except for a few of the ship's officers. The ship was again bombed whilst it was being towed to Alexandria for repair. All patients and staff of the *Vita* reached harbour safely but on 30 June *Waterhen* was sunk by enemy action.[6]

For nine months during 1941 Tobruk was under siege, held as a fortress behind the enemy's lines. During those very hot months the 'rats of Tobruk' held at bay a greatly superior force and smashed heavy attacks which were launched against them. That scarred and shattered shell of a town and its surroundings – the area about the same size as the Isle of Wight – was maintained and supplied by merchantmen and hospital ships sailing from Alexandria, often harassed by aerial bombardment and shelling by German artillery.

Sometimes, after dive-bombers had dropped their bombs, they would return and machine-gun the deck. The hospital ship *Somersetshire* suffered a particularly vicious attack when they had 539 patients from Tobruk on the way back to Alexandria and dive-bombers returned to riddle the deck with machine-gun bullets.

On another occasion, when there were no patients on board, ten nurses clearing wards below were flung off their feet by a terrific explosion which had a most unusual effect, as Colonel J.V. McNally, officer commanding medical personnel on that hospital ship, later related:

It was caused either by a mine or a torpedo striking the starboard side of the ship, causing ballast from the ship's bottom to be blown up over the ship's bridge. The Master sent out an SOS immediately for the ship went down 12 feet at the bow straight away and took a list to port. Boats were ordered away and all but 18 of the ship's crew were sent away. A roll call revealed 6 RAMC Medical Orderlies were missing. They were known to have been in the vicinity of the blast. After a short time the Master noticed that the ship was not settling any lower in the water so he halted the lifeboats and told them to keep close to the side of the ship. It was then safe to believe that the ship would sink no further and all personnel were told to get back on the ship. Boats were winched up on the davits. Some little time later a Greek destroyer came alongside and all the women – Matron, Sisters, Stewardesses and a few passengers – were transferred by motor launch to the destroyer. The *Somersetshire* accompanied by a tug eventually reached Alexandria.[7]

The harbour and town of Tobruk were constantly under attack. General Rommel, Commander-in-Chief of all German troops in Libya, was anxious to prove himself by bringing Hitler an early victory. Relentlessly he used everything available to throw in one assault after another. He cursed his unit commanders for their lack of initiative and courage. With such fearsome orders coming down the line it is perhaps not surprising that Luftwaffe pilots, dive-bombing ships in Tobruk harbour, did not differentiate between military targets and hospital ships. Amidst the flak of anti-aircraft fire there was little time for them to do this anyway.

But why were hospital ships at sea on their own deliberately attacked? Sister Helen Luker ARRC (Associate of the Royal Red Cross), who was with an army hospital in Tobruk in 1941, recalled one such attack: 'It was horrible. The ship had just cleared the harbour when six dive-bombers came in low and one after the other deliberately bombed and machine-gunned the ship.'

Why bomb these hospital ships? Had German Intelligence told their pilots that hospital ships were breaking the terms of the Geneva Convention and actually carrying materials of war to the besieged troops of Tobruk? If so then they could not have been further from the truth. As soon as hospital ships got to the Tobruk jetty, the loading of patients began. Rarely was anything offloaded except for medical supplies, and within hours of arriving the ship would sail. Many medical officers and nurses have vouched for this procedure.

The hospital ships had to cope with more than enemy bombardment. There was also the bad weather. Occasional sandstorms hit the harbour, leaving the ship covered in sand heavily charged with salt. Eye trouble caused by sand and flies was common, and barked knuckles or abrasions took weeks to heal.

At this time, hospital ships and drafts of nurses were converging on the Mediterranean, ready for the fresh campaigns that were about to be launched. Those ships which were already there were very busy.

When nurses reached base at the end of each trip, one of the first questions they were asked was 'Any mail?' Letters took a long time to arrive for most of the troops in the Mediterranean then. They often came in batches because the postal service did not always know the location of units. Hospital ships posed a special problem because their destinations varied according to changing needs.

Nurses arriving on new drafts were plied with questions. 'What's it like in England now? What's it like with the bombing?' Everyone had a different story to tell. Sometimes it was about the social life and dancing, with so many different nationalities in London: the hand-kissing French, heel-clicking Polish officers and the ultra-polite Czechs with their floppy hats.

Those from London hospitals told of air-raid ordeals, how in recent raids London's Big Ben clock had been battered, its face blackened but still keeping good time, the House of Commons had been destroyed, Westminster Abbey left open to the sky, and five hospitals hit. Lord Haw Haw, the ex-British Fascist, in his nightly broadcasts from Berlin, had said they were reprisal raids for the RAF's 'methodical bombing of the residential quarters of German towns, including Berlin'. Whatever the reason, those air raids in the Spring of 1941 were the heaviest London had ever experienced.

During this time, Sister Reeves and her colleagues were having to treat an ever-increasing number of air-raid victims. She was astonished by the brave, uncomplaining way in which mutilated men and women accepted their lot and were so thankful for the care they were given.

One night, two civilian women were brought in, two sisters, Betty and Hazel, the only survivors from a family in which both parents and three of the five children had been killed in the bombing. Betty, who had lost both arms, showed cheerfulness and courage beyond description.

During another raid bombs fells so close to the hospital that nurses off duty took to the cellar. Rats scuttled in terror along the pipes as the building shook to the explosions. All I remember of the bomb that fell on top of us was hearing a rustling, then a mighty wind and a devastating endless sound of falling masonry. When all had stopped toppling down, those of us who could move picked our way through rubble and climbed out into the corridor. Peter, a friend and nursing orderly, painstakingly picked the pieces of glass from my body and put on a dressing before I went back to the ward.

Four days later, Peter, my kind friend, was killed.

Mary Kent (later Hughes) an Australian doctor who had just arrived in London, was so shocked it took some time for her to get used to the constant rush of bloody, mutilated bodies, whereas she found British nurses and VADs taking it all as though it were just part of a day's work. She recalled:

One night it was particularly hectic, culminating in our being turned out of the emergency medical post because a time bomb had been parked outside. Next morning I met one of my six VADs, looking as unruffled and exotic as ever as she carried a basin of water, nearly as big as herself down the corridor.

'Oh please,' she called. 'If you are going down to town, will you make an appointment for me to get my eyebrows plucked at four o'clock?'

I thought to myself, dictators come and go, but there is something eternal about the way the English refuse to have their routine disturbed.'[8]

Increasing numbers of German bomber crews were shot down and needed hospital care. The seriously wounded were taken to the Royal Herbert Hospital, Woolwich. The NCOs were on one ward and their officers on the one above. Sister Sheila McDermott (later Bambridge), was in charge of the Luftwaffe officers' ward. She recalled the remarkable behaviour of those patients.

Some of them had very strange ideas of what to expect from us. One Luftwaffe navigator lived in absolute terror. He believed that the nurses were really trying to poison him with their medicines. As I could speak some German I'd learnt at school, I was sent to talk to him. I managed to reassure him and by Christmastime he cheerfully pointed to the string above his head and said jokingly, 'Look! I've hung out my decorations on the Siegfried Line!'

On the other hand there were those with whom one could build up a special bond and, despite the unusual and rather awkward circumstances, one could not help but become rather fond of some of them. I remember Sonderfuehrer Nothelfer in particular. Everyone liked him, respected him. Before the war he had been an Olympic runner, and I recall the poor chap had received terrible burns to his legs and, despite his treatment suffered from septic absorption. But we got him better and walking again.

There were also amongst them those who could only be described as 'odd characters'. One in particular who stands out in my memory was Werner Bartels who told me many amusing stories. Then there was von Perthes. He died of his wounds in the ward and I remember his calm dignity as he lay there facing death. His plight so moved one of the nurses that she vowed to write to his next of kin (which I believe was his mother) when the war was over.

Another nurse remembered how some officers lost the will to live. 'They did not want to survive. Some of them just pulled out their intravenous tubes when they were having a blood transfusion and wanted to die for the Fuehrer, and they jolly well did.'

Yvonne Jeffrey still has vivid memories of the cold nights she spent in that hospital, where the only place to get warm was in front of an open fire in the nurses' restroom. It was then too that the Luftwaffe raids were at their fiercest. Many bombs fell around the Woolwich Arsenal but not one fell on the hospital. This naturally gave rise to speculation that German aircrew had been briefed to keep their bombs well away from the hospital where their comrades lay.

So good was the care and treatment given to those Luftwaffe patients that after the war many of them wished to return and say thank you to the staff involved. Sheila met some of them. One, Leutnant Julius Heger, told her his nurses at Woolwich were 'wonderful angels ministering to my every need'.

It is easy to see in retrospect how fondness and affection could develop into genuine love.[9] Forbidden 'relationships of an amorous nature' led, within months of the war ending, to 800 marriages between British women and German prisoners of war, which were summed up by Minister of War, Bellinger, in Parliament as 'the inevitable course of nature'.[10]

Lorna Bradey had just come through a very heavy raid at Southampton when she was called to the newly repaired hospital ship, *Llandovery Castle*. At last it was ready to sail to the Mediterranean.

'We were given a great send-off. And then we came down to earth with a bump. And from that day on things got worse.' Lorna shook her head and blew out a long sigh.

Never has a hospital ship had such an awful complement of patients. They were not battle casualties but men with arms and legs broken in road accidents and drunken brawls, men with painful backs and stomachs and other ill-defined disabilities.

Our hearts sank when we finished our first rounds of these 'patients'. Mainly they were Australians who'd been sent to England for service in the British Expeditionary Force. But now we were to take them to Cape Town and from there they were going home. They thought for them the war was over. They would not co-operate at all.

When the Commanding Officer did his rounds it was the custom for 'up patients' to stand by their beds dressed in their hospital blue jackets, blue trousers, white shirts and red ties. But on the command to stand by their beds the Aussies wouldn't budge. They lay on their cots, black boots on white sheets, smoking and talking whilst the CO and doctors walked round with the ward nurse. One soldier, when told by the Regimental Sergeant Major to remove his pipe, told the RSM to go to Hell. He was arrested and went on hunger strike.

Other hospital ships reported having difficulties with Australian patients. The officer commanding troops on the *Somersetshire* had trouble with them on his ship and wrote in his Unit War Diary:

They resented being at sea and hospital discipline and were somehow obtaining illicit alcohol. We also had problems with mental patients on the voyage. The heat going through the Red Sea upset them. One tried to kill himself by jumping overboard but we stopped and picked him up after twenty minutes. The man was too good a swimmer to drown himself. He gave up the idea of suicide but he had then put thoughts into the minds of other patients. We had five other attempted suicides.[11]

At least the *Llandovery Castle* did not have that kind of problem, but the discipline got worse each day. It reached such a pitch that signals were sent ahead to Cape Town for Military Police to be there in force. But the Military Police either had other ideas or perhaps

Australian Army Headquarters thought better of the plan for these men to be returned to Australia. Consequently the plans were changed. The men were to remain on board and go to reinforce fighting units in the Western Desert.

Lorna and her colleagues groaned with despair when they heard that they were being saddled with them for another six weeks.

Naturally the men themselves were angry when they heard they were no longer going home. They were not allowed shore leave in Cape Town but some of them bribed their way off the ship. They became roaring drunk on Cape brandy. When the manager of a department store asked some of them to leave because they were molesting a young female sales assistant, they took hold of him, wrapped him inside a roll of carpet and carried him out into the main street traffic. It was a miracle he escaped unhurt.

Others just deserted and were never found before the ship sailed. Perhaps no one looked seriously for them.

The people of Cape Town were very generous in offering hospitality in their clubs for dances. Unfortunately for Lorna and her nursing colleagues many of these invitations had to be declined on orders from their Matron who was strangely antagonistic towards such socializing.

She forbade us to wear our lovely veils with our Number One uniform at night. One girl with lovely blonde hair used to flaunt these orders, but not for long. Life became very unpleasant for all of us. Matron even ordered us to leave our letters home opened to be censored. We refused. That Matron became increasingly introverted and peculiar even after the ship sailed from Cape Town. She was found one evening, sitting rigidly at the stern of the ship, staring out to sea. A ship's officer, alarmed at her condition and possible intentions, tactfully led her away.

We tried hard to approach her as she sat huddled in a corner on deck. She was put under medical care, sedated most of the time. Cables flew back and forth. We were very sad. Two senior ladies came to collect her at Suez and we never saw or heard of her again.

For the next fourteen months Lorna Bradey sailed to and from Alexandria in the hospital ship *Llandovery Castle*, and never knew where they would be sailing next. More often than not, though, it was the hazardous shuttle run from Alexandria to Tobruk and back.

On that run to Tobruk, they liked to arrive at dawn and load the casualties in half-light hoping to clear the port before the dive-bombers attacked. Usually they would embark over 500 casualties and be out of harbour again within four hours.

We operated on the severe cases on the return voyage and it was at this time that the 'Tobruk splint' was born. It was a long plaster of Paris splint to immobilize a wounded and fractured limb until we could get the casualty back to base.

One of our sister ships was attacked by dive-bombers. She was sailing with all lights on and red crosses brightly illuminated when the bombs hit her and she began to sink. Later I talked to one of the survivors, a theatre sister. She told me they were in the middle of a serious operation – a casualty with terrible abdominal wounds – when the captain gave orders to abandon ship. Can you imagine the quandary? No surgeon, anaesthetist or sister would leave a patient. Hastily they closed the wound, bound the patient to a stretcher and jumped into the water together, hanging on to the stretcher and patient. In the rough seas they were separated. The sister was picked up still with her operating gown and gloves on but she was haunted by their patient. Did he ever survive? I was never able to find out about this.

On one of our journeys from Tobruk we brought back some Italian prisoners. One Italian officer called me over and in English said he was being neglected and would report me to the Red Cross. He had on a 'Tobruk splint' with the wound packed with vaseline gauze then plaster of Paris over everything else. The idea was to let the wound 'stew in its own juice'. It proved to be a very successful treatment. When the stinking plaster was removed the wound would be half the size. Indeed I have seen maggots crawling out of old plaster and the wound healing beautifully. This Italian thought he was being neglected and even the assurances of the MO would not convince him. He had a nice surprise in store for him when the plaster was removed at base.

In winter the sea was often rough and grey with white tops whipped up by a bitterly cold wind. All portholes were closed and often it was difficult to keep our meals down. Imagine how it was for us in that stuffy operating theatre taking off stinking plasters in a rough sea. I remember how we used to rush out, spew over the side and then go back to the operating table. One day I couldn't face food and the Chief Steward saw me sitting on a chair taking deep breaths. 'I've got a remedy for you,' he said, 'a large pink gin and a slice of ham.' I heaved but he stood over me and watched every bite taken. 'Now sit still,' he said. I saw the skyline dip and come up again. But it did work.

After a year and a half at sea on the hospital ship, I felt I'd got my sea legs at last. It was therefore time for those powers that move us all like pieces on a chess board to send me from the sea altogether. I didn't realize then just how desperately I was going to be needed by an old friend.

5   A Nurse for All Seasons

The aim of the Army nursing service was to keep everyone
moving around, especially when they thought they were
settled.

Sister Yvonne Jeffrey, QAIMNS

The same month that Lorna Bradey was posted to the hospital ship
Llandovery Castle, embarkation orders also arrived for Sisters
Yvonne Jeffrey, Freda Barnfather and Vera Bryan. They were all
bound for a much hotter climate than they had ever imagined would
be the lot of a wartime nurse.

Vera was to join the small trooper ss *Abossa* bound for Nigeria. It
had been for her a month of tragedy. Her family seemed fated to
suffer one appalling misfortune after another. Her eldest brother,
gassed and shell-shocked in the First World War, had died when he
was only 25, and another brother, the one in the Royal Navy who
had caught brucellosis in Malta, had died aged 21. Sadly, just before
she sailed, she had more terrible news. A German bomber had scored
a direct hit on her home, killing her father. Her mother was on the
danger list in hospital, being visited by Vera's sister, Emily.

They had been so happy when Vera had left them on her embarkation leave, and so pleased that Vera was posted to a West African
hospital where part of her duties would be to teach local stretcher-
bearers and medical orderlies the rudiments of nursing care for
casualties. It seemed a safe posting which made the elderly couple as
content as anyone could be in wartime.

Vera was still in a daze when she boarded the boat. But there was
nothing she could now do. She would just have to face whatever
might come, as millions of others were doing.

They sailed away in fine style. Vera stood at the stern rail of the old *Abossa* looking back down the river at the other ships about to begin their long voyage round the Cape of Good Hope to Bombay. Along the quayside she could see wisps of steam thrown off by windlasses at the bows of ships as they weighed anchor. And from their smoke-stacks thin grey columns rose into the shafts of the setting sun.

Emotion welled up as Vera gazed at this last scene of her homeland. Would she ever see it again? Or was she, too, going to be afflicted by the same fate which seemed to plague her family? She had an odd sensation or foreboding, a feeling she later recalled almost as some kind of psychic phenomenon.

She shivered, a cool breeze had sprung up. The *Abossa*'s captain had increased the revolutions on the ship's engines to keep his allotted cable lengths from the ship ahead. Grey leviathans rose out of the sea: cruisers, destroyers and merchant ships. The land faded into the twilight mist.

Still shivering, Vera held onto her hat in the stiffening breeze and walked towards her cabin. That hat was important. It was new – a completely new type designed specially for the QAIMNS. It had been issued to Vera and two of her colleagues for a recruiting press photo session and had appeared in all the national newspapers.

The first few days out of England were very pleasant. Even the boat drills were carried out in good humour. The ship's captain gave some amusing advice over the ship's speakers – amusing but pertinent – such as: 'Ship's officers and men wearing dentures should keep them in their mouths or in their pockets because men in open boats have suffered much from leaving them behind.'

Vera would often be up early, walking briskly round the deck, taking deep breaths to aerate her lungs after a night in the fug of her cabin. On one of those mornings a black dot appeared in the sky, high above the convoy. It looked innocent enough but veterans of the Atlantic run recognized it right away as trouble: a German Condor. Based at Bordeaux, its flying range when carrying extra fuel tanks made it a good long-distance reconnaissance plane. Sailors saw it as the inevitable prelude to disaster. Now as it flew above, it would be radioing details of the convoy to its base: the number of ships, speed, course and precise bearings.

There was hardly any warning. A solitary Heinkel 111 came in to attack from the beam, low in the sky. Four 500 lb bombs fell in close succession as the plane thundered across the ss *Abossa*. The bombing could not have lasted more than a minute but it was vicious, and the noise deafening. Every ship nearby opened fire. Huge fountains of water rose alongside the *Abossa*, drenching everyone on deck. Miraculously not one of the bombs made a direct hit on the ship, though near misses caused a few casualties and minor damage. One bomb exploded so close that it felt to those on board as though the stern of the ship had lifted under a huge wave. And that was that. No more bombers. 'I was told that deckplates in the engine room had been lifted and the propellor shaft dislodged,' Vera recalled. We were disabled for several hours and left quite alone as the rest of the convoy sailed on. Eventually the ship's engineers repaired the damage and when the *Exeter* returned to escort us back to the convoy, a message went up on our ship's notice board: 'Well done *Abossa*'.

Their first port of call was Freetown, the only watering place on the west coast of Africa for Middle East convoys. Shore leave was not allowed. Within minutes locals were rowing out to the ship bringing green oranges, bananas and pineapple, for which the soldiers bargained. Each day they struck harder bargains by adding at the end of each transaction, 'And one for the King', 'And one for the Queen.'

Few, if any, of the nursing sisters knew why Britain should be stationing troops in such a 'God-forsaken place' as West Africa. It was not generally known then that every British possession in the area was entirely surrounded by pro-German, Vichy French territory, and there was always the alarming possibility of the Germans filtering into French colonies bordering the British ones on the route to the Cape.

On the fourth day the *Abossa* left Freetown and the day for disembarkation at Lagos neared. Vera was excited at the prospect of soon settling into her new hospital at Ibadan.

Then the unexpected happened. The ship was heading directly towards Lagos harbour when a signal from the shore turned her away. It was not difficult to see why. The harbour and adjacent jetties presented a scene of almost incredible destruction. The water between the wharfs was a graveyard of sunken ships showing a forest of masts and funnels above the surface. It would have been almost impossible for the *Abossa* to pass beyond the breakwater.

'Don't worry. We're going to dock at Port Harcourt,' Vera was told. She was not in fact worrying but she might have done if she had known what kind of journey that change of plan would cause her.

And she was just beginning to feel that this particular posting already had a jinx upon it.

Port Harcourt had been spared the bombing given to Lagos and the ship docked there without hindrance.

Vera got her first surprise when she met the British Railway Transport Officer (RTO) and his staff. They were all yellow skinned, thin-looking and stooped. They moved slowly, as if they had no energy to spare. A year or two earlier they had arrived in West Africa fresh from Britain, pink-cheeked, laughing and boisterous. But after a few weeks of indifferent meals, at which they picked rather than ate, enervating heat, humidity and the compulsory daily yellow anti-malarial mepacrine pills, their vitality had faded into the simple desire to do nothing but sit and rest.

Many of them had their faces and arms painted in rainbow hues of gentian violet, yellow acriflavine and other colourful unguents applied as desperate measures to heal old sores, skin rashes and grazes which refused to heal in that sweaty heat.

Vera and her colleagues then heard the next instructions. The hospital at Ibadan was not ready for occupation but they would be going there nevertheless. They were to take a three-day train journey, inland to Kaduna and down to Ibadan.

As she waited on the platform for the train, a storm was brewing. It started with an ear-splitting clap of thunder that startled everybody. Heavy raindrops spattered the earth, then it came down in a drenching downpour. It hammered continuously on tin roofs and water literally sheeted down.

The downpour died as abruptly as it had started. The whole area was like a steaming Turkish bath as the sun blazed down with surprising force, raising a mist that clung to the ground like a silvery wet haze. Then every gasping breath taken felt like a choking, throat-constricting ball of heat.

The train drew into the station. Vera and her fourteen fellow nurses were helped onto the train with their luggage by two soldiers, a scarecrow pair in their frayed shirts and shorts, who looked hardly strong enough for physical work. The climate had stripped their bodies of all surplus flesh.

The train threaded its way through countryside now criss-crossed by rushing rivulets and rivers swollen into muddy-looking floods carrying fallen boughs and brushwood. In the late afternoon the heat seemed to increase and the atmosphere grew more stifling. With dusk the mosquitoes were more noticeable, their whirr and ping audible above the rattle of the train. There was no air-conditioning; it was going to be a tiresome journey. Vera wondered what they would all look like by the time they reached the half-built hospital at Ibadan.

Somehow, though, when the train pulled into the station at Ibadan, the fifteen nurses on our draft stepped proudly off, pristine fresh in our white tropical uniform.

The wooden huts which served as hospital wards were built in space hacked out of the bush from which every form of unwelcome wildlife emerged to plague us. There were snakes, scorpions, bats, frogs, and of course the ever-present mosquitoes and sandflies.

The heat and humidity, the sickness, stomach cramps and flies made everyone long for home, with its fickle climate of showers one day and sunshine the next. We used to revel in English sunshine but not that of Nigeria. There the sun was never greeted as it is at home, it became a threatening, unbearable assault upon the senses. It was many years later that I discovered to my horror a melanoma which a surgeon had to remove, and realized just how seriously life-threatening that sunshine had been. But then we worked on, counting the days to the end of our tour and repatriation.

She did not know she was counting the days to another disaster.

Yvonne Jeffrey's hot posting was to No. 1 General Hospital Kantara, between Ismailia and Port Said in Egypt.

We were in tented wards and received casualties from the Western Desert. It was difficult to keep dressings and instruments sterile as there was only one tap with running water in the hospital. All water had to be carried into the wards. The 'up-patients' were wonderful in helping. But somehow we managed to make the most of our short stay. We swam from Africa to Asia across the Suez Canal, which was quite a feat. Our work was one long, hard slog in the heat.

However, just as we thought we were settled, we were posted again, this time to PAIFORCE – the Persia and Iraq Force. We boarded the ss *Bergensfjord*, sailed down the Red Sea and went up the Persian Gulf to Basra. We had Indians on board and the smell of curry permeated the entire ship. It had been built for cruising round Norway and had no air-conditioning, and as the portholes had to be shut after dark, our cabins were so unbearably hot we did not know whether to sit, stand or lie down. Our white dresses were soaked within minutes of donning them.

At Basra, the Venice of the East and home town of Sinbad the Sailor, we disembarked and took a train to Tehran – a journey of 150 miles through high mountains and fifty tunnels.

The nurses found it difficult to understand why they should be sent to such an outlandish part of the world when the war seemed to be elsewhere. In fact a British brigade of 2,250 men had landed at Basra on 18 April 1941 to challenge the pro-German government which General Rashid Ali had set up in Baghdad. Two weeks later 9,000 Iraqi troops attacked the British but were repulsed, and a month after that Rashid Ali surrendered.

The situation in Persia worried the Allies, and to safeguard the oilfields Russian troops occupied the northern and British forces the southern part and forced the Shah to accept Allied 'protection'. The Allies could not afford to lose those oilfields at Abadan and Bahrein.

Yvonne and her companions joined the tented No. 35 Combined British and Indian Hospital in the desert outside Tehran. At an altitude of 6,000 feet the air was thin but much cooler. There were six QAIMNS Sisters and a few Anglo-Indian ones.

We were nursing Polish patients, soldiers captured by the Russians when they occupied part of Poland after the pact with Germany. Later, when Germany attacked Russia, Polish soldiers were released to fight for the Allies against Germany. They were in a pitiable state, as thin as the victims released from German concentration camps in May 1945. We did our best to nurse them fit enough to fight the Germans they hated so much.

Off-duty nurses occasionally went into the centre of Tehran, which must have been one of the most cosmopolitan cities of the war. There was international gaiety in sophisticated night-clubs next door to ancient wrestling booths and Turkish baths. It was not always safe to walk through Tehran though. In previous disorders, British citizens had been shot. The Seaforth Highlanders were camped on the Tehran Racecourse to safeguard British interests. They celebrated New Year in fine style by holding a Hogmanay dance in the Totalisator for which they 'borrowed' 120 Polish ATS (Auxiliary Territorial Service) girls and a few nurses as partners.

The Persian officers were not pleased with the situation. As British trucks passed through the city streets, the Fifth Division historian noted: that 'Persian officers, powdered and scented in their mustard-coloured uniforms solemnly turned their backs to express their anti-British feelings, and there was a distinctly Teutonic smell in the air.'[1]

Yvonne recalled:

When the colder weather came and snow fell, we moved from the tents to a newly built hospital on the outskirts of the city. It sounded ideal but we found there was no running water, electricity or heating. It was too small to take all our patients and the overflow was housed in tents. When I was on night duty I had to trudge through deep snow holding a lamp.

True to the habit of the Army 'keep them moving', another sister and I were despatched to look after a group of Axis nationals – old people, women and children who were being repatriated to Germany. In a hospital train we travelled, back to Basra, then by another train to Baghdad – city of minarets, mosques, magic carpets and thieves – and from there up to Mosul on the Turkish border. We returned to Tehran and were told to wait a few days in a hotel for our posting orders.

The 'few days' was changed to a month's leave, so Yvonne cruised by coach across the desert to Damascus, then to the Sea of Galilee and Jerusalem, across the Sinai desert and back again to Jerusalem. Driving up the steep winding passes was a terrifying experience, for the driver had to compete with local drivers who drove like demons possessed, with little fear of the steep ravines that lay beyond the barrierless roadsides. A glance over the edge revealed quite a few that had shot over the side. It was nerve-racking for the passengers.

In Jerusalem an Irish monk showed me the holy sites by day and his friend showed me the less holy ones by night. The summer passed and we were posted to No. 6 BGH in Egypt. I was on night duty straight away. A few nights later there was a great commotion and the King of Egypt, Farouk, was admitted with injuries from a car accident. We put him in the officers' ward and I was one of the sisters who attended him. He seemed to enjoy having British nursing sisters to look after him so much that he asked for us to go to the Abdine Palace for three weeks until he recovered completely. There he entertained us to a sumptuous Christmas dinner but, being a Moslem, he did not drink any wine.

The high life was now about to end for Yvonne Jeffrey. The King presented her with the gold medal of the Egyptian Order of Merit and she went back to hospital duties, for another Mediterranean offensive was about to begin. The Eighth Army's victory at El Alamein had opened the way for it to push on to Tunis. The Russians at Stalingrad had decimated the German divisions that were to have driven through the Caucasus into Persia and Allied troops there began to withdraw to Egypt.

Arriving in Egypt at that time was Freda Barnfather, with a small draft of Army nursing sisters originally bound for the Sudan. By this time they were not surprised to find that their postings had been changed. They were to proceed to No. 7 BGH in Crete. The next day the orders were changed yet again. Fifteen hundred German aircraft had dropped the elite German parachute regiments on the island and British troops faced another Dunkirk. Freda and her colleagues would just have to stay in Cairo a little longer.

The Matron looked at her orders and smiled. 'Your quarters are in the Citadel. It's a beautiful building. You'll be sleeping in the harem.'

Off they went to explore their bizarre new home.

The harem was splendid, the marble floor was exquisitely patterned in mosaic, the windows were shielded by painted shutters, and in them were cleverly concealed peepholes. We giggled as we imagined the ladies of the harem peering through them to see what was happening in the world outside.

We unpacked and then went out to see the sights of Cairo. The shop windows were full of magnificent goods, the like of which we hadn't seen in England for years. We spent evenings in the two main hotels, Shepheards and the Continental. We ate strawberries and cream and mouthwatering pastries in Groppi's.

Freda was truly amazed by all the fripperies of prewar luxury living available for the rich in Cairo, and the cocktail and dinner parties. Women would emerge from hotels and headquarters in elegant evening gowns, bedecked with jewels. The war could have been a million miles away.

At last posting orders arrived. Six of us were to join the No. 16 BGH in the Sudan. We asked Matron what sort of a country the Sudan was. She told us it was a huge country, ten times bigger than Britain with a fifth of the population. We'd be looking after casualties from the Abyssinian campaign. She said it would be an interesting experience for us.

It was in fact going to be a trip of a lifetime – part of it usually reserved only for millionaires, the other half for hardy desert explorers.

Another cruise at His Majesty's expense,' said the witty one of our six.

The houseboat in the film of Agatha Christie's novel *Death on the Nile* was not more glamorous than the one waiting to take the nurses on the first part of their journey to their hospital, close to the combat zone on the border of Italian East Africa.

We were entranced! Everything was so dazzlingly white and richly gilded in parts. Our cabins were superb, fitted with every conceivable luxury and no sharing. In the fabulous dining room the food was unbelievably glorious, with exotic combinations of herbs and spices, and served by dark-skinned *saffragis*, each dressed in an immaculate white *galabieh* with a red cummerbund round his waist and a crimson fez on his head.

We tucked into spicey lamb tagines, succulent with prunes and apricots, exotic vegetable dishes of aubergines and marrow subtly flavoured with cumin and cinnamon the like of which we'd never had before. For the first time I tasted couscous with hot meaty sauces, a combination I've loved ever since.

I just could not believe I was still an Army nurse as the houseboat glided effortlessly along, scarcely rippling the surface. In the evenings we sat in deck chairs, beguiled by the hour just before sunset when the sky paraded a spectacular range of colours – orange, pink, scarlet and crimson. The river turned from muddy brown to silver grey. And when the sun sank altogether behind the rocks, the colours faded from the sky and everything darkened into a deep grey. It was magic!

We revelled in all the unexpected luxury of the journey, and we readily agreed with the Egyptian captain who said to us one evening: 'This is a millionaire's trip in peacetime.'

That luxury came to an end when the boat drew in to a palm-tree-lined jetty at Wadi Halfa, where an RTO met them. He was an old sweat who had got himself a nice little job for the duration. He escorted the six nurses to the railway station and put them on a train to Khartoum.

'You'll each have a compartment to yourself,' he said. The nurses looked at each other. More luxury? 'If this is active service, long may it continue,' said Freda.

Now they were in the Sudan, though, and about to cross the Nubian desert on a single-track railway subject always to drifting sand and subsidence of the track itself. They were six young women on their own, but there were some consolations. Darkened glass in the windows offset the glare of the brilliant, relentless sunshine and fans in the ceiling of the dining car freshened the air somewhat. Meals were served again by *saffragis* in spotless white *galabiehs* and red cummerbunds.

They made us feel like royalty, for when they were not serving excellent food to us in the dining car they were rearranging our compartments according to the time of the day – after lunch for the customary afternoon siesta, after dinner for bedtime. As we sat in the restful sitting room, we could press a button and one would appear like Aladdin's genie ready to grant our request for a cool drink, tea or coffee.

Nevertheless, it still seemed a long journey. The train steamed steadily through plains of sand, sandhills and sandy-looking rocks occasionally dotted with camel-thorn bushes shimmering in the heat haze. Stations were few and far between. There we saw small groups of dark-skinned men and women with black curly hair and ugly blotches on their shrivelled faces.

At one of those station stops a nurse in the party, pointing at one of those wrinkled faced women asked, 'Shall we look like that by the time we leave here?' It was a question Freda was to remember some forty years later when a doctor advised immediate surgery on a melanoma on her sun-damaged face.

Little did the nurses at that time know what problems the harsh sun would bring. Freda Barnfather and Vera Bryan were far from being alone amongst nurses who served in climates such as the Sudan and Nigeria in being scarred by operations for skin cancers and invasive melanomas later in life. It was not that they deliberately exposed their skin in sunbathing. That was to risk a court-martial; to be unfit for duty through sunburn was regarded as a self-inflicted wound. But there were parts of the body – on the legs below the dress hemline, on the wrists and lower arms and on the face – which did catch the sun.

Eventually the train arrived at Atbara, where the RTO met the nurses and took them to a small officers' mess for refreshments whilst they waited for the once-weekly train which ran as far as Port Sudan. Atbara was a comparatively new town developing in an area better known once as a hunting ground for slave traders during the Turco-Egyptian period – although slave trading still continued well into the 1920s under the Anglo-Egyptian Condominium Agreement.

The final stage of their journey to No. 16 BGH ended at six o'clock the next morning when the train stopped at Gebeit where the Unit Orderly Officer met them with baggage-handling troops and an ambulance to drive them to the camp.

The Matron welcomed them and showed them to their quarters in a row of sparsely furnished four-bedroom bungalows. There were no beds; they would have to use the folding camp beds issued to them before they left the UK – so long ago it seemed then.

Soon they settled into a routine of duty. Wards for other ranks were in marquees but officer patients were accommodated in huts. By this time the flow of casualties from troops who had been fighting the Italians had dwindled. Most of the patients were suffering from dysentery or typhoid fever.

Once again, Freda and her six friends found themselves in a funny kind of war. A leisurely nursing routine was balanced by a busy programme of physical and social recreation. They learnt to ride camels, and at five o'clock each morning a man called Ali called for them to go riding.

I discovered the most comfortable way to ride was to cross my feet over the camel's neck and ignore the stirrups. The only way of guiding the creature was by pulling on a rope tied round his jaws. Never could you relax, once mounted, for the camel was a wily animal; if it spotted a clump of camel thorn, off it would trot then down to the bush would go its head and down you would go too – right over its head and into the prickly thorns.

After an energetic ride we were ready for breakfast and then a day on the wards. In off-duty hours we often had the choice of several invitations to neighbouring Army or RAF officers' messes for dinner and perhaps dancing to records of Victor Sylvester's band played on a wind-up gramophone, or we could go to the local village of Sinkat, which had one general store. On the outskirts of the camp were a few civilian bungalows occupied by British officers who were overseers of the Sudan Railway. They were very hospitable and often invited us to use their swimming pools and join them for dinner.

At weekends we could travel further afield to Khartoum or to Omdurman, where the White Nile meets the Blue Nile. And so the months passed. There was always something happening. Nursing with the armed forces during the war was anything but humdrum.

Memories linger long. Freda remembered the day so vividly when she was just sitting down to her afternoon tea break and an orderly came into the mess and called her name quietly. 'There's a telephone call for you in the admin office, Ma'am.'

Like many of her colleagues with elderly parents at home, Freda feared the worst. Had one of them had an accident, become ill or died? Who else would telephone her in this God-forsaken place? She rushed to the office phone.

'Hold the line please. There's a call for you from Port Said.'

The man's voice immediately threw her into a turmoil. The Newcastle intonation unmistakeable. It was her penfriend Alex! Here she was in a barren wasteland of rocks and sand and yet able to speak to Alex.

'Where are you? What are you doing?' Questions tumbled over themselves in her excitement. After a short stay in the UK he had volunteered for service with the Royal Artillery in the Middle East, hoping by this means to meet Freda. Now at Port Said he was waiting to be posted to an Eighth Army unit.

Feverishly Freda thought of ways in which she might get to see him. So near and yet no chance of meeting. Or was there? The Air Force perhaps? She had met some Blenheim pilots over dinner at their mess nearby at Wadi Gazouza. Perhaps one of them could fly her to Port Said. No! She remembered, they were all grounded for making mock bombing runs over the hospital. Fate again decided that they should have to wait a while longer.

Disappointed yet elated that he had taken the trouble to find her by telephone, she walked back to her ward. Work would help to ease her disappointment. Work, she believed, could cure almost anything. And she was happy to know she really did have something to look forward to once the war ended. Then it was that she realized just how fond she had grown of this man she had never seen.

Putting on her usual cheerful act – she had found long ago that nursing demanded a good deal of play-acting – she went from bed to bed, having a word with Italian as well as British patients. By this time the six nurses who had come down from Cairo were quite used to nursing under canvas and in the intense heat. The worst part of their lives was night duty. In the long hours they had time to think and wonder, as did their patients, what they were doing in such a far-off place.

For the twelve months since we'd joined No. 16 GH we felt we nurses had been living on the sidelines of a drama called war. The campaign in that part of Africa was virtually at an end and now we felt our services could be put to better use elsewhere. Scarcely had we put such thoughts into words amongst ourselves when the CO brought news which made us all excited. We were all to move north.

Soon a real and arduous life would begin again for us.

6 In Peril on the Sea

Year after year, with insufficient guard,
Often with none, you have adventured thus;
Some reaching harbour, maimed and battle-scarred,
Some, never more returning, lost to us.

John Masefield, 'For all Seafarers'[1]

The Captain of the cargo ship *Britannia* woke at the shout, when most men would probably just have stirred uneasily in their sleep. But a year on the Atlantic run had changed all past habits; new patterns had now taken over, which called for lightning assessment and response, which brought every razor-edged faculty instantaneously from sleep to full consciousness.

He slid from between the blankets and pushed his feet into the shoes waiting by his bunk. Fear, anger and surprise moved him quickly from his cabin, where he had snatched a mere two or three hours' rest, to the bridge. He sounded the alarm: six short blasts followed by one long one. And he thanked God that he had insisted on regular and disciplined boat-drill practice. This time he hoped there would be no silly ones who forgot their 'panic bags' of small valuables and essentials for survival, and tried to get back below whilst others were struggling desperately to climb up to the boat deck. Time and time again he had berated individuals about that stupidity, ever since the first practice in the Clyde before they met the Atlantic swell and their first bout of sea-sickness.

In their small cabin below, Sister P.L. Shipton and her two QUARNNS colleagues woke quickly when they heard the alarm, but groaned inwardly. Surely there was no need for boat drill so early in the morning. But still, it was a small chore for them to endure compared with the enjoyment of the rest of the voyage. They had sailed from Liverpool bound for India, leaving behind the dismal, damp weather, the nightly air-raid warnings, the rationing, the queues for anything from a No. 9 torch battery to an unexpected orange from the greengrocer's. On board ship they were passengers with no duties. Indeed, they lived like pre-war tourists on a cruise ship and had settled into a routine, determined to enjoy their unexpected passage to India at His Majesty's expense.

Their day began with an old-fashioned English breakfast of bacon, eggs, sausage and fried bread served by polite, white-coated stewards who moved swiftly from one table to another making them feel like ladies of leisure. Already the three-course lunches and four-course dinners were making dresses feel tighter than they used to be.

In between meals they could stroll about the deck, getting their sea legs, breathing in and tasting the salt tang in the air. What did it matter if they had to take boat drill at odd times of the day or night?

It was when they heard the crack of a gun and felt the ship shudder that everyone pushed all other thoughts from their mind, finished dressing, grabbed their 'panic bags' and hurried upwards to the boat-deck.

It was 25 March 1941. In Germany, Admiral Doenitz, *Fuehrer der U-Boote* and Commander-in-Chief of the German Navy, had despatched special messages to all commanders of submarines and surface raiders to redouble their efforts against Allied shipping convoys.

Ironically Doenitz, a German U-boat commander himself in the First World War, had lost his own ship on its first operation, and spent months of captivity in a Manchester Lunatic Asylum until he returned to Germany in 1919. Now he was obsessed with the one passionately held belief that Germany's only hope of ultimate victory lay in the destruction of Allied shipping on the trade routes leading to the UK – something Prime Minister Churchill feared could happen.

To increase the U-boats' effective range off Freetown, West Africa, Doenitz had stationed a fleet of supply ships in the Canary Islands which could replenish six or seven U-boats with fuel, food and torpedoes. Their impact on shipping was enormous.

Furthermore, those U-boat commanders had the benefit of Doenitz's intelligence agents in Africa and the expertise of Germany's B Dienst cryptogram analysts, who had been reading the Admiralty's convoy codes since the beginning of the war. The Admiralty had long suspected this and were able to act accordingly, arranging evasive routing of the convoys. Even so, Allied shipping losses were reaching a critical level.

In London, just two days before Doenitz had sent out his latest orders to submarine commanders, Churchill had called the first meeting of the Battle of the Atlantic Committee to consider ways to stem the appalling loss of shipping in the Atlantic, which was now threatening Britain's ability to survive. After two years of war it was frighteningly apparent that if the deadly attrition of the British merchant fleet were not arrested then Britain would inexorably be starved into surrender.

Fortunately for their peace of mind, the three nursing sisters aboard the 8,799-ton cargo ship did not know just how hazardous their voyage could be. They knew it would take them round the Cape, a trip of 11,600 miles or thereabouts, depending on the extent to which the convoy had to take evasive action against German submarines. However, they were under the protection of the Royal Navy, and wasn't it the biggest and most powerful in the world?

It was not. For the Royal Navy, unlike the Army, there had never been a 'phoney war' period. They had been at battle stations in the Atlantic from the day the Second World War started, when German U-boat U30 torpedoed the passenger liner *Athenia* with 1,103 passengers on board. From then on Royal Navy losses were terrible.

The myth of Britain's mighty naval power had been kept alive, however, for the sake of morale. It had never been reported in the newspapers that within the first four months of the war the German Navy had sunk a third of the entire British battleship force. Losses had mounted steadily, month upon month, leaving the Admiralty with never as many ships to protect convoys as they would have wished.

And now, as the nurses and other passengers assembled on the boat deck the reality of war at sea shocked them all. Now they were in that war they had hitherto only read about in newspapers. Their war now and not somebody else's. And the reality of being attacked on that grey choppy sea left them stunned.

Sister Shipton remembered exactly when it all began. 'It was just quarter past seven in the morning. Suddenly the ship's siren blasted below decks. Six short blasts followed by one long one. The warning had barely finished before shells were hitting the ship.'[2]

Following her own personal drill, learnt from her student nurse days when speed was imperative and half a minute late meant a bad mark, Sister Shipton dressed quickly, taking clothes from a neat pile folded in the right order and ready to slip on.

She stood by the door, took one quick look round, grabbed her 'panic bag' and hurried out into the moving flow of troops hurrying to their appointed boat deck.

The German raider's guns thundered again and the *Britannia* shuddered as shells struck her broadside on, sending shards of jagged metal flying through the air. Boat-drill ranks scattered as everyone took cover behind whatever was solid and near.[3] Salvo after salvo shattered the superstructure and lifeboats, as Sister Shipton recalled so vividly.

They shelled us continually for nearly an hour. And then suddenly the shelling stopped and the guns fell silent. The ship had been hit below the waterline and began to list. A radio message from the enemy raider, aptly named *Thor*, to the captain of the ss *Britannia* then gave us half an hour to take to the boats. From the bridge came the order to abandon ship. Lifeboats were lowered but some were so very badly damaged by the shelling they were waterlogged as soon as they touched the sea. Quite useless. When our own lifeboat was lowered we saw it was holed too. It filled with water immediately. 'Find any boat you can,' bellowed an officer on deck with us.

Now with the listing of the ship and with a heavy swell running, the lifeboats were swinging some distance from the ship. The only way of reaching the boats was to go down the rope ladder. This was very difficult and when they tried to leap from the ladder into the boat many people fell shrieking into the sea. I was lucky and managed to judge the right moment for my jump and landed safely in the boat. It was an awful scene, people gasping and spluttering in the sea, shouting for help, and clinging onto whatever wreckage they could see.

By this time the ship was foundering and well ablaze, spewing burning oil on the water. From the lifeboat I saw the prow of that magnificent ship suddenly rear upwards, standing vertical out of the water from the funnel and the whole ship then sank slowly beneath the surface of the sea, stern first in a billowing of smoke and flames followed by a hissing as the water flooded the engine room.

All that now could be seen where the ship had been was a nasty grey sea, strewn with a pathetic scattering of wreckage – baulks of timber, a few battered Carley rafts, bits of hatches, spars, oil drums and debris floating amongst the burning oil.

The survivors in the lifeboats thought the German armed merchantman would come over and take them aboard as prisoners but it did not risk being attacked itself by destroyers returning to the scene.

Those survivors in Sister Shipton's lifeboat were immediately faced with difficult decisions.

There were fifty-six people in our overloaded lifeboat but there were still others in the water, desperately trying to keep afloat as oil and water washed into their mouths from the choppy sea whenever they took breath or shouted.

Our boat was already awash with water and we were afraid it would capsize if we tried to pull any heavy person in from the sea. But we could not leave them.

Carefully we hauled another seven men into the boat, grabbing their life-jackets or oil-soaked clothing. Once aboard they collapsed from sheer exhaustion.

Now there were sixty-three of us, sixty men and three women. Of these, twenty-five were Indians. The remainder were Navy, Air Force, Merchant seamen and a few civilians. Many still lay where they had landed in the boat, heaped across each other.

Sister Shipton saw that it was time for someone to take charge. An army officer commanding the Indian party started organizing personnel whilst she took charge of their medical treatment and welfare. Quick action was needed because the floor of the boat was filling with water and more was still coming in. Sister Shipton and the officer decided their best plan would be to stay close to the spot where their ship had been attacked so that if a wireless message had been sent out by the *Britannia* giving the bearings, any ships or Coastal Command aircraft sent searching for survivors would be able to find them. Meanwhile she organized groups for bailing out water from the lifeboat.

Sailors from the *Britannia* estimated their position as about 700 miles from land. But they said that to try and make headway towards that land against the trade winds and with only a limited amount of water would be impossible.

Sister Shipton took stock. She found that they had 10 gallons of water. It did not take much mathematical know-how to realize that no matter how it was rationed it would not last long.

In addition to the water there were some hard biscuits and a few small tins of sweetened milk. A big problem with the rationing was that there were only two enamel dippers with which to dispense milk or water. It was no easy task for a round of 63 to be served with only two dippers.

Sister Shipton explained how the problem was solved:

At first we used to spread the sweetened milk on our biscuits but then we found our mouths were getting too dry to swallow the biscuits. We just did not have enough saliva in our mouths. The next stage was to pour the thick sweetened milk onto the palm of everyone's hand. They could then lick up the glutinous dollop slowly. In this way, more empty milk tins became available for use as cups.

Some people found sucking a button helped to produce saliva. Then one day, magically it seemed, someone produced an apple. Where it came from we never knew. We broke it up into tiny fragments. I've never tasted anything so good. We longed for our morning and evening water ration. Our thirst was acute.

Sister Shipton knew they were all in danger and that although people could go without food for weeks without permanent harm they could only survive for a very few days without any water at all. Her boatload of survivors were now losing far more fluid through perspiration and even exhaled breath than they were taking in.

Many were in a very bad way, suffering from heat stroke and sunburn. Few had been able to bring adequate covering for their heads or limbs. Those without any head covering at all went down with sunstroke from the terrific heat within the first two days and legs swelled up from being so cramped and unable to move. Any abrasions or cuts turned septic.

With so many people packed together in the close confines of the lifeboat most people suffered from the constant pressure of other bodies, and the aching of bruised muscles and the pain from sleepless, bloodshot eyes was common to everyone. Several of the weaker survivors were lying semi-conscious in the bottom of the boat. Older merchant seamen were particularly at risk. After years enduring living conditions barely above subsistence levels, in atrocious, damp quarters, bereft of any comfort, with scarcely 12 square feet of sleeping room per man, without heating, and living on a diet little better than that served in homes for the destitute, it was not surprising that they were amongst the first to need special care.[4]

With great difficulty, she managed to get round her patients each day. Apart from those made ill by the sun there were others with injuries sustained in the shelling and also in leaping from the ship into the lifeboat. Unfortunately the first-aid outfit in the lifeboat was irritatingly inadequate – no doubt provided by some penny-pinching accountant.

There was nothing for our burning skin. Our faces were getting blistered and scabrous from both the sun and salt water and were excruciatingly painful. After our evening ration of water we prepared for the night as far as we could in our cramped positions. It was so difficult to sleep without something to lean against and it was just impossible to stretch out. No matter how they tried to lie, on the back, the side or face downwards, something always hurt. There was never the briefest respite from the relentless discomfort. And how long those nights seemed to be. No one slept. All they had were snatches of delirium, brief flits in and out of consciousness which left them wondering at times if they were alive or dead.

The weaker they got the more depleted became their reserves of will. It was here that Sister Shipton played an important role. She boosted their confidence. She knew from newspaper reports that men had survived after three or four weeks in an open boat.

By this time everyone was finding it hard to speak, their lips and tongues were swollen and throats parched. Their minds were also being affected. A thought which came to many was how cool and peaceful it would be to slide over the side of the boat and drift away. One man in such a deranged state stood up and stepped into the sea as if he were getting off a No. 66 bus. Two men pulled him back and he was then very sick from swallowing salt water. He did not attempt to do it again. Concentration was difficult. Some people were getting confused, others delirious. The effects of the heat and dehydration were now beginning to show. Something had to be done. Sister Shipton started a cooling down routine.

On the third day we had a dip beside the boat, immersing the body but holding onto the side of the boat whilst someone kept a look out for sharks and the stinging Portuguese man-of-war. One Indian got very badly stung. Despite the risks involved the dip in the sea refreshed and cooled us very much and also passed the time. It gave everyone something to do. Some of us sat on the edge of the boat and dangled our feet in the sea.

By the fifth day they were getting to the bottom of the water barrel and they had to accept the thought that no one was looking for them. They had seen no sign of any other ship or aircraft. Once they thought they heard the throbbing sound of a submarine but regretfully had to accept that it was probably just their imagination.

Sister Shipton had the unenviable task of distributing the meagre ration of water. Even though the prospect of rain seemed remote, she had everything ready to catch whatever might come down with a shower. Not a cloud appeared in the sky.

On the next day, however, hopes were raised. Looming above them and towards the horizon was a dark black cloud. At the back of someone's mind was a bit of childhood hearsay that the colour of clouds indicated their content. A cloud turned black when it was full of water and ready to spill. This cloud certainly looked like one of those low rainy clouds formed of water particles that would drench a cricket pitch before the covers were up. Hurriedly they hauled down the sail and got it ready to catch the downpour. They waited, praying silently. But they were unrewarded. Not a spot of rain fell.

Now people began seeing things, things that were not there. Often smoke was reported. They sent up distress flares but again had to accept the fact that what they believed to be smoke was in fact just low cloud.

However, the Army officer, acting as boat commander, then played a more prominent role. He gave instructions for everyone to keep a sharp look-out for ships passing on the horizon. 'I do believe we shall see something today,' he said, with a confident note to his voice which was caught by those in the boat. Hours passed slowly. Dusk was falling and hope of seeing a ship faded rapidly. So much for the Army officer's hunch. Night came. Sometimes they thought they saw the lights of a passing ship. Then they regretfully agreed that they were looking at low stars.

We had seen nothing even of the other lifeboats from the *Britannia*. Nevertheless the officer commanding the Indian troops kept the survivors who were still alert enough watching for lights of ships which might be called by emergency rockets. On that evening of the fifth day we were settling down for our night-time rest positions when suddenly there was a shout.

'Did you see that, Sir?' asked an Indian soldier. 'Over the port bow there was a light. It looked like a searchlight but very far away.'

Right away the officer was on his feet. He grabbed a boat hook, strapped a flare to it and waved the blazing flames aloft.

Now everyone in the boat waited anxiously, all afraid to be too optimistic. The flare petered out. No response came from the far horizon on which all eyes had been fixed.

'Put another one up, Sir,' shouted a seaman who had been shipwrecked himself before.

The officer held up another blazing flare. Again all eyes concentrated upon that dark spot where the suggestion of a light had been seen. It could have been ten minutes later or less, no one could say for sure, the searchlight appeared again but from a different direction. Again some time later a much smaller light appeared from as far away as the eye could see.

'Look, yes, yes, it's coming this way,' shouted the Indian soldier. In a fervour of excitement arms waved and fingers pointed. The lights were definitely getting bigger and nearer by the minute.

From a hand-held lamp the officer flashed onto the lifeboat's sail the international distress signal, SOS, three short flashes, three long and three short. Immediately came a reply a seaman interpreted as, 'We are coming to pick you up.'

'It was a wonderful sight,' recalled Sister Shipton.

We watched the rescuer's light getting bigger and bigger in the darkness. Then, frighteningly close to us, they switched on the bright searchlight and stopped their ship. Our men eagerly took to the oars and rowed the lifeboat to the side of the ship.

Our greatest fear then was that the Indian troops would get so excited, clambering clumsily about, they would upset the boat. But a few words from their officer brought perfect order.

It was a ship from a neutral country and the crew lowered a ladder down to us. Whilst some were climbing out of the boat, those waiting their turn finished off the last of the water from the barrel. As we climbed slowly up the ladder, the passengers kept cheering and helping us onto the deck. Waiting for us there were trays of hot drinks and food to eat.

What a thrill it was later to have a whole glass of water to drink and then a bed to stretch out in. And perhaps what pleased me as much as anything was that there were still sixty-three of us. We had not lost one during our ordeal.

Though she would be the last to mention it, probably one of the main reasons that all sixty-three survived that distressing experience was the professional nursing care so many received from a seemingly tireless Sister Shipton.

Everyone grew stronger during the next few days, before they arrived at their first port of call – Tenerife in the Canary Islands, where they were received by the British Consul who made arrangements for them to be taken on to Cadiz. From there they went as passengers on a very old bus bumping along the road towards the frontier. That brought surprises for Sister Shipton.

We never realized there would be such a shortage of food in the neutral country through which we had to travel. We tried to buy some food at an 'inn' but they had no food at all. They told us people were dying of starvation in the streets. We tried again at another inn along the road and this time we were more fortunate. They produced fried eggs but they had no bread. Eventually we reached the frontier and crossed into the British Territory of Gibraltar and were taken to a hotel. We waited a few days there until we got a ship to Liverpool.

Sister Shipton and her fellow survivors were amongst the few from the ill-fated SS *Britannia* who lived to tell the tale. Of the 203 crew, 122 were missing and of the 281 passengers, 127 were logged as missing. A later official report showed that one lifeboat sailed 1,600 miles to the coast of Brazil.

Although it had not been so long since Sister Shipton had left Britain on the *Britannia*, she saw her homeland again with fresh eyes as she walked with doctors, men with flat caps and bulging pockets, through the dock gates and into Liverpool.

In her bedraggled, water-stained uniform, she began to feel embarrassed when she got into the city centre. Women there had taken heed of those notices on the boarded up windows of bombed shops: 'BUSINESS AS USUAL'. Young and old women were going to work in smart outfits of 'utility cloth'. They had heeded the oft-repeated advice in women's magazines, such as 'There is no excuse for a woman to get slack just because her man is away serving at the front or in camp. A woman who is unkempt and ill dressed soon loses her morale. It takes courage to carry on as though nothing out of the ordinary is happening but that is the kind of courage women must have if we are to keep alive the vital thing Hitler has menaced – civilization.'

The much-bombed Liverpool women were certainly showing that kind of courage and enjoying it. But Sister Shipton, who had drawn a railway warrant but little else from the RTO at Lime Street Station, boarded a London train and somehow felt as though she had arrived in a different world, a world in which women were living normal lives.

She was more aware now of how many women were in uniform, and as she turned the magazine's pages she realized how difficult it was to find an advertisement which did not feature a woman in smart uniform. And here she was so scruffily dressed in her nurse's outfit. It made her feel even more unkempt.

Her only reason for going to London was to visit the Matron-in-Chief for instructions as to her next posting. She was just leaving Euston Station when she saw approaching her two sisters of the QARNNS. They looked as though they had stepped out of a tailor's nursing uniform catalogue. This was just too much for Sister Shipton. The courage which so recently had stood her in so much stead evaporated. Quickly she turned in her tracks and hid in a side-street doorway until the two smart sisters had passed.

Her interview with the Matron-in-Chief was brief. A posting order would be sent to her whilst she was at home on leave. She would also be sent a grant to cover the cost of a new uniform. She had done well to survive her ordeal. Very well. Now she could go. And that was that.

Her ordeal was at last over.

Shortly before Christmas she received the award of Commendation. By that time she had also received a cheque which was barely enough to pay for a new uniform.

Parsimonious though this payment was, it was bountiful indeed when compared with that which the seamen from the same shipwreck were given. They received nothing. Incredible though it might seem today, their pay was stopped from the moment they jumped into the sea from the sinking vessel. They were deemed to have broken their contract and had 'left the ship'![5]

Being shipwrecked was an experience that many nurses had to face. Of the hundreds who lost their lives during the Second World War, most did so as a result of enemy action at sea. This is not the place to recount all of those experiences, although some can be found in accounts of the assault landings on the beaches of Sicily, Salerno, Anzio, Crete, the Far East and Normandy which are given elsewhere in this book and also in the companion volume, *Front-line Nurse*.

One other incident, however, the sinking of the SS *Laconia*, deserves a special mention because hundreds of people needlessly lost their lives when it went down, not because of the actions of the German submarines but as a result of the stupidity of Allied airmen. At least it looked that way when all the facts became known at the Nuremberg War Crime Trials, where German U-boat captains gave evidence on oath. The story of the tragedy also deserves telling because of the amazing fortitude of one nursing sister, Doris Hawkins of the QAIMNS and it is the subject of the next chapter.

7   Humanity in the Midst of War

Even in the Midst of a war one must recognize gratefully the humanity shown to us survivors by the personnel of the German submarine which picked us up. I shall always feel grateful for it, even though I know that the German captain who was so courteous and humane in his treatment of us was also responsible for our plight.

Sister Doris Hawkins, QAIMNS

It was a scene which could have come straight out of a film. The young mother standing on the hospital steps held baby Sally up to her face, murmured a few words and then gently offered the child to Sister Doris Hawkins. At the last moment she pulled the baby back for a final cuddle and then quickly put her in Doris's arms.

'She'll be all right with me now. I'll get her home safely for you,' said Doris.

The young mother said something then which Doris Hawkins never forgot. The exact words echoed for ever in her memory; she had not been expecting such a remark. 'Never forget,' said the child's mother, 'if anything happens and Sally has to go, that you must do all you can to save yourself . . . we cannot replace you, and you have work to do.'

After five years in the British Military Hospital in Jerusalem, Sister Hawkins had been looking forward to going back to the UK. But she had never for one moment thought she would be going home in charge of a 14-month-old baby. However, as with all her other duties, Doris Hawkins just accepted the situation and there would be her friend Mary on the ship, who could help her to look after Sally. She was a contented child, ate well and slept through the night.

It had been hard work at Jerusalem, with battle casualties coming up from Cairo, Alexandria and the Canal Zone. Many were recovering from serious war wounds and some were medical cases – malaria, sand-fly fever, chest trouble and the awful tropical bilharzia disease, said to be one of the greatest plagues of the world. Soldiers caught the disease by drinking or swimming in infected water. Parasites entered the body's organs through the stomach or by penetrating the skin and entering the blood stream, and laid eggs which hatched into moving larvae. Patients had to be given regular injections, otherwise the disease could go on for years or lead to a slow death. Doris was not sorry to be leaving all that behind.

The posting had come without warning. Suddenly one day, she and her friend Mary were told to pack one small suitcase, send off their heavy luggage and be ready to move at a moment's notice for the next boat home.

When they finally boarded the ss *Laconia*, their cabin was big enough for Doris and the baby even though the rest of the ship was packed with soldiers returning to the UK and 1,800 Italian prisoners of war. The meals too were much better than those in the Jerusalem hospital and consequently the long voyage home started off pleasantly enough.

They were almost halfway home when, on 12 September 1942 Doris came up from dinner and, as was her usual habit, looked in her cabin to see if Sally was all right. She was asleep alongside the 'panic bag' everyone had ready in case of submarine attack.

In that summer of 1942, Admiral Doenitz was basking in the glory of his huge success in the Western Atlantic. In seven months his U-boats had sunk 4 million tons of Allied shipping. Adolf Hitler was greatly pleased and sent him glowing messages of praise. Amongst the officers on the look-out for suitable targets in the Western Atlantic then was Werner Hartenstein, Knight's Cross, commander of U-boat U156. It was in the late afternoon of that same memorable day, 12 September, that he was alerted to the looming grey shape of what looked to him like a British armed merchant cruiser. This was not surprising because that was exactly what the 19,000-ton ss *Laconia* had been before it was converted into a troopship. Indeed, it still carried some armament and was therefore a legitimate target.

Quickly and efficiently, Hartenstein gave orders for it to be attacked. He was not to know that aboard were nurses from a British hospital, the civilian wives and children of servicemen returning to the UK, and also nearly 1,800 Italian prisoners of war – German allies – on their way from North African prison camps to internment in the USA. Torpedoes were fired.

Doris Hawkins had just reached her cabin when the first torpedo hit the engine room. The whole ship shivered, and the cabin seemed to lift in the air and sway curiously. An odd noise, discordant and frightening, came from the bowels of the ship. Doris's first thought was of the baby. Hurriedly she wrapped the sleeping child in a blanket and forced her way through the crowded passageways onto the boat-deck. Terror gripped her. But her training came to her rescue, as she remembered the tight-lipped Matron of her training hospital admonishing young probationers to 'get a grip of yourselves'. The words echoed in her mind: 'Get a grip.'

At the boat station, waves were hitting the ship's side, soaking everyone. Some of the lifeboats had been swept away. Sailors were having difficulty in swinging the remaining boats over the listing side of the ship. In the dark, noise and confusion reigned. There were not going to be enough lifeboats.

Doris nuzzled her face into the warmth of the blanket round baby Sally's face. She was lying quite still, making only little cooing noises. At that moment Doris felt a firm hand upon her shoulder. A voice spoke into her ear. She turned and saw a young Fleet Air Arm officer she had met once or twice before. Without waiting for permission he took the baby from her and hurriedly, with the help of another officer, wedged it into the back of his greatcoat. He tied a blanket round his waist to hold the baby firmly in place at his back and then clambered down the rope ladder into the mass of people packed into the swaying lifeboat. Doris followed. A strong wind was now blowing. It whipped the spray off the grey and heaving sea.

Doris tottered from her unbalanced position amongst the arms and legs of the panic-stricken mass of humanity sprawling on the bottom of the lifeboat. She reached for the child. The officer held the baby in his outstretched arms. Doris had almost got her hands round its small body when a huge wave crashed against the side of the ship. The lifeboat tipped and then capsized completely, flinging everyone into the rough sea.

Baby Sally was never seen again.

Doris Hawkins felt herself sinking lower in the water. Her lungs, filled with a mixture of air and oily water, reacted, making her want to cough. She pressed her lips close together and fought her way to the surface. Her hand touched a floating wooden spar. She clung to it desperately, spluttering and gasping for air. Two Italians pulled her onto a raft. There she lay, retching violently, her stomach trying to rid itself of all the thick, oily water she had swallowed. Time passed and she was able to get her bearings on the raft. Near to her was an RAF Squadron Leader she knew. His name was Wells. Now he seemed to be taking charge, reassuring the shivering groups on the raft that they would be all right as it drifted away from the sinking ship, and that they would all be picked up in the morning.

It was broad daylight when the U-boat surfaced. Its commander approached closer to the lifeboats and raft to inspect his handiwork. He saw soldiers in Italian uniform and perhaps wondered what damage he might have done to the already strained relations between Hitler and the Italian Duce, Mussolini.

Touched with remorse, perhaps, he then set in motion a chain of events the effects of which very nearly culminated in the execution of his commander, Admiral Doenitz, himself.

What he did was certainly humanitarian in intention. There were a great many women and children in the lifeboats, hundreds of miles from land, and his U-boat was a large one. At obvious risk to its safety he ordered his men to bring the survivors on board, regardless of whatever uniform they wore. Those who could not be accommodated in the U-boat were put into the biggest and most seaworthy of the lifeboats which were then roped together so that they could be towed.

Incredible as it might have seemed to any of his enemies then listening, and to the reader today, he compounded the risks he was taking by transmitting the following message on the international emergency wavelength:

If any ship will assist the shipwrecked *Laconia* crew I will not attack her, provided I am not attacked by ship or air force. I picked up 193 survivors 46'52" south, 11'26" west. German submarine 0600hrs Sept. 13th.'

The story of what happened next becomes even more like a far-fetched novel and less like the real wartime world. However, the fact remains that Admiral Doenitz, on reading the signal, ordered two more German submarines and one Italian to go to the rescue at full speed. As if this were not enough he went as far as to order the Vichy French at Dakar and on the West African coast to do what they could to help.

Whilst these signals were flashing to and fro across the South Atlantic, Hartenstein in U156 was cruising at a snail's pace with 200 survivors packed below deck, another 70 clinging onto the rail of the narrow deck of the submarine at sea level and four lifeboats in tow. Others on rafts he tried to shepherd as best he could.

Within twenty-four hours the first of the rescue U-boats arrived to pick up survivors. It helped to distribute them more evenly and take them to a rendezvous already arranged with a Vichy French ship. For the next thirty-six hours Hartenstein proceeded at little more than a walking pace. For his own safety he bedecked the U-boat with a huge Red Cross flag.

Sister Hawkins was then on the U-boat and remembered vividly how it was for them all.

Our legs were swollen and stiff from the salt water and sunburn but we were looked after very well – in fact better than the 150 Italians with us. Our clothes were taken from us and dried and we were given hot tea and coffee, black bread and butter, rusks and jam. The Germans treated us with great kindness and respect the whole time; they were really sorry for our plight. One brought us eau-de-Cologne and another cold cream for our sunburn, which was really sore. I did not hear 'Heil Hitler' once and I saw no swastikas. The commandant was particularly charming and helpful; he could scarcely have done more had he been entertaining us in peacetime.

A message then came from the Vichy French which brought great hope to the survivors. A cruiser was on its way at high speed and would rendezvous with them within two days and would take the survivors to Dakar.

Amazingly, it seems in retrospect, several German submarines surfaced and then set about the task of shepherding lifeboats together by towing them in turn to the rendezvous. They collected fourteen. It seemed to Doris then that the worst was certainly over. Unfortunately it was only just beginning. Far worse times were to follow.

The U-boat look-out spotted a four-engined aircraft with US markings approaching – a B24 Liberator bomber. After sending out so many signals about his rescue efforts, the U-boat commander was not particularly worried; indeed, as he later said in the Nuremberg War Crimes court, 'I felt secure with the proof of my peaceful intentions shown by the Red Cross flag stretched across the bridge facing the aircraft's line of approach.'[2]

The aircraft flew off. An hour later another four-engined Liberator bomber came swooping in, making five low-level runs, bombing and strafing the boats. Hartenstein's submarine was hit, several lifeboats smashed and overturned and, as blood spread over the water, sharks swarmed to the scene.

Doris remembered how it was then: 'The submarine shivered and shook and one end compartment was damaged. It was a dreadful sensation; we knew that one direct hit could send us to the bottom. The explosions through the water were tremendous.'

Hartenstein reported the attack to headquarters and was immediately ordered to submerge and abandon all attempts to rescue the survivors of the *Laconia*. But he could not submerge with all those additional people on board and was forced to put them into the shark-infested water. Doris Hawkins recalled how distressed he and the crew were. They took the survivors as close to the lifeboats as possible. 'We were, once more, swimming for our lives,' recalled Doris.

They swam for fifty minutes. Doris, a very weak swimmer was towed for most of the time by Squadron Leader Wells, a strong swimmer but ill himself. Eventually he had to leave her treading water whilst he swam off to tell one of the lifeboats to row towards her and her friend Mary. Slowly the lifeboat came over and picked them up.

When daylight broke he started the survivors singing to keep up their spirits. When he waved his arms as if conducting a choir, Doris noticed blood trickling from under his greatcoat sleeve. She asked to look at his arm. There was a very nasty gaping wound near his shoulder. She looked for some material to tear up and stanch the flow but realized there was nothing anyone could do for such a pulped mass of flesh.

Later, slowly and with obvious pain, the Squadron Leader took off his watch, turned it over to show Doris the address inscribed on the back. He looked at her and said as clearly as he could muster the energy to do, 'To my mother.' Doris, surprised at the way he had so suddenly weakened, told him she would take the watch to his mother if she survived.

In that 30-foot lifeboat with Doris and Mary were sixty-six people. 'Most of the others who were in the submarine failed to reach a boat and perished there in the Atlantic when rescue was almost at hand,' recalled Doris. 'Squadron Leader Wells died ten days after he had helped me into the boat.' Most of those in the lifeboat were destined not to survive.

One can imagine Hartenstein's feelings upon being attacked after taking so much care of the survivors. Admiral Doenitz was so angry about the ruthlessness of the Allied airmen that his reaction to the episode was equally harsh and ruthless. He radioed all his U-boat commanders:

No attempt must be made to rescue members of ships sunk, and this includes picking up persons in the water and putting them in lifeboats, righting capsized lifeboats and handing over food and water. Rescue runs counter to the most elementary demands of warfare and the destruction of enemy crews and ships. The only personnel to be picked up should be captains and engineers when interrogation would be of value to U-boat crews.

His message ended with the words: 'Be severe. Remember that in his bombing attacks on German cities, the enemy has no regard for women and children.' This order was the basis upon which a war-crimes charge was brought against Doenitz at the postwar Nuremberg trials of leading Nazis.

So it was that on 17 September 1942, just as Sister Hawkins and the other survivors from the *Laconia* believed they were being brought to safety, they were abandoned. By order.

The lifeboat into which Doris and Mary were hauled was crowded, and during the next twenty-seven days everyone became gradually weaker. Their pores closed up completely, they became light-headed and dreamed of water, the sun and salt water rotted their clothes until they hung in shreds on their thin bodies. Sores on their arms, legs and bodies discharged pus, fingers and toes became septic and ugly boils erupted and discharged pus freely.

To their amazement, out of the mist of dawn one day, a long grey shape rose out of the sea close to them. It was a German U-boat. The commandant asked what they needed. Hurriedly he gave them some water, hot coffee and bandages. Just before he submerged again he told them to head north-north-east, where the nearest land lay. 'It's six hundred miles away,' he said. He looked hard at them all in the boat, shook his head and added, 'You'll never make it.' Then he was gone.

Doris's friend Mary shivered all through the cold nights. Doris lay close to her, trying to make the most of their combined body heat. One morning, whilst she was still asleep, Mary just stopped breathing; she was dead. Those near to her in the boat tried to sing a verse of 'Abide with me' as they lowered her body into the water, but the effort was pathetic.

Now Doris felt very much alone. She was now the only woman amongst some sixty men; the others had all died. As a nurse she felt helpless too; she had no drugs, no dressings, no stimulants and her only surgical instruments were a razor blade and a penknife. With these she opened septic fingers and toes, cleaned them in sea water and tried to explain to everyone the importance of not infecting each other.

A doctor named Pursglow, who had tried hard with Doris to help those who were suffering, developed a deep infection in his left hand and arm, and also in his right foot and leg. Doris used her razor blade to open his finger and this discharged pus well, but nothing came out of his foot. The next day his glands began to swell, and red lines streaked his arm and leg. He was now too ill to move. He lay there, not even taking his small ration of water. More septic places appeared all over his body. Blood poisoning had set in firmly.

It was on the nineteenth day after the ship was torpedoed that he came to a decision. He heaved himself painfully up the side of the boat and then, in a voice stronger than anyone had heard for days, he said: 'I cannot do anything more for you. I am a source of danger to you all. It is better I should go.' He took a long look round everybody, said 'Goodbye' and stepped over the side of the boat.

After the third week at sea few people had enough saliva to eat the small ration of biscuit. Only a miracle could now save them. They prayed for rain.

A torrential downpour drenched them the next morning. Almost deliriously, they collected 6 gallons of water in two tins as it ran from the sail. It was bright yellow from dye in the sailcloth, but no one cared. The rain poured down until sunset and by that time the bottom of the boat was inches deep in water.

New hope came not only with the rain but with the appearance of birds, new birds in the sky. Then a leaf floated by in the sea. Could land be near?

On Thursday, 8 October, one of the naval ratings became excited. His eyes brightened. He beckoned to Doris. 'Sister, can you see anything over there?' He pointed. 'Don't disturb the others in case it's nothing, but I think I can see a ship.'

For half an hour, as they gazed intently ahead, the shape seemed to multiply. Perhaps it was a convoy. But the ships did not move as a convoy would. They knew then that their prayers had been answered again. It was land!

By the end of the day they could make out trees and hills. They dropped their sea anchor for the night. The next morning an off-shore breeze blew them gently but steadily away from the land. Towards the end of the afternoon the wind direction changed. Now they had an on-shore breeze. It was about this time too that a small flying boat with the Union Jack painted on its fuselage came down and circled overhead. It flew low and dropped a lifejacket to which was tied a pillowcase full of fruit. Unfortunately it broke on impact and only an apple, one pear and a banana were saved. But on the life-jacket was scrawled quite clearly: 'OK. Help coming.'

Night fell and the boat continued to drift. Ahead they could see walls of spray. Then it happened. Two waves took hold of the boat and washed it firmly onto a sandy beach – the only sandy beach for miles along that rocky coastline. Anywhere else and they would have perished on the rocks, for no one would have had enough strength left to swim.

They crawled on hands and knees beyond the reach of the tide. Sixteen of them had survived the 700-mile voyage in an open boat. Sixteen only out of the original sixty-eight.

Some local people led them to an African village where they discovered that they had landed in the West African republic of Liberia, formed in the mid-nineteenth century as a home for emanci-pated slaves. Some of the locals spoke English. They took Doris and her companions into their homes and brought oranges, huge bananas and ripe plums for them to eat. The survivors boiled water from the creek and ate sparingly of the fruit, fearing harmful effects after their long fast. The next morning some women brought more food: coconut milk and raw eggs warmed in the sun.

From one man who spoke better English than the rest they learnt that there was a small trading town, Grand Bassa, further down the coast. There the Dutch East Africa Company had its store. Three of the men from the lifeboat who could walk set off slowly for the town to ask for help. Four days later they arrived back with a boat to take everyone to the little town.

From Grand Bassa cables were sent round the world and soon, via a trawler and then a destroyer, Doris Hawkins reached Freetown where she was examined by a doctor and immediately admitted to hospital. It was then that the inevitable nervous reaction set in.

Nightmares came with awful regularity. She dreaded the nights, for as soon as she closed her eyes she could see the faces of all those who had been her companions in the lifeboat. When sleep came, scenes of horror were relived with increasing intensity. Such night terrors were to haunt her for months. It was six weeks before she was fit enough to board the *Laconia*'s sister ship. It sailed unescorted for 3,000 miles through those same U-boat-infested waters, a nightmare voyage for Doris, in which every bang made her leap from her bunk.

She landed in London exactly four months after leaving the hospital in Jerusalem, thankful and wondering how it was that she had survived when so many had not. It was much later that the real cost of the sinking of the *Laconia* and the attack by the US aircraft came to be known. The official figures show that over 2,200 people died.[3]

What impressed Doris about the whole experience was the fact that the German officers and men of the submarine which torpedoed them had not been corrupted by the Nazi policy of brutality. They had shown genuine compassion and a desire to save as many lives as possible after they had done their duty in torpedoing the ship.

It is worth noting that there were other instances of German naval officers showing compassion in saving lives after sinking a ship. Two Army nursing sisters had a truly remarkable experience of this when they were returning to the UK from Australia after having escorted children from Britain there under the government evacuation scheme in 1940. Most of the escorts went home direct from Sydney, but Sisters Betty Sandbach and Geraldine Edge sailed via New Zealand.[4]

They left Auckland on the *Rangitane* on 24 November 1940 and were enjoying almost peacetime luxury cruising when they were wakened by a strange sound, more like a scraping than a shell or bomb. They wondered whether they should go up on deck or not but decided that everything must be all right as the lights were still on, the ship was still moving fast and no alarm had been sounded.

They were about to settle down in bed again when there was a tremendous blast and a clamour which reverberated throughout the ship. This time the two young women leapt from their bunks and had just got trousers over their pyjamas when a shell went clean through their deck, bringing the whole cabin crashing upon their heads. Flying glass cut Betty Sandbach's head and eye, falling timber knocked Geraldine Edge out, but she came to her senses on the boat deck, not knowing how she got there but with a lifebelt someone else had tied around her.

What she saw then brought a rush of dismay and fear. Close to their ship was a big black vessel flying the crooked cross of the swastika and alongside that were two smaller ships flying the Japanese flag of the rising sun. No one panicked. All passengers took their places in the lifeboats as if it were a routine practice. Once on the water each lifeboat was visited in turn by a German officer in a motorboat. Courteously and in perfectly enunciated English he directed each lifeboat to one or other of the waiting ships.

The two nursing sisters were sent to the black German ship. Once alongside it, they looked up at a rope ladder which seemed to stretch endlessly upwards. They had to climb up to the deck and from there were sent down to a large room in the hold. Fifteen women gathered there. An hour later a German sailor came down with a jug of black coffee and one cup. Another came with slices of black bread spread with lard.

It must have been night-time, for men came down and spread a few mattresses on the floor. As they took their time arranging them there was some good-natured banter, some in German and some in English. An observer would never have thought that here were two enemies, said by the newspapers to hate each other. 'The German sailors were kind and never rude, and obviously bore us no hatred whatever. The officers questioned us a great deal but were always courteous. The medical attention was excellent,' recalled Geraldine Edge.

A heart-rending experience came next morning. All the women were taken onto the deck where they saw a stretcher with the body of a woman lying under the Union Jack. One of the female escorts had died that morning. The ship stopped. All 150 crew members lined up and the swastika was ceremoniously lowered to half-mast. The German Captain spoke at length, pausing as he went along for his words to be translated into English. Sailors came to attention, officers saluted and men removed caps. The end of the stretcher was raised, pivoting at the rail side and the body slid over the side. Within a few days a message from the Red Cross would bring the news to the girl's parents.

The next day they were rowed over to a bigger ship, more like a peacetime liner. More sad news awaited them there. They met more of the escorts and heard that five of those young women who had volunteered to accompany the evacuee children had been killed outright by the torpedo explosion. Two nursing sisters had been badly wounded; one of them had to have an arm amputated.

The new vessel was a German supply ship commanded by a real character – an elderly salt with a beard, a cigar and a dog. He made his rounds of the ship every day and always made time to chat to the nurses. He told them he had many American friends, for he had been with his shipping line for twenty-five years.

It was an extraordinary time for the women imprisoned on that supply ship. Hardly a day passed without some incident. The raiders caught small cargo ships going with Christmas traffic to various islands in the Pacific, and every time this happened four or five women and about fifty crew would be taken on board the supply ship. Whenever one of these operations was about to take place the nursing sisters and other women were always locked in their cabins, but they could roam freely about the deck at other times and again there was cheerful chaffing between the German crew and the women; the Germans said Britannia no longer ruled the waves but cheerfully agreed that their turn could come next.

For three and a half weeks the raiders carried on taking ships and crews until, with over 700 prisoners on board, the German captain decided food and space were running out. The next surprise for the nursing sisters came when they were told that all prisoners would be put ashore on an island with enough food for four days, but with no cooking equipment. In charge of them would be Captain Upton, the senior ship's officer from the *Rangitane*.

The great day came; everyone was excited. Was it going to be a Robinson Crusoe life? It was not. Waiting for the lifeboats coming ashore were two white men and their wives, who lived on a planta-tion 10 miles from the beach and had not seen any white people for nearly a year. The women were taken to the plantation by the only truck on the island, in groups of twenty at a time. The men had to walk. A tea of bread and butter, coconuts and pawpaws was waiting for them when they arrived.

It was a beautiful island. The women slept on the floor of the plantation house and the men built wigwam-like structures. There was a lot of boisterous tomfoolery, and it resembled a scout camp.

Before leaving their prisoners on the island the Germans gave them one of their lifeboats and told them there was another island 80 miles away which had a wireless. In return for the boat the prisoners had to promise not to use it for forty-eight hours. If that promise were broken the raider would return and pound the island with shells.

The lifeboat was not used. Fortunately, unknown to the Germans there was a motorboat on the island, which set off as soon as the forty-eight-hour period was over. It returned on Christmas Eve at 11.30 in the morning with food and a message saying a liner would arrive the next day to take everyone to Australia.

From then on there were welcomes all the way. At Brisbane a formal welcoming party took the women to a hotel to have a hot bath and lunch. First-class railway sleeping compartments were there for their trip to Sydney and a package of underclothes and dresses was left for all the women. On every carriage seat were chocolates, cigarettes, fruit and handkerchiefs.

At Sydney there was yet another official reception. The ordeal for the two nursing sisters had turned into an amazing adventure holiday, the like of which they would never experience again.

They had nothing but praise for the officers of the German raider, who had treated them with such courtesy and care for their well-being. They would certainly have agreed with the sentiments of Doris Hawkins when she said: 'Even in the midst of a war one must recognize gratefully the humanity shown to us survivors.'

8   Third Time Unlucky

We were the remnants of our damaged ships
And we were homeward bound,
We possessed what we stood up in,
Some begged, some borrowed, some found.

Bernard Hallas, Corporal Royal Marines,
HMS *Warspite*, 'The Rabble Comes Home'[1]

The awful news came without warning.

During the war, the nurses serving in West Africa could send a message home to the United Kingdom and receive a reply by means of a cable, which cost half a crown. Messages were restricted to those listed against a code number so that for 'I am well' for example, there would be a corresponding number. Vera Bryan sent one every week and received some occasionally herself. Like telegrams, though, cables from home were usually received with some apprehension.

I opened mine one day, looked at the number and then at the list to see what the message was. Against my number were the words, 'Your mother has died.'

She had been living with my married sister Alice after my father was killed in the bombing, but the injuries and the shock had undermined her health. She was never well again.

It was a shock for me, but being so far away from England it did not seem real. Also there was with me all the time I was in Nigeria a strange feeling of foreboding. I can feel it all now as I read letters I wrote to my sister, which she kept.

Typical of that feeling was my mention of knitting in those letters. I used to knit a lot in my spare time because British customs regulations then prevented anyone from importing wool when they returned from an over-seas posting. You could not take in balls of wool, but you could pack knitted woollen garments. Perhaps it was to do with clothes rationing. There was plenty of wool in Ibadan so I knitted a lot of cardigans. In letters to my sister Emily I often wrote, 'I hope after all this knitting we don't get torpedoed on my way home and lose all my work and wool.'

There was plenty of time for knitting. Life was boring in the extreme, with very little real nursing to be done, and our efforts to train natives to become efficient orderlies was an unrewarding task, Occasionally, though, we would have a patient who needed all our 'tender loving care'.

One of these was a corporal suffering from blackwater fever. The death rate from this fever, which was often a sequel to malaria, was high, for there were not the drugs available then that there are today and survival depended upon constant care and attention. Rather illogically, the patient's water was not black; his urine was in fact red. This was owing to the breakdown of the red blood cells by some malarial toxin. Intensive care was needed to ensure that the patient drank as much fluid as possible and was kept away from quinine and other anti-malarial drugs.

When possible, patients were nursed in a darkened and mosquito-proofed room. The foot of the bed had to be raised, and all movement of the patient in bed had to be done with utmost care. Any sudden exertion could cause instant death.

Vera remembered well how her patient responded to treatment. In a letter to her sister she wrote: 'It was touch and go whether he would recover. So few people did. Fortunately my patient did get better and was sent back home to the UK. He was such a good patient he deserved to get better.'

Many of the patients in that hospital were casualties of the hot and humid conditions. In the skin ward were patients with faces disfig-ured by red blisters filled with yellow pus and other, older, blisters encrusted with the yellow scabs of impetigo. There were many other examples of terrible blistering allergies in the skin ward but scabies predominated. The treatment meted out to those patients by nurses might today seem rather vicious, as Ann Radloff (née Reeves) recalled.

The soldier had to strip naked and stand before the nurse whilst she scrubbed his entire body with a stiff brush, getting into every crack and cranny. She then painted him all over with a stinging solution of Benzyl Benzoate. One can only marvel at the way those soldiers accepted such ignominy and degradation, standing without any covering whatsoever whilst we sisters carried out this horrible procedure. I felt depersonalized doing it but it must have been much worse for them.

Much worse it might have been but it was then the only treatment available to relieve the awful itching which drove many frantic as the small scabies mite, almost invisible to the naked eye, burrowed under the surface of the skin. It was commonly found between the fingers and on the front of the wrists, and became a troublesome, prickly tickle when the body got overheated, particularly in bed.

Most nurses disliked giving a scabies patient his treatment but they got on with the job and just counted the days until their repatriation date. Boredom was the bugbear. Vera said:

In the Sisters' Mess itself there was little to keep boredom at bay. One sister was heard to say of the hospital, 'Our casualties here are mainly those suffering from foot rot, skin rot, gut rot or nut rot.'

It wasn't easy to get far away from the hospital for a break because there wasn't much in the way of transport apart from the rare dilapidated taxis with incompetent, swashbuckling drivers fancying themselves as racing drivers, who scared the living daylights out of you in the short ride from the Sisters' Mess to the European Club, where we might get a game of bridge or tennis. Occasionally there would be a dance.

When all else failed there was always letter writing to fill the spare time. But even that was not easy. Apart from having little news and not having regular letters to which she could reply there was also the actual physical problem of putting pen to paper. Before she started she put blotting paper under her wrist to stop the paper sticking to her sweaty hand and mop up any drips that fell from her forehead.

In a letter to her sister Emily, dated 11 June 1942, Vera mentioned her rather unusual romance with a man called George, which had begun in England years earlier. She had received another letter from him. He was a businessman in a reserved occupation in Birmingham who had met Vera shortly after her eighteenth birthday. She had been looking after the baby of a friend of her sister's, and the friend had said to her one day: 'You'd like my brother, George.' A meeting was arranged. Afterwards the friend asked her brother what he thought of Vera. 'Not much. A bit thin. Not impressed at all.'

Despite his apparent lack of enthusiasm, George kept in touch. They wrote to each other regularly and became fond of each other. Another bit of news from Vera in the same letter was another good reason for coming home soon. 'It would be lovely to be in England after living in my little wooden hut in the bush,' she wrote.

We can almost watch the bush growing up around us now that the rains have started. The sand flies and mosquitoes are such a trial, I spend my days scratching bites. We are continually being bitten by all kinds of flies, big fat ones, small ones and mosquitoes but they do not raise the same big bumps as they did at first and now I hardly notice them. But I did feel a small lump on the back of my head the other day and I thought it might be a pimple or boil that needed squeezing. My friend Joan said she'd help me and started to squeeze. She got so far and then saw something coming out. It was a maggot waving its head to and fro at her. Very skilfully she got the whole thing out alive. We put it in a matchbox. These jumbo maggots are fairly common out here. They usually come in a batch. Luckily I haven't had another.

She had been worried about the fact that she was losing weight, and with her nursing experience imagined fearful causes. It was therefore reassuring when one day she went to a modern lavatory and glanced down to find she had passed a huge tapeworm.

We never knew what we might find lurking for us next. I was doing the rounds of the ward, talking to each patient by his bedside as I went, when suddenly the native orderly with me put out his arm and stopped me in mid-pace. He pointed down to the foot of the bed. There, wrapped tightly round the leg of the bed was a snake. He motioned me to stand still. He dashed out of the ward and came back moments later with two other orderlies, each of whom carried a machete. They raised them ready to strike then one took two swift paces forward and brought his sharp machete down on the snake's body. It partly unrolled and the other man then struck with his. Within seconds there was blood and bits of wriggling snake on the floor.

You can imagine how we longed to be away from West Africa.

Every week Vera wrote to Emily and it was clear from her letters how much she was looking forward to being back in the UK. But she did not like the thought of the sea voyage at all.

By August 1942 she had bought presents for relatives and friends at home, mainly leather bags, belts and native ornaments. She had been knitting non-stop in every spare moment. On 13 September she wrote to Emily and once again echoed her long-standing fear: 'I have knitted three jumpers and one vest in the last few weeks so hope I am not torpedoed and lose all my luggage. I should be annoyed!'

Annoyed?

Vera was now very run down and weighed only 6 stone. Her legs ached for no apparent reason and she was bothered by back pain. 'I look a bit scraggy and I do envy anyone on their way home,' she wrote. 'A year in this country is about as much as anyone can stand. They said when we arrived that fifteen months would be the longest we might have to stay,' she wrote.

One day the magic piece of paper arrived. She held it at arm's length and danced around the ward. Even a soldier who had been desperately ill with blackwater fever smiled. All the rumours about the home leave ship were now confirmed.

All the way back to the Sisters' Mess that lunchtime she sang to herself with gusto the hopeful song of all time-expired troops – 'Bless 'Em All'.

> They say there's a troopship just leaving Bombay
> Bound for old Blighty's shore
> Heavily laden with time-expired men
> Bound for the land they adore.

Eleven of us were selected for various reasons, some because they were genuinely 'time-expired' and ready to return to the UK but I think the doctors and the Matron were beginning to worry about my health and thought I had better get back to Britain before I faded away completely. I was all skin and bone.

Nurses and medical officers began to rush around trying to buy more last minute presents. I took care to fold and pack all the cardigans, jumpers and twin sets I had knitted, and when I saw them all together I had once again that strange feeling of foreboding I had often written about in my letters home: 'I hope we're not torpedoed and lose all this hard work.'

In a flurry of activity the remaining days passed quickly and in the last week of October 1942, Vera arrived in Lagos ready to embark – except for one last thing she had to do.

I had not been to a hairdresser for months and months so I looked for one near the port. My eye was caught by a sign outside one shop saying 'Ladies' hair straightened'. Impulsively I went in and asked if they could make ladies' hair curly as well as straight. I was assured they could. And they did – with too much success!

I took one look in the mirror and shrank back in horror. My hair was twisted, crimped and curled into a frizzy mass!

Fortunately for her peace of mind, Vera had little time to worry about her new hairstyle. Earlier than expected, they were called forward to embark on the Blue Funnel passenger and cargo ship *Stentor*. At last, thought the nurses, we are now really on our way home after all those false starts and rumours of the last few weeks. They would not have felt quite so relieved had they known the *Stentor*'s run of bad luck so far in the war. It was one of the first ships to be involved in a convoy collision, which it survived only to be bombed and machine-gunned by British aircraft in Jeddah.

Third time unlucky? The crew could be excused if that thought occasionally crossed their minds.

But to all the new passengers, and particularly the eleven nursing sisters, that October of 1942, *Stentor* looked good. Designed for the Far East passenger and cargo trade and built in 1926, she had some unusual characteristics. She had two decks – a feature which would save Vera's life – and five holds with watertight bulkheads. Curiously in the middle of these was a huge, deep tank, filled with palm oil.

We heard the ship was called 'the bachelor ship' because there were only four other women – stewardesses and wives – on board besides ourselves. Shortly after embarkation we sailed for Freetown, where we stayed for three days whilst the convoy assembled. During that time we felt as though we were incarcerated in an oven which was getting hotter with each passing hour. There was no air-conditioning. However, we felt better with the good news of Montgomery's desert victories.

They would not have felt better if they had known the full story of the North African campaign strategy – a plan which would bring the lives of so many young men and women in that convoy forming up in Freetown to a premature and tragic end. With hindsight it appears that both the British and the German High Commands were making plans that would place Convoy SL125 in grave jeopardy.

Admiral Doenitz was ordering a pack of U-boats to concentrate near the Canary Islands, while the forty-two ships of Convoy SL125 cleared the port of Freetown and headed towards those same islands. Amongst them was the Blue Funnel ship *Stentor*, carrying 125 passengers and a crew of 121.

Vera, having talked to naval officers of the Corvette K53 on escort duty with the convoy, was later sure that the departure was deliberately timed as a decoy. Because at that very same time as the Freetown convoy was about to attract the attention of the German submarine pack, the largest amphibious invasion force in the history of warfare set sail from Britain into the Atlantic and on south to the invasion beaches off French North Africa. In that force were 300 warships, 370 merchant ships, and 107,000 assault troops.

A few days later, when Vera's convoy approached the Canary Islands, the U-boat commanders must have rubbed their hands with glee when they saw over forty merchantmen steaming towards them.

The first thing we on the *Stentor* knew of the submarine attack was at 7.30 p.m. There was a tremendous thud amidships near to where I was standing with my friend Joan Moon. After that things moved rapidly into a lurid hell. Joan ran to our cabin to pick up her 'panic bag' but I decided to go straight to our appointed lifeboat station. As I drew aside the thick blackout curtain at the top of the companionway, a wall of flame gushed straight towards me. I dropped the curtain and stumbled towards the alternative exit, slipping and sliding on palm oil that had somehow got all over the decks. I fell full length and the crowd of passengers pushing behind me carried on trampling over my back until someone helped me to my feet.

I heard later that the torpedo had hit the deep tank which was full of palm oil and it had been spattered all over the bridge structure, setting it ablaze. Captain Williams was severely burnt and the Vice-Commodore of the convoy was blinded by the flames.

The lifeboat drill at first went smoothly. Five boats were lowered. The ship was sinking very quickly. By the time I got to the lifeboat station, owing to having been trampled in the panic-stricken crush, our boat had already gone, lowered into the sea. 'Go down to the second deck,' shouted a ship's officer. 'You'll get a boat there.'

First Radio Officer R. Borrer sent a message to the convoy Commodore's ship, received acknowledgement and then, hearing the order to abandon ship, left his radio room. Only four minutes had passed but he saw the ship was doomed, for she had a marked list to starboard and had settled so far by the head that the sea was already lapping the centrecastle deck at the after end of the bridge house. The whole of the bridge structure and Nos 1 and 2 lifeboats on the captain's deck were ablaze.

Topping this awesome picture on the monkey island above the wheelhouse, surrounded and illuminated by the flames, were the 3rd and 4th Mates, Hearn and Lewis, busily throwing overboard live ammunition from the Oerlikon gun regardless of the imminent fate of the ship. It had not been possible to launch the port lifeboat on the centrecastle deck due to the list but the starboard boat had been swung out and although it had not been lowered it was already waterborne owing to the combination of the list and settling by the head. This boat was crammed with passengers and some crew but it seemed that nobody was doing anything to release it from the falls. It was with the intention of activating the patent release gear that I made my way towards the boat. I reached the ship's side by the boat, which was being bumped to and fro against the ship's side by the swell, so I jumped into the water just abaft the boat and pulled myself round to its outboard sides by the grablines. Just as I was about to climb into the after end of the lifeboat to release the falls, the ship upended as if on an axis, the stern rose high in the air and I could see the funnel horizontal against the darkening sky. The ship seemed to hang in this position for a few seconds before starting to slide slowly beneath the surface.[2]

By this time Vera had run as fast as she could towards the boat, leaping down iron ladders until she came to the side of the second deck. She recalled vividly what happened next.

'Here. Take a hold of this rope! Slide down it. There's a boat below!' shouted a sailor in my ear. To my joy and surprise I landed in the lifeboat. By this time the forward part of the ship was under water and the stern was rising up crazily above us. And we were still attached to the davits. 'Look out below,' came a shout, then a thump. A sailor landed next to me. He slashed at a rope with a knife. The boat was free. But it looked as though we would now be sucked under the ship as it sank. At that moment I saw my friend Joan. She jumped from the top deck into the sea near our boat. The *Stentor's* stern towered above us for a brief moment, its propeller above our heads. Then with a frightening noise it slid down into the depths. Our lifeboat bounced up in the air, throwing us all into the sea. Frantically we struggled back into the boat and then began to pull in other survivors. I don't know where I got my strength from because I had nothing on my bones that could be called muscle before the voyage began.

The Radio Officer described the scene.

I was pawing on the ship's side as she was going under when something caught in the shoulder of my life jacket and dragged me under. It did seem that my time had come, but, surprisingly, in no time at all it seemed I found myself on the surface again. By this time the ship had gone and I was surrounded by other survivors, all looking for something to hang on to in the palm-oil-covered water.

All this happened so quickly that the ships which had been in line astern on the *Stentor* in the convoy were still passing us in the water at the spot where she had sunk.

I joined a group hanging onto a Carley float but this was just about submerged and after a short time the Second Radio Officer and I found and took hold of the wreck buoy. This wreck buoy was a 40-gallon drum with the ship's name painted on its side and a long length of wire spot-welded lengthwise around the drum, the other end of the wire being secured to the ship's structure – the idea being that if the ship sank in shallow water the drum would float to the surface and indicate the ship's position.

We manoeuvred a wooden hatchboard parallel with the drum so that he could lie across the hatchboard and hang onto the strop around the drum. After a time we became aware of the corvette some distance off picking up survivors. We could not make any headway with our rig so we let the hatchboard go and struck out towards the corvette, each holding onto the strop around the drum and swimming with the other arm.

As we came within hailing distance of the corvette we heard her engine start and a faint cry of 'We'll be back' before she disappeared into the night.

We were now out of sight and sound of any other survivors, apparently alone in the Atlantic.[3]

They were not alone, in fact. The lifeboat with Vera in it was not far away from them as she recalled:

From the time the ship was hit until it slid beneath the waves a mere eight minutes had gone by. I was sitting in the bottom of the boat and almost up to my waist in water. The bung, they said, was missing. I found a dipper and began to bale out. Eventually we found the bung and blocked the hole.

In that wet, overcrowded boat we drifted about in the darkness for about four hours and then there was a great noise of engines from behind my back and a grey shape loomed out of the darkness. We thought we'd rather be in a German U-boat than drifting in the Atlantic. What a joy it was to hear the voices of British seamen. It was the corvette K53, HMS *Woodruff*. But suddenly our hopes were dashed.

The corvette's captain shouted through the loud hailer that he had to leave straight away to hunt a submarine reported in the area. 'Cling to the wreckage and rafts. I'll be back soon.'

The whirl and wash of the corvette's screws churned the water and I had visions of a few luckless swimmers being drawn into the maelstrom and pulverized into pulp.

Hours went by. Radio Officer Borrer and his mate were in a bad way by this time.

When we heard the sound of the corvette's engine we were unable to swim because of the cold and the sea having become rougher, so we lifted our lifejacket lights higher and blew our whistles hard. After a while we were picked up by a lifeboat from the corvette and taken alongside the ship. The lifeboat had already put a full load of survivors aboard and we were the last two to be picked up in a final sweep of the area. I could hardly manage to climb up the scramble net hanging down the side of the corvette and I just tumbled onto the deck which was already strewn with survivors. Sailors were giving out mugs of tea and tots of rum. I saw people spewing up their first drink so I contrived to have a mug of tea first and having got rid of that was able to keep down the warming tot of rum.[4]

That final climb up the scramble net just before dawn proved too much for Vera. But she smiled as she recalled how she actually 'flew' up the ship's side. 'Two burly sailors reached down for my wrists and gave a mighty heave as if they were pulling up a heavyweight boxer instead of an emaciated 6-stone weakling. I literally sailed high over the rail and onto the far side of the deck!'

The next few days are indelibly printed upon her memory, not just because of the frightening events but also because of the kindness of the corvette's officers and seamen.

They could not have been kinder to us during the next seven nights, in coping with an extra 202 people on board such a small ship. We had at least one hot meal a day, albeit on occasions this might only be a bowl of hot Navy chocolate.

During that time U-boats chased and torpedoed the ships of the convoy. The corvette's men not only fed us but clothed us. They told us where to sit and not leave that place at any time when the crew were on action stations firing weapons. It was a terrifying time because we could not tell whether the ear-splitting thuds and bangs were from depth charges being dropped or further torpedoes hitting the ship.

In those seven days the Germans sank thirteen of the thirty-seven ships in the convoy, with heavy loss of life. It made us realize just how lucky we were to be picked up by the corvette. In all, 202 persons on board the *Stentor* were saved. Twenty-one of the crew and twenty-three passengers were lost. Amongst those passengers lost were four of our nurses: Joy Walters, Eileen English, 'Taffy' Davis and C.D. Manfield.

Incidentally we heard that the Captain went down with the *Stentor* but came up again and swam clear! The ship's doctor, who was so busy attending to badly burnt sailors, lost his life. He was posthumously awarded the Albert Medal.

The Captain of the *Woodruff* gave up his cabin to four of us nurses, whilst he slept in the wheelhouse. Our wet, oil-soaked clothes were collected and we were given a motley collection. I had a pair of the Captain's trousers, his tie as a belt, a pullover from another officer and a pair of decorative native slippers from a sailor who'd bought them as a present for his wife.

When the survivors docked at Milford Haven on the evening of 5 November 1942, no welcoming party from the War Office establishment awaited the seven survivors from the eleven nurses who had set off so joyously on that journey home. There were, though, some very kind ladies from the Women's Voluntary Service who fixed them up with enough clothes to get them all back to their homes, and one very kind lady took pity on Vera and Joan and took them back to her own home for the night. Vera still remembers what bliss it was to sleep in a bed again after all those nights on the deck of the Captain's cabin.

The next morning the Railway Transport Officer took us into his office and began to write out railway warrants. 'Where's your home railway station?' he said to me. I looked at him blankly. I had not yet thought about that. My home? It was a pile of rubble somewhere. And both parents dead. He must have thought I was barmy as I stumbled over my words. I did not know George well enough then to throw myself upon his hospitality so I took a warrant to the home of my uncle. Perhaps he would look after me until ... well until I got to my next unit. In those days, there was no point in looking too far ahead.

9   Armada to Africa

We run normal wartime sea risks but these eight fearless
girls never turn a hair. They just carry on with their jobs as
though they were in a hospital ashore.

Surgeon Captain RN of HMHS *Oxfordshire*[1]

On 7 November 1942, the Navy's hospital ship *Oxfordshire* nosed
quietly into position off the port of Algiers. Somewhere, through the
darkness towards the shore, a few lights twinkled.

For the last twenty-four hours, since passing through the Straits of
Gibraltar, the *Oxfordshire* had been sailing into a high-risk zone.
Now attacks were to be expected from German bomber aircraft
based on nearby Sicilian airfields and there was always the threat
posed by U-boats of the German Mediterranean Fleet, vigilantly
patrolling the route from Gibraltar to Malta.

But for both the German Navy and the Luftwaffe there were now
more attractive targets than usual from which to choose: an incredible number of warships and troopships in the largest amphibious
invasion force in the history of warfare – 300 warships, 300
merchant ships and 107,000 men. The BBC correspondent Howard
Marshall, who was sailing with them, was clearly awestruck and
wrote: 'Such an armada had never sailed before, and in London and
Washington those who knew what was afoot waited anxiously for
news. The U-boat packs were prowling from the Atlantic to the
Mediterranean, and here was their richest target.'[2]

In that high-risk situation all personnel, including nurses, were on
special alert, but despite the known hazards, the *Oxfordshire* tried to
be as close as practicable to the combat zone so that specialist medical

care could be given to wounded personnel with minimal delay. Casualties then had a far better chance of recovery than if they had to be ferried to a hospital further away from the fighting.

No one knew how many wounded there might be from this North African operation, but the nurses had checked and rechecked that everything in the *Oxfordshire*'s wards was ready for them. Now there was nothing more they could do but wait. No one felt like talking. Deep in everybody's mind was the knowledge that soon, very soon, their time of real danger would come.

All the nurses aboard the *Oxfordshire* were new to nursing duties at sea. They had sailed from the Clyde on 26 October and steamed straight out into rough Atlantic weather. Most of them were seasick. Sister Anne Griffiths of the QARNNS recalled being a 'ministering angel' to her retching colleagues during that first week of the voyage.

Unfortunately the old *Oxfordshire* did not take kindly to rough seas. The whole ship seemed to rise on gigantic waves, poise herself at their peak and then fall away into the next trough. For the nurses it felt as though they were going up in a lift and then dropping without control. As they lay on their bunks feeling awful, the storm had been incredibly noisy. Waves crashed and thudded against the side of the ship and the wind howled almost as if it wished to terrorize anyone stupid enough to be sailing in such violent weather.

They had received little consolation from the crew's reassurances that rough weather was something for which they should be thankful. Experience had taught the veteran sailors that stormy weather was a form of insurance against German submarine attacks. Torpedoes were difficult to launch in bad weather and in any case, with high seas running submarines had difficulty in seeing ships. Definitely, gales suited the convoy crews.

The *Oxfordshire* had been built in 1912 for use as a small cruise ship on the Far East run and had been converted to a hospital ship in November 1939. It had well-planned, spacious wards so that medical staff could move freely round the fixed cots. In addition to the medical and zymotics wards there was a surgical ward with a well-equipped operating theatre, an X-ray department and a dental surgery. The ship was generously staffed with eight QARNNS sisters, six from the Reserve, a principal medical officer, six medical officers, and a dental surgeon, very well supported by experienced sick berth staff.

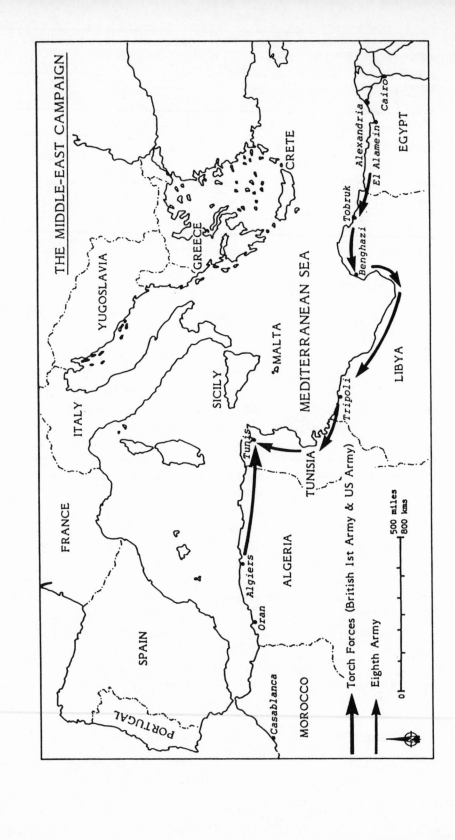

THE MIDDLE-EAST CAMPAIGN

FRANCE

SPAIN

PORTUGAL

ITALY

YUGOSLAVIA

GREECE

CRETE

MOROCCO

Casablanca

Oran

Algiers

ALGERIA

TUNISIA

Tunis

SICILY

MALTA

MEDITERRANEAN SEA

Tripoli

LIBYA

Benghazi

Tobruk

Alexandria

El Alamein

Cairo

EGYPT

Torch Forces (British 1st Army & US Army)

Eighth Army

500 miles
800 kms

0

The ship's Captain and medical staff ate together in the dining room and this, to nurses used to the meagre rationed fare of UK hospitals, was a treat indeed. Fruit was plentiful but bread was scarce and not without the odd weevil. However, compared with some hospital ships life on the *Oxfordshire* verged on luxury.

Now the last stage of the critical voyage had arrived. Slowly, almost gliding through the calm sea in the wake of the assault ships, HMHS *Oxfordshire*, approached the invasion beaches.

From somewhere behind and above their heads, the nurses leaning on the ship's rail heard the whirr and tinkle of engine-room telegraphs on the bridge as the Master rang 'Stop engines'.

Ahead of them, as zero-hour approached, men of the assault battalions waited patiently on the troopships' decks, alongside their landing craft. It seemed as if they were overburdened with kit: buoyancy lifejackets under their equipment, haversacks bulging with forty-eight hours' rations, pouches packed with ammunition, rifles slung, Bren light machine-guns ready to be shouldered.

For most of those soldiers it had been a relief to emerge from the nerve-racking claustrophobia of the horrendous lower troop decks and breathe fresh air again. A quiet order passed through the ranks. Awkwardly men began to step across the deck rails into the assault craft which swung on the davits, where lifeboats had once hung. Then there were anxious moments as the craft were lowered into the water.

Suddenly there was a startling roar as the landing-craft engines started up and were revved hard as they cruised round until every assault craft had been lowered and was in position. Then they roared away, heading for the beaches and an uncertain welcome.

The nurses had been 'put in the picture' to use the vernacular of the time. What it amounted to was that nobody knew what kind of welcome those troops might get from their former allies, the French; it was anybody's guess. The attitude of the French Army was uncertain, that of their Navy less so, for they had not forgiven the Royal Navy for sinking their ships at Oran in July 1940 to prevent them from falling into enemy hands.

In Algiers, cars fitted with loudspeakers toured the streets, blaring out the *Marseillaise* and broadcasting a proclamation from General Giraud saying:

Germany and Italy intend to occupy North Africa. Today the United States is forestalling them and have assured us of their loyal and disinterested support. We cannot neglect this chance to rise once more. I am back with you in the battle line. Now, the fate of France is in the hands of the Army of Africa.

Again and again, throughout the city streets, the *Marseillaise* was played along with rousing military marches. And yet on that pale and hazy yet sunny November day, the population was far from convinced. Nobody knew exactly what was happening. Rumours ran wild.

Neither the waiting nurses nor the troops had much idea of what the object of the operation was except the vague notion that it was all part of the fight to maintain freedom for ordinary men and women threatened with the tyranny and brutality of Nazi domination. It was simply a job that had to be done. And if there were going to be casualties then the nurses would be on the spot to give the best professional treatment available.

For the generals in charge of that invasion force, the main aims of the operation were to secure French Morocco and Algeria, from where the British First Army could rush to join up with Montgomery's Eighth Army advancing confidently from Libya and so complete the destruction of all the German and Italian forces in Africa. Tunisia would then provide a strong base from which to launch a long-awaited attack upon the European mainland.

Part of the strategy was that the French should believe the landing craft were filled with Americans and not with British who, to quote the Vichy French Foreign Minister, Laval, should be defeated for sinking French warships at Oran in 1940 and killing hundreds of French sailors.

So it was that, when the first United States assault craft approached the shore, an American officer stood up in the prow of one of them. He put a megaphone to his mouth, licked his dry lips and began to shout in execrable French with an American nasal twang: '*Ne tirez pas. Nous sommes amis. Ne tirez pas. Nous sommes Americains.*'

His garbled, almost farcical, requests for the defenders not to shoot were ignored. Shells and bombs rained down upon the whole Allied force. On HMHS *Oxfordshire*, waiting off shore, the nurses of the QARNNS found themselves in the midst of fire from French artillery and German dive-bombers. On each side of the ship, bombs sent up pluming spouts of water but not one made a direct hit. Two bombs found their mark on a merchant ship carrying trucks and ammunition. After the first explosion there was a second one, a great orange flash which lit up the whole convoy and all of the sky above in one ghastly bang. The ship, with a cargo of ammunition, disintegrated completely and all that was left was a sickening succession of splashes as torn pieces of metal fell back into the sea. The entire crew died in one moment. So quick. So brutal.

The nurses took cover as the bombing and shelling went on. From his vantage point on the bridge of the *Oxfordshire*, the Captain kept a watchful eye on everything. There was nothing to be done. Then, about a hundred yards away he saw a flash and great gushes of smoke from the middle of a merchant ship. It was sinking fast, stern down, almost to sea level. Men in the water cried out in pain and fear.

As soon as the bombardment had subsided, crew and hospital staff came up from below, and a boat was lowered. The men in the water struggled to keep afloat, the weight of their clothes dragging them under the waves, thick oil drifted around them, choking their cries. The men in the boat took hold of whatever limbs or clothing they could reach.

A fortunate few, shivering and black-faced in their oil-soaked clothes, were brought back to the hospital ship. Some had lacerated scalps from which blood streamed, one or two from the engine room had arms and faces gruesomely scalded by steam, one man had caught the flash-back from the boiler full in the face, and his flesh was shrivelled and his eyebrows and eyelashes seared. All were dazed by the suddenness of their ordeal. They looked about them, coughing and vomiting fuel oil and salt water. Some stood silent in wonder at being saved and in even greater wonder when they saw the nurses.

The discipline of their training drove the Navy nurses. No longer did they stand in shocked amazement. They forced themselves into action; there was so much to be done.

The *Oxfordshire*'s Captain then received orders to move a little way down the coast. The ship had just arrived when the destroyer *Partridge* was torpedoed. It began to sink stern first, and its depth charges rolled off rearwards and fell into the water where they began to explode. The Master of the *Oxfordshire* knew well enough what that could mean for the men in the water. He had seen what the tremendous pressure of an undersea explosion could do. They would be pulped out of all recognizable shape. Even men on the fringe of the detonating depth charges would be gravely injured and require special care.

Fortunately for many of those sailors from the *Partridge*, there was on board the *Oxfordshire* a man who knew more than almost any other medical man in the Royal Navy what could be done for men suffering from immersion blast. He was Surgeon Commander E.R.P. Williams, and he had been engaged on research work upon immersion injuries earlier in the war, before joining the *Oxfordshire*. He was able to direct the nursing sisters in their care of the survivors. Most of them presented the picture of 'blast syndrome' in varying degrees, including symptoms of intrathoracic and intra-abdominal catastrophe.

Methodically, the nurses, keeping as far as possible an impassive expression upon their white faces, dealt with each survivor in turn, taking the severest injuries first. Four of the blast cases were fatal but the remainder survived.

Under the supervision of the medical officers, they also cared for men wounded before entering the water. They stitched gashes, immobilized broken limbs and coped with those whose horrific burns had rendered them insensible with pain.

As had been expected, many of the casualties brought on board were in a state of shock. For them as many hot-water bottles as possible had been placed in readiness, hot drinks were available in the wards as also was morphia and anti-tetanic serum. The accepted practice then was to give 3,000 units of anti-tetanic serum to every man who had sustained a wound of greater penetration than an abrasion.

In their preparations before going into the combat zone, the nurses and medical staff had checked to see that a stock of anti-gas gangrene serum was to hand in the operating theatre as well as in wards. It was the practice then to administer 4,000–8,000 units of anti-gas gangrene serum to all cases where muscles had been injured or where a compound fracture was present.

As soon as the opposition at Algiers had been overcome and casualties taken on board, the *Oxfordshire* sailed for Gibraltar. Further surgical treatment was given on the way there.

The nurses did what they could to ease the pain of the wounded. But for some, their efforts were in vain. Those tormented by the pain of their burns and still shivering in shock lost the will to live and slipped out of life without warning.

Once the *Oxfordshire* had docked in Gibraltar, the Reuters correspondents soon got to hear of the hospital ship's part in the North African invasion and their reports made much of the fact that women of the Royal Navy's nursing service were close to the action to care for casualties with minimal delay. Gone were the days when wounded men travelled long distances in blood-soaked clothing.

But the North African experience was only the beginning. Henceforth every major operation in the war was to be a seaborne affair in the first instance and the only possible evacuation route open for most of the casualties was by sea. Consequently the Navy and Army hospital ships formed an essential part of all future combined operations assaulting beaches in Sicily, Salerno, Anzio and Normandy.

In the evacuation of casualties, mention must be made of the part played by stretcher-bearers. Theirs was a vital and often self-sacrificial role in getting wounded men from the battlefield for treatment. The first Victoria Cross to a stretcher-bearer was awarded in North Africa to Private Eric Anderson, a young Bradford man serving in the East Yorkshire Regiment. Three times he left the safety of his cover to bring in wounded men from a bullet-swept slope. He went out a fourth time but by then he was the only target left for the enemy to shoot at. He was hit and mortally wounded as he was administering first aid.

Regimental stretcher-bearers were often in action when the fighting soldiers were taking cover. Without the stimulus of a gun in their hands with which to hit back, the stretcher-bearers needed a special kind of courage in bringing badly wounded men back to the care of the medical officers and nurses. The red crosses on their armbands never guaranteed immunity.

Nor, as we have seen, did the red cross always safeguard the hospital ships. To minimize the danger for nurses and medical personnel serving on them, in compliance with the terms of the Geneva Convention, they were painted white with a broad green band round the hull. Large red crosses were much in evidence on the sides of the ships and also on the upper decks so that aeroplanes should have no doubt about the ship's role in evacuating wounded from the combat zone. At night the ship was ablaze with lights on all sides. At short intervals all round the ship, electric light bulbs shone from their frames of green glass and spotlights illuminated the red crosses. But it did not take long for nurses on hospital ships to become somewhat disillusioned with all those safety precautions. Even when fully illuminated and with red cross markings plainly visible, once a hospital ship entered a combat zone crews and medical staff got used to the idea of being prepared for an attack.

The wounded men have never forgotten their first sight of women nurses in the combat zone, and how it uplifted them. Indeed, one commander of a field hospital noted in his Unit War Diary the beneficial and therapeutic effect a woman nurse in a dress had upon wounded men. 'It was astounding. The touch of femininity, the knowledge that a woman was around, gave the wounded man courage and confidence and a feeling of security. And the more feminine she looked the better.'[3]

Some critics of the recent film *The English Patient* took issue with Juliette Binoche's use of make-up in her role as the nurse in that film. But Second World War nursing veterans such as Brenda Fuller, who had read such criticisms in the *Daily Telegraph* wrote emphatically: 'Girls who wore lipstick and face powder in civilian life continued to wear them in uniform. Any device to keep up the spirits of casualties and ourselves was welcomed.'

Of course, certain modifications to dress were necessary for some duties. Nurses on hospital carriers and ships, as well as those in the field, very soon discovered that trousers were the only suitable wear. 'Flimsy grey cotton frocks, Army modesty capes and floating veils do not go well with the wind on a boat deck, bending over stretchers or climbing up to top bunks, nor, if the worst should occur, with floating in the water complete with lifejacket,' said Mary Johnston, Sister-in-Charge of the hospital carrier *Leinster*.[4]

By 9 May, when German forces in Tunisia surrendered to the Allies, those nurses knew all too well what to expect from war and their efforts are recorded in the companion volume to this, *Front-line Nurse*. It seemed a long time since they had first touched the shores of North Africa and experienced with surprise the cold, relentless rain, the hostility of the local Arabs and the unfriendliness of the French. In their hospital wards at sea and on land they had seen not only the grim side of war but also the nobility of the human spirit and how men and women could, even in the midst of all the horror, enjoy times of gaiety, good humour and a certain feeling of exuberance.

They were more than ready to make the best of the brief interlude between the end of the fighting in Africa and the landings in Sicily and Italy. It was a strange, tense two months, during which almost everyone, including the nurses, was able to make a pretty good guess at where they would be going next, and that thought was never far from the back of their minds.

Incredible though it might seem today, it was the Supreme Commander of the operation himself, General Eisenhower, who first told people the destination of the invasion fleet gathering in African ports. Early in June 1943 he summoned all war correspondents in Algiers to his headquarters and told them that Anglo-American forces would attack Sicily early in July. This frankness in taking the press into his confidence was either courageous or stupid. Many thought it was asking too much of newspapermen who lived by exchanging information, to keep the secret for weeks of inactivity before the invasion.

Whether or not his confidence was abused is open to debate. The fact remains that Germany sent its crack Hermann Goering Division into Sicily in June 1943 and its bombers and submarines attacked the invasion fleet. Amongst the losses were several hospital ships and carriers with nurses on board. During the interlude, Luftwaffe bombers also raided African ports where ships were gathering.

Despite these raids however, the nurses found time for socializing. Invitations came from shore units nearby and also from ships anchored close enough to each other in the bay. On one free day, nurses from Hospital Carrier *Leinster* paid a visit to an American hospital ship which had just arrived after being newly equipped to cater for 400 bed patients. Mary Johnston and her colleagues were astonished at the size of the American ship's staff – thirty-three nurses, twenty medical officers and numerous 'corps boys' or medical orderlies and technicians.

Another remarkable aspect of that ship was the way preparations had been made for the reception of mental cases. There were wire cages, iron doors and padded cells. The whimsical thought which crossed Mary Johnston's mind when she saw this department was whether the American Medical Corps expected their soldiers to cope with the stress of war less well than the British or whether it was just that they were nearer the border line when they left home.

As a means of reciprocating the Americans' generous hospitality, the Captain of the *Leinster* flashed an invitation to them to celebrate 4 July at a cocktail party on the *Leinster*. This was accepted and so it was with barely concealed pride that the *Leinster* sent one of its water ambulances for the US nurses and when they arrived alongside the ship, swung them up in it to the boat deck in true hospital-carrier style.

Some time later, Sister Mary Johnston and her colleagues from the Army's hospital carrier *Leinster* received a pressing invitation to lunch aboard the Navy's hospital ship *Oxfordshire*. Both ships were at that time anchored off the North African port of La Goulette. Four of the younger nurses had already accepted an invitation to dine on a large tank landing craft and had been fetched by a smart launch manned by two sailors and with a naval officer escort.

Apart from the lunch, just going aboard the *Oxfordshire* was an eye-opener for Mary. She began to feel pangs of jealousy, for the *Oxfordshire* looked so big and stable that her own hospital carrier seemed more like a ferry boat in comparison, as she later recalled: 'The QARNNS sisters and medical officers were all dressed in immaculate tropical white, the decks looked much larger and, it must be confessed, cleaner. The whole appearance gave one the impression of spotless efficiency.'

Lunch was served in the style of a luxury liner, even to the provision of menus! 'I felt,' wrote Mary, 'that I had stepped off the *Brighton Belle* into a very exclusive yacht club.'

Generally, the hospital ships of the Royal Navy tended to be bigger than those of the Army and much bigger than hospital carriers such as the *Leinster*, which was a 4,000-ton motor vessel originally built as a luxury cross-Channel ship. In its conversion it was fitted with an excellent operating theatre, anaesthetic room, dispensary and X-ray plant. On the boat deck were three officers' wards and on the next deck below were two wards of thirty-five beds each for the more acute cases. One of these had stands to facilitate the administration of blood transfusions. Each bed was also fitted with oxygen cylinders.

Once back on the small hospital carrier *Leinster*, the nurses had no time for a post mortem on the day's entertainment. Orders were received, putting them on stand-by, and whilst they were all getting ready for action, German bombers came over to see what damage they could inflict upon the ships massing in the harbour. 'It was the best firework display we had ever seen and we were full in the midst of it, well blacked out so our ship was as good a target as any other,' commented Mary Johnston.

But what worried them more than their own situation was that of the four young nurses who had gone aboard the tank landing craft. Its Captain was more worried still. Every one of his guns was blazing away as the bombs rained down and he knew they were all sitting on 60,000 gallons of petrol. His problem was whether it would be better to send the nurses back across the water in a small boat whilst shrapnel was falling all around or risk keeping them on top of the petrol. He decided to send the girls back and hope for the best.

They crossed the harbour looking very vulnerable in their small boat lit up by gun flashes and flares dropped by the bombers, and climbed back onto the *Leinster* apparently unaffected by their experience, although full of graphic details of their perilous journey back. Not one of them had a steel helmet or lifejacket and there was a ceaseless rain of shrapnel falling. 'It was a grim lesson for all to see how essential it was in a combat zone to be always prepared,' commented Mary.

Then suddenly, the peaceful interlude was over. Orders came again for everyone to be on a four-hour stand-by.

Mary remembered how the nurses felt when they listened to their orders for sailing. 'Everyone on board was full of enthusiasm. We felt we were about to begin the real thing.'

From ports all along the African coast, from Algiers to Alexandria, troopships and hospital ships were getting ready for the next mighty assault, and nurses were being posted – with orders marked 'MOST IMMEDIATE' of course. Amongst them was Freda Barnfather and her friend Sally, who, after baking in the Sudan, had moved on to Palestine. Their 'Urgent and Most Immediate' posting sent them hurrying gleefully to Alexandria to join Army Hospital Ship No. 34, the *Somersetshire*.

So the Allies left North Africa as swiftly as they had arrived, going to fight another war on another continent, leaving only a few to gather up the dead and bury them – men who had fought and died for a forgotten cause. Today there is hardly a trace of them left, save for their graveyards in Tunisia – some 9,000 British and 3,000 American.

10   Choices and Decisions

> If I were fierce, and bald,
> and short of breath
> I'd live with scarlet Majors at the Base,
> And speed glum heroes up the line to death.
> And when the war is done and youth stone dead,
> I'd toddle safely home and die – in bed.
>
> Siegfried Sassoon, 'Base Details'[1]

After fourteen months on a hospital ship, Lorna Bradey was looking forward to working in a real hospital in Cairo, in charge of the officers' ward. Very soon after arriving there she was having second thoughts.

It was infested with bugs! They hid in the cracks of furniture and ceilings. At night they came out in force, dropping onto beds, crawling into creases of bedding and then found the warmth of a body. They bit in clusters leaving five lumps together. No remedy ever got rid of them.

I had a folding table for my desk and I asked my orderly to give the table a good scrubbing getting into all the cracks. He did this enthusiastically and then in a moment of inspiration put paraffin in the cracks to ward off the invaders. I arrived for duty that night immaculate in white drill, scarlet epaulettes, white shoes and stockings and the beguiling veil. The table looked beautifully clean but smelt powerfully. I started my charts and soon began to scratch. I looked down and let out a shriek. My lap, legs and feet were a black mass of heaving bugs. They had cunningly hidden in the cracks and the paraffin and the warmth of my body had done the rest.

Despite the bugs I found my work in the officers' ward satisfying. Most patients were wounded Army officers brought back from the desert. One patient, though, was different. I shall never forget him.

He was an RAF pilot, an emergency admission. He'd crashed at Heliopolis airfield. I was sitting with him as he came round from the anaesthetic. He didn't know the extent of his injuries and kept crying out that his legs were hurting him. The Medical Officer came and said there was no easy way of telling him the truth. I've rarely seen a man weep so bitterly. He kept repeating, 'It can't be true. I can *feel* the pain in my legs.'

Both legs were amputated at the thigh. His eyes pleaded with me to contradict the doctor. The pain he felt often happens after amputation. The nerve endings stay alive as if he could still feel his legs. He was so young. I sat with him and tried to comfort him. As soon as possible he was sent home.

Such cases had an unnerving effect on our sensibilities. We tried to detach ourselves and be objective but it was not easy.

It was even more difficult with a naval officer who looked like a monkey. The maxillo facial team [plastic surgery section known affectionately as the Max Factor boys] were trying to rebuild the havoc fire had wrought of his face. The surgeon had brought down a flap from his scalp over his nose to get the skin to take and black hairs stuck out on either side.

We learnt never to show shock or alarm on our faces. When I talked to him I looked straight into his eyes and smiled. He was tall and slender, his hands were like talons with no flesh on them at all. He hid in his room and we encouraged others to go in and talk normally. One day he told me his story. He had been torpedoed on his destroyer and had fought his way out, tearing at the blazing bulkhead. His face and hands were the worst. The rest of his body was only slightly scarred. He pulled out a photograph of a beautiful girl and a handsome naval officer. They had just got engaged. I tried hard not to show my shock. Sadly he said, 'Sister, you couldn't blame her. She'll never have me now.' He was passed on to Sir Archibald McIndoe's unit in Ward 3 of East Grinstead Hospital. I hope and pray that his girl had the courage to welcome him back home.

It was here that love came to Lorna; she was swept off her feet. It was, to use a wartime expression, a whirlwind courtship, at a time when war acted as an aphrodisiac, fanning passions more fiercely and quickly than would have happened in peacetime. In her officers' ward she met a very attractive Major who had been wounded in the desert fighting. He was not only handsome but also a charming companion. The inevitable happened; Lorna found herself wanting to spend more and more time with James. To be on the safe side, however, having met men in France who had said they had no ties but were in fact married, she looked up his records: 'Next of kin, Mother'.

Whilst he was convalescing they spent all their spare time together. 'We had a hectic social life,' she recalled with a smile.

One of our favourite restaurants was Groppi's, partly because it was renowned for good food and partly because the hospital hygiene department inspected the kitchens regularly. Whenever the cockroaches and other insects became too numerous, it would be closed. But then it would be opened again after a thorough blitzing of the insect life.

James soon was graded fit for active service and was posted back to his unit, 'up the blue' as the desert front line was then called. Soon after he rejoined his unit, his division was brought out for a rest in a reinforcement camp close to Cairo and he was able to see Lorna frequently. He took leave and spent the whole time with Lorna, dining and dancing.

A few weeks earlier, Mona had begun to work with Lorna. She was a Roedean-educated Egyptian VAD. Her mother, a Glasgow-born Scot, had married a very rich Egyptian who lived in a Geziera mansion. Soon Lorna, who had shown no favours to Mona, was their favourite weekend guest. They provided expensive civilian clothes for her visits, a masseuse to wake her up on Saturday mornings, a visiting hairdresser, exquisite night clothes and even handmade shoes.

It was after a party at the Geziera mansion that James asked Lorna to marry him. They became engaged and Mona was so very excited she wanted to make arrangements to hold the wedding reception in their marvellous house.

What a wedding it was to be. Cairo cathedral was booked. James went back to his unit in action up the blue again and the days flew by. Suddenly one evening I got a telephone call from a complete stranger, a Major who was a friend of James. He wished to see me urgently but did not want to say more over the phone. He asked if we could meet for dinner. Puzzled and anxious for James, I agreed. He was a nice man and wasted no time before delivering the shocking news – a real bombshell. The Major knew James very well, had known him in England – and his wife and children. He'd just heard the news of the wedding plans and felt he must tell me. I was shattered.

When confronted later, James admitted the truth. He had given his mother's name deliberately so he could have fun and it had got out of control. He begged me to believe he loved me. Angry almost beyond belief I sent him away. I then had to face all my friends.

It was then I learned I was not the only one to have been taken in by romantic officers. I heard of a nursing sister who got married and in her joy retired from the QAs and took a flat in Cairo. She took up voluntary work and her husband went back to his unit fighting in the desert. Her blissful state lasted a few months and then his letters stopped arriving. Anxious, she made inquiries and discovered that her husband had faked a nervous breakdown, had committed bigamy and was on his way home. The news was broken to the 'wife'. She rejoined the QAs and like me she found forgetfulness in hard work.

The work for Lorna was more than hard. One part of it turned out to be hair-raising. She got a call from an old friend who had served with her in France in the Dunkirk days.

She rang me out of the blue, saying she was on leave from Eritrea and could I come at once to the hotel where she was staying close to the hospital. More than that she would not say. I was baffled. How had she found me? And why? After duty that day I hurried to the hotel. When I enquired at the reception desk I was guided up to her room, which surprised me.

As soon as I opened the bedroom door I saw her lying on the bed, white as chalk and bleeding like a pig. Haltingly she told her tale. A very senior army officer had got her pregnant but without telling him she had taken a week's leave, came to Cairo and had an illegal back-street abortion.

Now the mattress was soaked through with blood and her pulse was pretty thready. Fortunately I was a midwife and worked fast, massaging her abdomen until I could feel the flabby uterus harden under my hands. She was terrified and of course my first reaction was to get her into hospital without delay. But she begged and wept and asked me to help her. No one must know. I wrapped her up with towels and packed her as tight as I could and, satisfied that the bleeding was under control, rushed back to the hospital.

What should I do? I was in a complete quandary. Should I insist on handing her over to a British hospital or should I do what she begged of me?

The black market flourished in Cairo, so by dint of heavy bribing I obtained sulphonomide tablets. Sepsis was the thing I feared most. Back I rushed and made her swallow a good handful of these.

I stayed with her all that night. No one would miss me as I was not on duty until the next morning. I plugged in the fluids, took her pulse constantly and made up my mind that if she got weaker I'd act on my own, regardless of what she said.

The night wore on – bits of placenta and other muck came away. I kept massaging her uterus and slowly the bleeding was normal. I never want to go through such an experience again – ever. Loyalty to a friend or a death on one's conscience. But luck was with us. The antibiotics got hold.

She was there a week. It was a nightmare for me, but the improvement was dramatic after the first forty-eight hours. I visited her every moment I was off duty, checking her temperature and pulse, and by the end of the week, she was sitting up in a chair every day. She regained her strength enough to return to work, weak but alive. She spun some tale of 'gippy tummy' to account for her pallor. She promised undying friendship and gratitude for life.

It's not surprising, but after the war I stopped hearing from her and wrote to her home. Finally I received a reply. She would never forget what I had done for her but had married a very rich man – something to do with the sponge business in Cyprus – and thought it better if we corresponded no longer. I knew too much so I was to be forgotten. It hurt me terribly at the time.

Lorna Bradey did not have long to serve in Cairo. The war was moving on rapidly up the desert and a move to Tripoli was already planned for the hospital. Before she went, however, she had one further experience that she was never to forget.

I was walking down a darkened corridor one night when suddenly a door was flung open and a man jumped out and grabbed me. I screamed. In seconds men on crutches and sticks came to my aid. The poor man had suddenly gone mad. He'd been wounded and had bottled up his feelings, never thinking his mind was going. He was taken away in a straitjacket.

Hospitals for such patients were increasingly needed, and were being opened for men of all three fighting services in every theatre of operations. Unfortunately there were always some Tommies who tried to take advantage of the situation and feigned being mentally ill.

Some nurses thought the psychiatrists – quickly nicknamed 'trick-cyclists' – could be very unsympathetic, and uncaringly despatched mentally ill men back to their units in battle when they would have benefited from a week longer in a rest area.

Nobody ever told Lorna Bradey the name of the unit to which the man was sent who grabbed her, and for a very good reason. Those special units were never openly talked about. It would not have been good for public morale, nor for the resolution of men in the fighting services, to know that so many psychiatric hospitals were being established at home and abroad for the treatment of men who broke down under the stress of combat.

By the end of the war, in Britain alone there were eighteen hospitals specializing in the treatment of disturbed neurosis, five centres for mild neurosis, four psychiatric centres and thirteen for those whose documents carried the label 'NYDN' (not yet diagnosed neurosis).

Once a unit medical officer came to the conclusion that a man was not fit for front-line service, he would refer him to a neuropsychiatric specialist. The Navy, Army and Air Force each had their own specialist hospitals and recovery units. Treatment at first depended on the decisions of the psychiatrists, and these varied considerably between those who considered such men to be cowards and malingerers and those who recognized that there were genuine patients with minds disordered through excessive exposure to terrifying experiences in which they had narrowly escaped death.

Treatment at No. 6 Base Psychiatric Centre attached to No. 95 BGH, Algiers, no doubt frightened many patients. It was frightening too for the medical orderlies, as the commanding officer recorded in his War Diary. 'Orderlies are knocked about and given black eyes in the exercise of their duty. I asked for them to be paid "danger money". We had 85 acutely insane cases cared for in wards equipped for only 68 beds.'

It was frightening too for soldiers to hear harrowing tales from fellow patients about electric shock treatment. The War Diary of the psychiatric centre gave details:

Convulsive therapy by intravenous Phrenazol was used to a large extent at first but was later supplanted entirely by electrical convulsive therapy. Pentothal abreactive and prolonged narcosis have also been considerably employed. With other patients occupational therapy in various forms – metal work, carpentry and gardening for example – has been considerably employed.[2]

The mental disorder problem then was greater than was generally known. In No. 6 Base Psychiatric Centre alone, in the three-month period between 9 December 1943 and 8 March 1944, there were 818 in-patients admitted (659 psychoneurotics, 149 psychotics, 10 'mental defects') and a further 688 treated as out-patients. Of these 398 returned to duty; the remainder were evacuated to the UK on the hospital ships *Amarapoora, Anra, Llandovery Castle, Oranje* and *Oxfordshire.*

Not surprisingly, the problem of combat fatigue got worse the longer the war went on and the longer fighting troops were at the sharp end of it. Colin Welch, a 20-year-old platoon commander of the Lincolnshire Regiment recalled what it was like for young men in the front line towards the end of the war. In June 1944 he looked at the drawn faces of 18- and 19-year-old lads in his platoon: their weary bloodshot eyes, faces haggard through lack of sleep and ill from poor food and constant fear.

They had seen many of the men they had trained with killed or badly wounded. He was angry that casualties in his unit had been so very high yet he could see back at base headquarters many fit officers and soldiers who could have gone to the front themselves. 'But,' he said, 'as the campaign wore on and losses mounted, they were callously passing on mere children to be minced up in the front line, bewildered. In Holland we got a big draft from the King's Liverpool Regiment. They looked mostly like the original Beatles at the start of their career.'

Welch felt strongly about the way psychiatrists who had little idea of the trauma some of those young lads had been through made quick decisions to send them back to the front as cured and labelled *'malades imaginaires'*. Nor did they know, he said, that often those same shell-shocked lads – for 'lads' is what most of the reinforcements were after D-Day – endangered their own lives and everyone else's by their tragic antics in full view of the enemy once they were back in the line, as if they had given up all hope of surviving anyway and wanted to get it over with. Welch's opinion of decisions made by psychiatrists never altered. He had no faith in them. 'No blimpish colonel of either war would have behaved with such idiotic inhumanity,' he wrote.[3]

Welch's battalion sustained 100 per cent casualties and their replacements 70 per cent in the ten months from D-Day until his own number came up in the horror of the Reichswald Forest.

At one time, when they were going back to the front where the battle raged fiercely, they paused for a meal break in a staging area.

Marjorie Aston (later Mathews) in mess dress of QARNNS 1943. She volunteered for flying duties with the Royal Naval Medical Air Evacuation Service in the Pacific

Lorna Bradey (later Kite), theatre sister on hospital ships and field hospitals in the Middle East, Italy and, later, Germany

Yvonne Jeffrey served with the British Expeditionary Force in France, in 1939–40, and later served in Persia, Iraq and with the Central Mediterranean Force

Sheila McDermott (later Bambridge) saw duty with German POWs at Woolwich during the height of the blitz, and later in the Far East on the Arakan front with the 14th Army

Right: **Agatha Dampier-Child** (later Tinne) served on the Royal Naval hospital ship, *Vita*, in the Italian campaign and later in the Indian Ocean tending a wide range of patients from the war-wounded to those suffering from leprosy and tuberculosis

Freda Barnfather (later Reid) served north of the Arctic Circle in the Norwegian campaign and then in the searing heat of southern Sudan. She went to Cairo and served on two hospital ships involved with the assault landings in Sicily, Salerno and Anzio. Finally she was on a hospital ship bringing casualties back from the beaches of Normandy and taking patients across the Atlantic to New York. Freda Reid today

Vera Bryan (later Dunnett) at King's Hospital, London, in 1938, just before joining QAIMNS. With Mary White and Ruth Daintree in a special press photo displaying new style QAIMNS cap

Betty Lawrence (later Halliday) delivered a baby boy during a heavy air raid on Plymouth and met him for the second time fifty years later. She also served in India and Ceylon. With Isabel Hyniers in India 1945

Anne I. Powis (later Cockburn) joined the QARNNS (R) after nursing in London during the blitz. She was posted to RN hospital Haslar and was 'blitzed' again by the matron for wearing brown shoes. Later she served in the Far East and at RN hospital Herne Bay, Sydney, Australia. She nursed casualties from the final sea and land battles against the Japanese and then the emaciated men returning from Japanese POW camps

Helen Vlasto (later Long) in VAD uniform 1945 wearing the Africa Star having served in the Libyan desert and at El Alamein

First Aid Nursing Yeomanry training in techniques of moving an ambulance bogged down in mud, loose gravel or sand. *Below:* Navy hospital ship, *Vita*, bombed at Tobruk

Nursing sisters of QARNNS with patients on the deck of a hospital ship

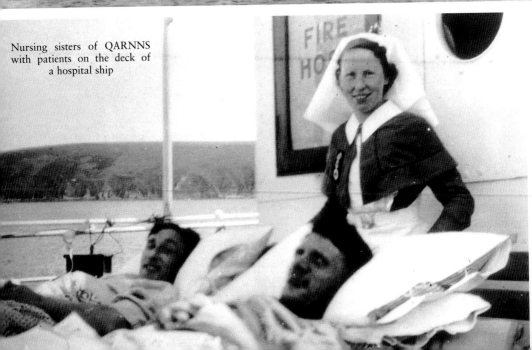

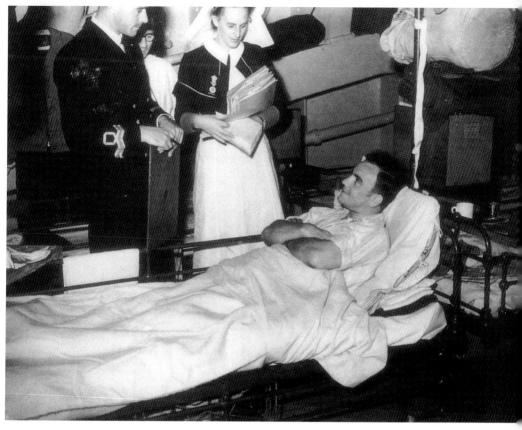

QARNNS sister on hospital ship with RNVR surgeon
lieutenant and patient

Femininity uplifts morale. Nurses and
women workers were encouraged to preserve their femininity in wartime. 'The more
feminine she looks the better,' wrote an
officer commanding a field hospital in his
unit war diary

Nurse on fire-watching duty on the look
out for incendiary bombs falling on roof-
tops. Armed with stirrup pump and sand
buckets they had to dowse incendiary
bombs quickly before they damaged the
roof timbers

HMHS *Amarapoora*

Hospital ship *Llandovery Castle*
on which Sister Lorna Bradey
served for fourteen months

The harsh reality of war seen on Admiral Doenitz's doorstep. He told all his U-boat commanders to remember that 'in his bombing of German cities the enemy has no regard for women and children'. His outburst came after Allied aircraft attacked U156 when it was rescuing survivors, including Sister Hawkins, from SS *Laconia*. He ordered U-boat commanders to make no further attempts at rescue

Identity card of
Vera Bryan

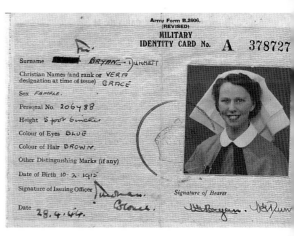

K53 Corvette, HMS *Woodruff* rescued Vera
Bryan and other survivors from MV *Stentor*
when it was torpedoed in October 1942

So impressed was Vera with the help
she and others received from the K53
Corvette crew and later from the
Corvette Association that, fifty years
later, she insisted her new car should
be battleship grey and have the
registration K53

One of the stately homes of England, Cholmondeley Castle, doing war work as an RN psychiatric rehabilitation centre. Wounded sailors were nursed back to health in spacious rooms and beautiful grounds where they could relax

Rockside Hydro, Matlock, one of the eighteen special psychiatric hospitals for casualties of combat fatigue. An airman patient jumped from the top window just beneath the spire

Hospital carrier *Leinster* in harbour

Stretcher cases being carried down the gangway from hospital carrier *Leinster*

Embarking American troops off Salerno beaches. There is a smoke-screen between HMHS *Vita* and the shore

Wedding day of Agatha and John. The troopship romance of Captain John Tinne and Sister Agatha Dampier-Child that led to a Golden Wedding celebration in 1996

Ambulance crossing the raging torrent of the River Volturno, Italy, 1943

Staff of the sick quarters of HMS *Garuda*, S.India. Sister Betty Lawrence QARNNS is second from right in front row

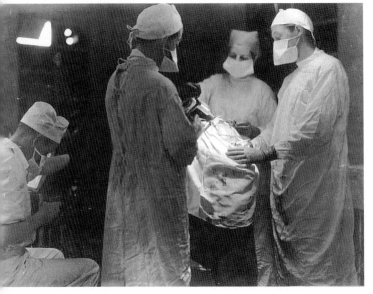

Theatre sister assisting the surgeon in a field hospital. Lorna Kite recalls helping with over eighty operations in one day in Italy

Mule companies took medical stores, rations and ammunition up the mountains to forward positions and often brought down wounded men on stretchers slung each side of the pack saddle

Mud! Mud! Mud! A typical scene which confronted Sister Lorna Bradey outside her operating theatre in Italy 1944

Vera Bryan *(back row, seventh from left)* with happy colleagues from her field hospital in Belgium, 1944, having recovered from her Nigeria experience and being torpedoed on the way home

Ann Radloff (*née* Reeves) after receiving maundy money from HM Queen Elizabeth at Westminster Abbey

Returning to the beaches fifty years later. Vera Dunnett and Brenda McBryde with Pat Stephens *(right)* who was one of the youngest nurses to serve right through the north-west Europe campaign

Wounded at a field hospital in Normandy. Note US army medical corpsman giving a cigarette to soldier on a stretcher. Doctors believed cigarettes helped to combat shock

Gas gangrene wound given the open incision treatment. Exposure to air helped to cure the wound

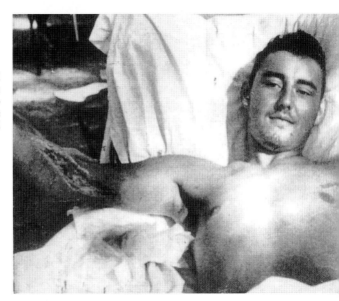

Bed in a slit trench with Sten gun and field telephone close at hand. RAF nursing sisters, Iris Ogilvie and Mollie Giles

Wounded arriving home, making use of whatever transport facilities were available

Patient from RN ambulance launch being carried ashore

Heinrich Himmler in black
uniform of the SS, to the right of
Hitler, Hess and Lutz.
Himmler's body ended up on a
post-mortem slab of 74th BGH
where locks of his hair were cut
off as souvenirs

Enjoying the luxury of shopping
for cosmetics in Bayeux after
fourteen days in the front line following D-Day. Sister Iris Ogilvie
MBE and shop assistant

Joan Loader, Margaret West and Marjorie Aston
on arrival in Sydney for duty with the RN Medical
Air Evacuation Service

Cecile Lake, Margaret West and Eileen Creane
QARNNS in flying kit of Medical Air
Evacuation Service

RAF nurses training to drop by parachute to tend to wounded on the battlefield. The war finished
before they went into action

SAFE CONDUCT

The German soldier who carries this safe-conduct is using it as a sign of his genuine wish to give himself up. He is to be disarmed, to be well looked after, to receive food and medical attention as required, and is to be removed from the danger zone as soon as possible.

PASSIERSCHEIN

An die britischen und amerikanischen Vorposten: Der deutsche Soldat, der diesen Passierschein vorzeigt, benutzt ihn als Zeichen seines ehrlichen Willens, sich zu ergeben. Er ist zu entwaffnen. Er muss gut behandelt werden. Er hat Anspruch auf Verpflegung und, wenn nötig, ärztliche Behandlung. Er wird so bald wie möglich aus der Gefahrenzone entfernt.

Safe conduct pass carried by Germans who sometimes walked into British forward casualty clearing stations. Vera Bryan kept this one as a souvenir

There they met a rag-tag group of soldiers coming back. The wreck of what had once been an impressive infantry major shrieked at the officers and men going forward, 'It's hell up there. Run for it while you can.' But Welch's men had no choice in the matter.

So after their meal and mugs of tea, they marched on through ground littered with dead animals – horses, cows, geese, ducks, chickens – and their blue-smocked peasant owners. It was a gigantic abattoir; there were bodies – Allied, German and civilian – everywhere, stiff and hideously swollen, covered with white dust or mud, men with faces blown away or dreadfully distorted, crawling with flies, rotting, giving off that terrible sweet-sour stench of death which, once smelt, is never forgotten.

No wonder that some men came into the care of the nurses mere wrecks of what they were when they marched proudly on the parade grounds of infantry training depots. It was clear to the nurses that those once so confident young men all had a certain stock of courage and when they had used that up they were in danger of a nervous breakdown. It was an opinion that Lord Moran, physician to Prime Minister Churchill was soon to endorse.[4]

What men suffering from combat fatigue needed most was sleep, rest and rehabilitation in a specialist centre. Sister Hornby of the QARNNS was in one of those psychiatric rehabilitation centres at the Royal Naval Hospital at Cholmondeley Castle in the heart of the lush pastures of Cheshire. Patients must have wondered where they were going when they entered the long drive which led alongside a mere and through extensive, well-kept parkland before reaching the impressive edifice of the castle itself.

In spring, daffodils bloomed prolifically on the grassy banks of the castle and later in the year the same banks were covered by Lord Cholmondeley's prize-winning azaleas. A more restful scene could not have been found for those men with minds mentally bruised by frightening ordeals.

Lady Cholmondeley was Superintendent of the Women's Royal Naval Service (WRNS) and she and her husband kept just one large room of the castle, on the ground floor, for their own use. Only occasionally could they use it, when they had a short break from their wartime duties. The castle itself housed two wards, one on the ground floor in two large rooms, and one upstairs in three of the larger rooms. There was a third ward in a converted stable block.

'Occasionally,' wrote Sister Hornby, 'nurses helped the more severe cases by administering pentothal, but each patient was seen privately by the Medical Officer at regular intervals.

It was sometimes a case of deciding who was genuinely in need of psychiatric rehabilitation and release from the service and of who was just 'working his ticket'.

The atmosphere at Cholmondeley was not one of restriction, even when potential suicides were known to be in the group. All were free to wander at will through the park. One patient who we knew had vague thoughts of suicide decided on the mere as his way out of his mental torment and nightmares. He walked into it one morning, found it was terribly cold and came back to the comfort of the ward.[5]

Suicide was an ever-present hazard with mentally ill patients who could no longer face the life they were leading, even in the hospital ships bringing men home from active service. Quite early in the war, when HMHS *Newfoundland*, heading for Liverpool, steamed slowly into the estuary of the Mersey, a patient jumped overboard. Another man jumped in to save him. A boat was lowered and both patients brought back to the ship. A week later another patient threw himself overboard, but he was not recovered. Two days later another patient tried to kill himself by cutting his left radial artery. The blood vessel was ligatured and the man made a complete recovery. Almost as if suicide were contagious, yet another patient attempted to kill himself that same day by cutting his throat – but not deeply enough. To finish off that black second week of March, 1942, another patient eluded his guard and leapt over the rail. A boat was lowered and twenty-five minutes later the man's body was recovered, but resuscitation failed to restore life and he was buried at sea.[6]

As the hospital ship *St Julian* was nearing home, two men killed themselves, a staff sergeant worried about his physical disablement and a sapper of the Royal Engineers. Neither could come to terms with the new life they were to lead.[7]

Some men were so severely wounded mentally they needed long and careful care from medical staff who understood how their condition had come about. After a long time spent continuously in the midst of terrifying noise and the carnage of battle it was not surprising that some men just broke down. It could happen to the bravest of men. RAF aircrew of Bomber Command, for example, came under tremendous pressure; their average life expectancy was fourteen missions over enemy territory.

Jean Caudwell, who looked after such patients in the quiet RAF hospital housed in the Victorian spa of Rockside, at Matlock, has never forgotten the pitiful state they were in.

Many of them had a facial tic, a winking eye, nervous flicking of the hands over the face, plucking at fibres in their clothing, hardly able to hold a conversation on one subject. One minute they would appear quite normal and the next they would be jumping about, starting an argument about nothing at all or bursting into tears.

Many of them worried about their future. What would they tell their families? Would they be sent back on operations? Would they have any choice at all?

Catherine Price, a nursing attendant at Rockside, remembered one man who was always worried and felt ashamed of himself. One evening he put an end to all his worries in a frightful way. It happened when Catherine Price was just going on duty. As she approached the front door of the imposing six-storey building, her eye was caught by the movement of something white right at the top, immediately below the roof. To her horror, the next moment a pyjama-clad figure came crashing down onto the hard concrete drive.

The episode was hushed up, as was the whole subject of neurosis in the armed forces in the Second World War. But at Rockside today (now a boarding school for girls) they still remember the tragedy. It is said that students sleeping on the top floor are sometimes troubled at night by a feeling of someone or something being there, and by the sound of footsteps that go one way – and do not come back!

Generally, patients in Navy, Army and RAF psychiatric rehabilitation centres responded well to a quiet, regular routine. On average about a third of them went back to their units and full duty, to the unremitting offensive on the sea, on the land and in the air.

By the autumn of 1943 the war had moved on from the desert after the victory at El Alamein into Tunisia where the Eighth Army met the First Army, through the bloody battles of Sicily and into a different kind of warfare altogether. The desert wadis and sand in which the Eighth Army had fought were replaced by the mud, mountains and rivers of Italy.

It was into the thickest of mud that Sister Lorna Bradey found herself setting up equipment for the operating theatre for that bitterly cold winter of 1943–44. That was also when Sister Freda Barnfather was posted to the hospital ship *Somersetshire*.

11   A Soft Under-belly?

> Working under very trying conditions in gales and in the
> stale atmosphere of wards through lack of ventilation, slip-
> ping on wet floors, and flung about by violent movements
> of the ship, sea-sick themselves, they met every demand
> made upon them and their cheerfulness throughout the
> voyage was an inspiration and a comfort to patients.
>
> Colonel H Foxton, RAMC, Officer Commanding Troops
> HMHS *Newfoundland*[1]

It was a thrilling sight. There she lay bright and sparkling white in the
brilliant sunshine, HMHS *Somersetshire*.

'It was enough to take your breath away,' recalled Freda Barnfather
some fifty years later.

Everything was freshly painted white with a broad green band from bow to
stern broken at intervals by great big, strikingly red crosses. Unmistakably a
hospital ship. And amongst the other ships it stood out like a sitting pigeon.

Anchored nearby was our sister ship, HMHS *Dorsetshire* looking equally
striking in its white, green and red identification colours. Wistfully, I hoped
the Germans would take the Geneva Convention markings seriously.

Freda had come across the *Somersetshire* when it had been evacuating casualties from Narvik at the time when she was also in Norway.
It had been torpedoed during its runs to Tobruk, and had been towed
into Alexandria for repair, which accounted for its pristine condition.

Whilst those repairs were being carried out some of the nurses
from the ship had had a most unusual posting – they were sent to
staff River Nile steamers – *Delta, Lolus,* and *Niagara* – transporting
patients from Shall Al and Wadi Haifa. When the repairs were

133

complete and the *Somersetshire* was ready for action, fourteen nursing sisters – Lowther, Egan, Avery, Garland, Kelly, Lawford, Lancaster, Deill, Fox, Ross, Wilson, Garnett, Williams and Freda Barnfather – joined the ship for one of the most hazardous periods of its duties in the Second World War.

It was a memorable day for Freda.

Once on board our ship we were taken to meet Matron and then shown our quarters. We had a cabin between us and in fact had everything we could possibly need for our home at sea. We even had a cabin steward for Sally and me. He was Ali, a Lascar with a limited command of English. Standing no more than 5 feet tall he was still an impressive figure in his white turban, white outfit, grinning white teeth and a huge black moustache as he came to our cabin every morning carrying a cup of tea for each of us. A few minutes later he would knock on the door again, bow to us both and say: 'Bath ready, memsahib.' Then he stood on guard outside the bathroom until one of us claimed the bath. After the Sudan this was absolute luxury!

Inevitably the warning came. All personnel to be on board by 2400 hours. That night, amidst great excitement, we moved off.

Our excitement was a trifle premature. We only moved to an anchorage further out in the harbour so that another ship could take on stores. This kind of movement went on until the harbour was unbelievably packed with ships of all sizes. By this time we nurses were taking orders and their cancellation in our stride. We never had time to be bored for we got so many invitations from the captains of neighbouring ships to join them and their officers for drinks or a meal. We did however spend some time listening to lectures about our hospital ship duties and we made thorough checks of the wards and equipment in them.

The cots for the casualties were of iron, two-tiered and slung between stanchions anchored to the deck. There was a fixture to hold each one steady or to allow it to swing to the motion of the ship. A short ladder was used to reach the upper berth of each cot.

Then it happened. And it came as a shock because the night had been quiet. We got up one morning, went on deck to fill our lungs with fresh air and looked around in amazement at blank spaces. Most of the ships had gone. Gone too was the *Dorsetshire*. Why were we still there, we wondered. Was there something special waiting for us?

Sister Helen Luker, on board the *Dorsetshire* had seen action with her for two years.

I had little knowledge of the sea but I soon realized how much we as a nation owed to the Merchant Navy and the longer I was at sea the more my admiration and respect for them all grew. We had accommodation for between 400 and 500 patients in cots. Most of these were of the twin-bunk type except in the acute wards, where we aimed to have single bunks. Needless to say, there were many occasions when we had to wash, feed, dress wounds and give infusions and treatments perched precariously on a ladder or stool. When it was rough we had to lash the dressings trolley to the side of the bunk.

What was always a problem for us on the hospital ship was the supply of fresh water. On a long trip it was cut off completely for certain periods of the day. Native patients and nursing sepoys [the grand title given to Indians straight from their primitive village] were the chief offenders; they used to be found literally sitting on the pressure taps, thus enabling their friends to enjoy a fresh-water shower. But some of these Indians were so devoted and faithful that one had not the heart to be angry with them for long.

The unit, run by a lieutenant-colonel assisted by three medical officers and a dental officer, had an operating theatre, and a plaster room where patients' dressings were often done to relieve the congestion of the wards and to avoid the heat. Particular attention was paid to these two rooms to make sure everything was to hand – plasma bottles, supplies of drugs, bales of bandages and dressings.

Night duty required careful organization. On the *Dorsetshire*, two sisters looked after seven wards, but in order for this to work efficiently, training had to be concentrated on ensuring that medical orderlies were proficient and capable of looking after a ward for short periods with a sister from another ward on call. Helen Luker believed this was a good idea: 'Some orderlies became very proficient, especially if they were left on a ship for several years.'

Helen had been on the *Dorsetshire* when it was the last hospital ship to leave Tobruk on 10 April 1941. The port and town was then surrounded by German troops. Once, during fierce fighting for the port, *Dorsetshire* loaded 400 stretcher cases.

While there, Helen saw the Navy hospital ship *Amarapoora* attacked and damaged by six German dive-bombers. 'It was a horrible scene. Six of them came in at low level just as the Navy hospital ship was leaving harbour. She was badly damaged below the water line and patients were taken aboard a destroyer. The hospital ship was towed to Alexandria.'

It was at this time that the Mediterranean was deemed to be too dangerous for hospital ships *en route* for the UK and so for the next eighteen months casualties were evacuated via the Red Sea to South Africa.

There were some strange and amusing situations for Helen on these safer voyages. Whilst taking on some native casualties wounded in the Abyssinian and Eritrean campaigns, the nurses discovered that one patient had smuggled his pet monkey aboard. The monkey escaped from his master just before the morning rounds of the Medical Officer and the ship's Captain. All the orderlies and 'up patients' joined in the hunt. With minutes to spare the monkey was caught and put in a locker with the door shut firmly upon him, and an orderly was placed on guard in front of the locker.

East African patients were usually delightful – so co-operative and appreciative. But there was one who proved to be a mystery to everyone. 'He was under the spell of a witch-doctor, but as we could not get him home for a consultation with his specialist, I regret to say there was nothing we could do to improve his condition and he died. A post-mortem examination revealed no cause of death.'

It was always a revelation to nurses, no matter how many times they had nursed badly maimed soldiers, to see how courageously they accepted their pain and disablement. Helen Luker kept a cutting from the *Daily Express* concerning one such patient. Beneath the photograph of a tall young man smiling with a bride on his arm in the church doorway, the caption read:

David Bell, a soldier at 18 came back from Africa a blind man without hands but with immense realism and pluck, to learn to type, to learn languages from records and learn to dance. Now he has married Miss Sybil Irene Page at Shrewsbury and will live happily keeping a tobacco shop provided by St Dunstans, where the couple met.

Now the *Dorsetshire* was sailing towards invasion beaches where they would load yet another batch of wounded young men for whom the future would be a challenge and often an ordeal in a society not always sympathetic to their needs.

In Alexandria, on board the *Somersetshire*, Freda Barnfather and her colleagues did not have very long to ponder the problem of why they had been left behind or where they would be sent. Their time came early on the morning of 5 July 1943. Immediately they sailed, there was a boat drill, followed by a briefing in the dining room. There the senior officer revealed the outline of the strategic plan for the invasion of Sicily and how Italy was to be knocked out of the war within the year. D-Day was to be in five days' time, 10 July 1943.

After the briefing the Unit Commander called the nurses back and told them the news he thought best to be given to them privately. Their sister ship, *Dorsetshire*, had been hit by bombs. There were no serious casualties, however, and she was limping back to port.

Ships joined the convoy as it sailed past various North African ports until it became a formidable invasion fleet, the like of which had never been seen before – an army moving forward in full war panoply. Yet Freda and her colleagues continued to live the life of peacetime cruise holidaymakers, eating meals of peacetime proportions, old-fashioned breakfasts of bacon and eggs, sausage and fried bread, served by white-coated Asian waiters. Only the colour of the diners' outfits – khaki – gave away the grimmer purpose of that voyage.

Quite suddenly, yet again, the good time ended. Loudspeakers crackled into life. Instructions echoed throughout the ship. This was it. The real thing. Life for the entire ship moved into a more urgent tempo. The invasion of Sicily was about to begin.

Then the wind freshened and grew in its intensity. After weeks of perfect weather a storm was brewing. Now the invasion fleet presented a far different picture as troop transports laden with seasick British Canadian and American soldiers strained to keep to the all-important timetable. Ships buffeted their way through gale-force winds and were tossed up and down as if on a giant roller-coaster.

As the 2,500 ships of the invasion fleet approached the Sicilian beaches the storm grew in fury to a force 7 gale! At dawn on 10 July the *Somersetshire* anchored off the port of Catania. Enemy aircraft attacked all shipping, dive-bombing, machine-gunning and roaring frighteningly, mast-top high over the ships, without any breaks in between. Freda recalled:

The noise was indescribable, absolute hell! Blazing ships sank in swirls of smoke and steam, ammunition exploded, anti-aircraft guns fired, shrapnel hurtled down, embedding itself in wooden decks. It was in this raid, a little further down the coast, we heard later, that the hospital ship *Talamba* was sunk. That too was in a deliberate attack, as the ship was loading stretcher-case casualties.

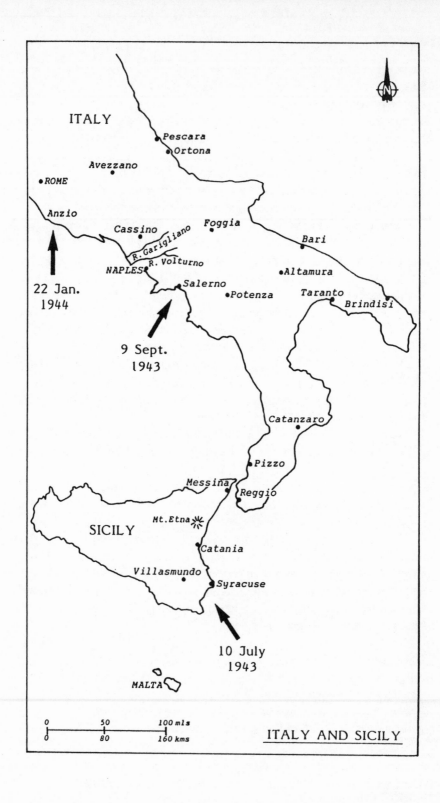

ITALY AND SICILY

Many had already been carried down to the wards when a direct hit from a dive-bomber wrecked the ship. It began to sink at an alarming rate and went down in twenty minutes whilst nurses, stretcher-bearers, doctors and crew rushed desperately up and down from the ward trying to get all the wounded off in time. One nurse did not make it and went down with the ship. Another was wounded but safely evacuated.

Mary Johnston, who was nearby on the *Leinster* heard how a surgeon on the *Talamba*, who had jut cut off a soldier's leg, could think of nothing better to do with the man than bandage his stump tightly, strap him to a stretcher and slide him over the rails into the water. 'He was picked up later and taken to hospital where he made an excellent recovery,' she recollected.[2] She was surprised to find how well stretchers floated and it made her wonder whether it was a wise procedure to transfer patients from stretchers to hospital ship cots when there was only a short journey in dangerous waters to be covered.

As the *Leinster* approached the appointed beach on the island, the nurses, who were all keyed up to tackle whatever task might come their way, were surprised to hear that they would be going close in to the beach at Licata which was being assaulted by American troops. The *Leinster* had been sent in their support as that particular US division did not have a hospital carrier of its own.[2]

The staff and crew of that small hospital carrier had a dreadful pummelling in the rough sea approaching the island. But Mary Johnston had an unusual attitude to wartime storms, as she was to write later: 'The more it thunders and lightnings, the happier one feels!' For Mary and her colleagues, a pounding from a rough sea was far better for them than one from German dive-bombers.

It was not so good for the small assault landing craft, though. They were tossed about like toy boats. Many of those with the US Seventh Army capsized at Licata, and of the men going in at Gela, twenty-seven drowned. Further down the coastline another nine men were drowned when a davit on a tank landing craft broke and dumped the soldiers into the heavy sea.

Leinster anchored just off the beach at Licata, where a US tank-infantry task force assaulted Yellow Beach. Surprisingly, there was scant opposition. And the whole affair gave the GIs a very amusing tale to tell in the bars afterwards.

It happened that most of the Italian defenders – reluctant allies of

Germany – had scattered, including those manning the Italian command post of that area. With the assault troops was a US war correspondent, Michael Chinigo of Italian descent, who spoke fluent Italian. Just as he dashed into the command bunker the telephone rang. He picked up the phone. A very agitated Italian general spoke: 'My adjutant says the Americans have landed at Liata. Please, I beg of you, say it isn't so.' Chinigo put on his most authoritative voice and assured the general that all was quiet on that front. *'Non preoccupati. Qui tutta va bene!'*

'Meno male!' said the general and settled down in bed again believing he had been misinformed by some nervous junior officer. Incidentally, Chinigo was later awarded the Silver Star for gallantry, a rare honour indeed for a civilian.

Nearby, US troops had met stiffer opposition and *Leinster* sent a water ambulance to the beach to pick up casualties. It had just returned at 6.30 p.m. with eighty stretcher cases, when a US patrol boat flashed a signal requesting an urgent despatch of water ambulances to the beach at Gela a few miles south of Licata.

Hurriedly, the *Leinster* crews finished off-loading the eighty casualties and by 9.30 the hospital carrier was nosing its way between the destroyers and supply ships lying at anchor off Gela beach. Apparently, the US 1st Infantry Division, the legendary 'Big Red One' – so named for its large red '1' on the division shoulder patch – had met stiff opposition and in fighting its way onto the beach-head had suffered heavy casualties.

Enemy aircraft droned overhead, and every few minutes anti-aircraft guns shattered the evening buzz of activity, bombs dropped and bright flares lit the scene momentarily. By this time it was dark and foggy. Orders came to send in water ambulances immediately.

The *Leinster* men had never operated water ambulances by night before. The Chief Officer gave instructions – simple ones, to follow him in line and obey his torch signals. The beach was strewn with wounded Americans and dead Italians.

Soldiers tend to be superstitious; Italian soldiers – and civilians – would walk round the dead and never touch them because they believed in the evil eye, which would bring death upon them too. British soldiers would sometimes dig graves for the dead, provided they were not asked to lift the bodies, even of their former pals, into the hole. They feared being tainted by death and being the next to go.

Mary Johnston also noted the curious attitude infantry soldiers had to death. When one of them died in the ward and the body was about to be taken out to be buried at sea the others would immediately realize what was happening. The Sergeant-Major came into the ward one day carrying a Union Jack under his arm. Mary Johnston glanced round the ward and there was not a man to be seen. They had all slid under the bed clothes and pulled the sheet over their heads. She dragged the sheet from one of them, and he said, 'Isn't he calling any of us yet?'

But the stretcher-bearers from the *Leinster* had no qualms about handling dead men. On that gruesome Gela beach they worked with hasty efficiency, sorting out the dead from those still alive and ferrying them speedily back to the hospital carrier. As soon as each water ambulance glided alongside the ship it was hoisted up to the deck with its load of wounded, who were then sorted out by the medical officers. A sister stood by, ready to give injections of serum or morphia.

Morphine was a great life-saver. Shock was the cause of so many deaths but if morphine were given to deaden the pain, shock cases could often be pulled through. Many infantry officers in both the British and the US Armies carried ampoules of morphine to give injections in the field of battle. British infantry platoon commanders often carried these ampoules and an indelible pencil to write a large 'M' on the forehead of anyone given an injection. This certainly helped to give wounded men a better chance. In the US Army, too, many infantry soldiers carried their own supply of sulphanilamide to sprinkle on wounds in order to reduce the risk of infection.[3]

An urgent signal sent the hospital ship *Somersetshire* to the bay of Syracuse, still packed with shipping which attracted all the dive-bombers the Luftwaffe could muster. The medical officers and eight sisters of No. 7 CCS had been working non-stop since the invasion began. Its CO, Colonel J.D.P. Macpherson explained in his War Diary how they coped:

We have a large reception ward capable of holding 50 to 60 cases at a time. From 'reception' the wounded go to 'resuscitation'. We have three surgical teams working a 12 hour tour of duty and one team always on call. The operating hours work out on average at 16 hours for each surgeon.

The mortality rate in cases of abdominal wounds, is 50 per cent. This is also the experience of other CCS.

Light wounds are dressed, given 24 hours rest and a bath, a change of under-clothes, a shirt and a haircut before being returned to unit. On arrival all cases that can manage it, have a cup of tea, a slab of cake and a packet of cigarettes.[4]

Sometimes casualties came directly from warships. The *Leinster* had been working non-stop for many hours when a destroyer signalled that it was coming alongside with sixteen severely wounded sailors. Dawn was just breaking and the nurses were taking their first cups of tea when the destroyer came close – too close. The hospital carrier's Captain shouted to the destroyer: 'Stand clear! I'll send a boat for the wounded.'[5]

They were a pitiful-looking group. A few of the wounded were on stretchers but most of the very severely burnt were walking because it was too painful for them to lie on a stretcher. All of them were terribly burnt about the face, arms and body.

One young lad being helped aboard was black with oil, his arms held out straight, too painful to hold down, his face and chest covered in huge blisters. From those that had broken, serum oozed and ran down in streams. But before being treated he offered to help with some of the other men. Six hours later he was dead.[6]

Six more of them died that night. Mary and the nurses watched from the bridge of the *Leinster* as, wrapped in their sacking shrouds and weighted so that they would sink immediately, they were carried out on stretchers and placed in a line on the deck. Each one was covered with the flag of his nationality and the stretcher-bearers, dressed as they would have for a drill parade, stood rigidly to attention, paying their final respects as the short burial service was read. It was a deeply moving ceremony that evening with the sun setting beyond a vast expanse of sea. The engines were stopped and over the ship was a holy quiet as those memorable words were spoken: 'Greater love hath no man than this: that he lay down his life for another.'

The nurses had to get used to the nerve-racked men having nightmares in their wards. The worst would need special treatment in specialist psychiatric hospitals. But generally they found that casualties did not complain much. They said that it was good enough just to be alive, as Agatha Tinne (then Sister Dampier-Child) of the Navy hospital ship *Vita* recalled: 'They were marvellously brave, and never grumbled.'

Once on board a hospital ship, casualties felt a surge of relief. It is easy to imagine the release from anxiety at being away from the terror of the battle, and how marvellous to be lying in a bed with clean white sheets and food freshly cooked for them. Freda Barnfather said that often they would fall asleep and not wake up for forty-eight hours. She did make the point though that hospital ships could often give the impression of calm normality whilst the reality of what was going on elsewhere in the ship was very different.

For example, in the operating theatre, when I was theatre sister, surgeons worked for hours on end, day and night as the hospital ship made its way from Sicily to Phillipville on the North African coast. Often they worked under very difficult conditions. A rolling ship in dangerous waters was not the ideal setting for an intricate operation. Only the really essential operations were carried out, those primarily directed towards the preservation of life and limb. Otherwise surgeons thought it better for the patient to rest as much as possible.

Resuscitation from shock was also one of the first considerations. Medical officers in the field of battle had two main aims; the first was to make the casualty stable enough to be transported and to preserve his life until a well-equipped hospital could be reached, and the second was to prepare a casualty to withstand any life-saving surgery that might be necessary and to prevent infection of the wound.

Surgeons with responsibility for the care of hundreds of wounded soldiers were confronted with a host of problems requiring decisions to be made, with little time for deliberation or discussion with other specialists. Yet, according to the Surgeon Consultant, Allied Force Headquarters, Edward Churchill, rarely was there any evidence of a hasty, slap-dash and bloody spectacle of an operation, with rapid evacuation of the patient to the rear.[7]

A fleet of ambulances waited for the casualties as they were off loaded from the *Somersetshire* at Phillipville. Straight away the nurses busied themselves preparing the wards for the next intake when they sailed for Sicily the following day.

A wireless message directed us towards the beach where the casualties were waiting. Some were sorted right away, others had to wait until they were hauled on deck. They were a pitiful sight, abdominal wounds, compound fractures, amputations of arms, legs, feet and thighs. Some of the casualties had had an arm or a leg either partially or completely blown off, so the surgeons had had no choice.

Stretcher-bearers bringing the casualties back to the hospital ships said they had never seen so many wounded and dying on the battlefield. Indeed, the official history of the Durham Light Infantry makes the same point: 'Men who had experienced the fiercest fighting of the North African campaign at Alamein and Mareth said they had never seen so much slaughter in such a small area.' The three DLI battalions had lost 500 killed and wounded.[8]

And this was what Churchill had called 'the soft under-belly of Europe'. It turned out to be a 'tough old gut'. Stretcher-bearers on the long back-breaking journey carrying casualties from the beach to the *Somersetshire*'s water ambulances, came back with tales of an area littered with broken rifles and machine-guns, bundles of blood-stained clothing, shattered anti-tank cannon and dead soldiers. Stretcher-bearer Stanley Mitchell remembered 'the sickly, all-pervading smell of unburied German dead, their sun-blackened faces like negroes, their bodies putrefying by the roadside, bloated and puffed up by the gases within'.

Somehow, those men and women looking after the maimed and mutilated bodies retrieved from the battlefield managed to carry on without breaking down with the stress of it all. It was the same story on the ships of the Royal Navy. Marine Corporal Bernard Hallas manned 15-inch guns on the battleship *Warspite* during the whole time it was engaged in battles at Narvik, Cape Matapan, Crete, North Africa, Libya, Sicily, Salerno and Normandy, during which time she was hit no fewer than 29 times by enemy shell-fire. He had his own ideas about the post-traumatic stress syndrome much talked about these days. 'It wasn't that we were hard-skinned and didn't feel sorry for our mates who had been killed or smashed up. It was just that we never had time to think about it then. We had to carry on with the action or grab something to eat or a bit of sleep if there was a lull.'

On hospital ships it was always a relief for everyone when the last casualty was aboard and the ship set sail for the open sea and its voyage across the Mediterranean to Phillipville. 'As we steamed steadily along that sea as blue as the sky above and so flat and calm after the dreadful din of naval big guns firing, and aircraft flying overhead, it was difficult to believe that we carried such a sorry cargo,' Freda reflected.

There would be many more of those 'sorry cargoes' before General Patton's American Seventh Army met Montgomery's British Eighth Army on the northern tip of the island. The generals and politicians then claimed a resounding victory. Alexander, the Allied Operational Commander for the campaign reported that 'the last German soldier' had been 'flung out of Sicily and all Italian forces on the island had been destroyed'. Newspapers in Britain carried stories about Sicily, the bastion of Hitler's 'European fortress' being in Allied hands and a great victory having been achieved over German troops.

The truth was different. The Germans succeeded in evacuating a large part of their army: 40,000 men, taking with them nearly 50 tanks and 10,000 other vehicles, 94 guns and 17,000 tons of supplies. Those troops had inflicted much heavier losses on the allies than they had suffered themselves, but what mattered more was that they had escaped to fight another day.

Afterwards General Eisenhower had the honesty to admit that with the Sicilian Campaign, the Allies had blundered. It had cost them some 30,000 men dead, wounded and missing. Furthermore, Montgomery in his memoirs added, 'If the planning and conduct of the Sicilian campaign were bad, the preparation for the invasion of Italy, and subsequent conduct of the campaign in that country, were even worse.'[9]

He was right. One bloodbath followed another as the Allies fought their way up the length of Italy. Each river line and mountain ridge was taken at appalling cost. And the nurses as usual would be close at hand to pick up the pieces. Fortunately, perhaps, they did not know what lay in store for them.

12   The Avalanche that Never Was

> It was a puzzling and most disappointing campaign. No doubt the authorities will eventually reveal that there was something wrong somewhere.
>
> Alan Moorehead, war correspondent in Italy, *Eclipse*[1]

Security was lax. If anyone heard any news they talked, whatever their rank. A general commanding an Allied division was sent home in disgrace when the censor read his letter to his wife. He told her he would be celebrating their wedding anniversary in Italy.

Sister Lorna Bradey then serving in a hospital in Tripoli, also heard the news.

We were invited to dances in neighbouring units. We also went to other ranks' dances and it was policy to accept. They were most enjoyable for they danced far better than the officers. It was when we were invited to a Sergeants' Mess party that I heard the news. A red-headed sergeant, full of his own importance and drink, told me the troop movements to Italy, including the date and the place where they would be going. I went back to our hospital in agonies of uncertainty, but then I thought of Tripoli teeming with spies, and that if anything happened to those troops I'd have to live with it all my life. So I reported the incident. I felt dreadful but he was court-martialled and reduced to the ranks. When I also went over to Italy not long afterwards and looked after the wounded soldiers from Salerno I was no longer sorry for reporting the sergeant.

Denis Healey, later Chancellor of the Exchequer and now Lord Healey, then a major and a beachmaster for assault landings in Italy,

146

recalled how he was sent to Tripoli three times, and there, he said, 'they were planning the landing at Salerno in conditions of almost total publicity.'[2] Rumours spread like weeds in a wet summer. Nurses in Phillipville exchanged the latest information over glasses of Tunisian red wine. Medical orderlies heard the name of the bay bandied about in the NAAFI. *Salerno*! South of Naples.

The Germans had already heard. They too were getting ready.

Operation Avalanche, the Salerno assault, was full of risks. The invasion beaches were too far away for effective fighter cover and defended not by indifferent Italian infantry but by highly trained German divisions. They were also at the end of a long sea crossing for both the troop-carrying and the hospital ships. In the first week of September 1943, close on 100,000 British and 69,000 American soldiers gathered for the invasion of Italy.

Meanwhile hospital ships ran a shuttle service clearing hospital wards in Sicily and North Africa, ready to receive casualties from the next operations. Said Freda Barnfather:

Usually we'd sail between Sicily and Phillipville and mostly at night with all identification lights blazing, but we never felt sure that some over enthusiastic German pilot would not drop a spare bomb on us.

As soon as we were no longer needed on the Sicily run we were sent to Tripoli to get the ship ready to leave at short notice. Meanwhile we were kept occupied with lifeboat drill, being lowered in the big wooden boats from the davits and then practising rowing and manoeuvering the boats in the sea.

At that time, more hospital ships were concentrating in the North African ports. In Bizerta the *Aba* arrived, then the hospital ship *Newfoundland* and the Navy hospital ship *Vita* with Sister Agatha Dampier-Child (later Tinne) of the QARNNS on board. She remembered that time well for a very good reason:

I'd been sent on the troopship *Almanzora* to Bombay, where I was to join the *Vita*. On board the troopship were 3,000 men and eleven women, six of whom were Navy nurses.

It was a memorable voyage out mainly, I'm sure, because of a romantic meeting. It happened that I got to know a very courteous Army medical officer, John Ernest. He was tall with fair curly hair, son of a Liverpool doctor. To our surprise, we shared the same unusual hobbies – collecting rare specimens of wild flowers and unusual sea shells. Soon, never a day went by without us meeting and talking excitedly about our flowers.

To pass the time and help in the entertainment of the troops I took part in a ship's concert and at the end of it my new friend came onto the stage and presented me with a colourful bouquet of flowers. They were made out of toilet paper and bits from his medical stores. He must have spent hours making them.

By the time we reached Cape Town we were almost inseparable. There, in a foursome, we went up Table Mountain and on top we roamed about picking flowers and came down as a twosome. That same evening we took dinner together in a small café before going back to the ship. We sailed round the Cape to Durban, where we all had to leave the ship; the troops went to a huge transit camp and the officers to a hotel. Whilst waiting for our next ship we made a few trips out of town on picnics. Once we went to a lovely beach at Amanzimtoti, where we collected some marvellous seashells. During this period of waiting John and I went out to dine several times. He called for me one evening wearing his best service dress and a Sam Browne belt. I knew he didn't have one of these belts with him, so I thought it odd, as though that evening was going to be special. It was. After dinner he asked me to marry him. I accepted right away.

He rushed into town next morning and bought an engagement ring which he put on my finger. It was just in time, for twelve hours later I embarked on a small ship going to Bombay. Just before the ship sailed, a large bunch of flowers arrived for me – real ones this time!

Agatha must have wondered how long it would be before she saw John again – if at all. As events turned out, she was still in Bombay when the second convoy from Durban came in.

I found out that John Ernest was on one of the ships so I stood on the quay-side in my white uniform staring up at the ship's rail, over which hundreds of Tommies lean. Then I spotted him. I felt very foolish shouting 'Hello' but it was so lovely to see him again. He managed to get off that ship before any of the others and we spent the rest of the day togther up in the hills – picking flowers again!

I joined the hospital ship *Vita* the next day and John went on to Burma. I wondered if we really would meet again one day, as the words of the popular song then reassured all young lovers.

For several months the *Vita* made short trips down the Red Sea and lay for ages in the stifling heat of Port Taufiq, Suez. We had a small isolation ward aft and on one occasion took on board some Army personnel suffering from leprosy. On another voyage we had an intake of tuberculosis patients. I felt so sorry for them down below in the ship where it was so airless, in spite of the blowers. The atmosphere was terrible, with fifty-one patients coughing and spluttering TB germs everywhere. In rough seas we closed all sea doors and it was even more hot and sticky.

It was really upsetting to see young men in their twenties with extensive bilateral tubercular infection. I felt angry that the disease was so far advanced before it was discovered. We buried some of those young men at sea. The others we disembarked at Durban.

However, to get back to the *Vita*, we were at Durban when orders came for us to go to Tripoli. We were delighted with our first view of the town. After the sweltering heat of Suez, Tripoli looked clean and fresh, with its well-kept squares bordered by trees and green grass.

Another interesting view was presented to the nurses on that day too – a destroyer moored alongside the *Vita* as Agatha recalled:

Suddenly young sailors, stripped to their birthday suits were appearing at the rails and leaping joyously into the water, not realizing there were ladies aboard the ship lying so close to them. We all had a good laugh at their embarrassment as they started to climb back to their destroyer whilst orders were being given for them to swim around to the other side.

We soon had work to do, embarking patients from Tripoli hospitals to clear the wards. We were all struck with how wonderful those wounded men were. Most of them were so cheerful and pleased to see us, even those who were terribly disabled. We took them to Alexandria and almost immediately we then set off for Reggio on the toe of Italy. The sea was exceptionally rough. Almost everybody was seasick and the Third Engineer had a mental breakdown. However, ill as we felt on arrival, we worked very hard embarking a full complement of patients at Reggio and set off for Phillipville in North Africa. Again I marvelled at the way they made little of their disabilities. In my diary I wrote: 'The men are magnificent, bless them.'

One after another Navy and Army hospital ships pulled into the harbours of North Africa. On 8 September 1943, at about five o'clock in the afternoon, a nurse came running to Mary Johnston's cabin on the *Leinster*, bursting to tell her the joyful news. Italy had surrendered! 'That night we had a celebration dinner,' Mary recalled. Those joyful nurses did not know then that soon, they would be in a far grimmer phase of the war than they had ever experienced.

Orkan – the code word flashed to all German troops taking their siesta around Salerno Bay. *Orkan* – prepare for Allied landing. German infantry and artillery regiments, and the 16th Panzer Division moved into position. Look-outs scanned the sea. Crack German troops commanded by Field Marshal Kesselring were waiting for the big seaborne invasion of which they had heard.

Somewhere beyond the horizon lay an armada of 450 ships, packed with men of the Allied Fifth Army, soldiers with orders to blast their way across the beaches and up the road north to the vital port of Naples. One of the fiercest, bloodiest actions of the Second World War was about to begin. It was to be an operation which turned out to be a painful tale of terrible confusion and horror.

The casualties were enormous. Under fire themselves, the nurses took the wounded from the beaches to safe hospitals in North Africa. The Allied assault troops were still fighting on the beaches when the hospital carrier *Leinster* sailed in for the first load of casualties. The bay was a mass of shipping – cruisers, destroyers, supply ships, minesweepers and landing craft. Just then all ships ran up the 'red' warning flags to indicate enemy planes overhead.[3]

It had not been the best time for Allied assault troops to go in, for they had heard of Italy's capitulation on the ship's wireless the previous evening. The momentous news had been received with incredulous cheers and a great sense of relief by the invaders. But it created a false idea that the enemy was disintegrating. They expected an easy landing since the Italians had given up. They did not expect the Germans to be waiting.

Somewhat off guard, the first assault troops were surprised by their fierce reception. Three days after the first wave of troops with their supporting CCS landed, the Allies were barely hanging onto a foothold on two narrow beaches, in grave danger of being thrown back into the sea instead of being in Naples as planned.

On the first day of the Salerno landings, the Navy hospital ship *Amarapoora* embarked over 300 casualties from the beaches. They were in a sorry state: dirty, bloody and plagued with black flies, which settled on oozing field dressings and on the tear ducts of men whose wounds prevented them from wafting them away. The wounded lay blinking in pain, waiting for their turn to be taken to beds in hospital ships.

Agatha Tinne vividly recalled the sight of hundreds of wounded soldiers being loaded onto HMHS *Vita*.

We packed stretcher cases in wherever we could find space; those not in cots lay on tables, hatches and in the chapel. It took us all our time to care for them. A bizarre scene sticks in my mind: a Sunday morning church service – God knows how we found time – we were singing 'The King of love my shepherd is', whilst guns thudded a base accompaniment!

I was on night duty on the way to Bizerta; the sea was very rough and although everyone was ill we just worked as fast as we could giving urgent medication on the way. One patient died and we stopped the ship to bury him at sea.

No sooner had we off-loaded all patients than we left straight away for Catania where we embarked 160 patients whom we took to Algiers this time. There the staff and equipment of the 65th Army Mobile Hospital came on board to come with us to the Salerno beach, where they were urgently needed.

Vita was continuously shuttling patients from one part of the Mediterranean to another. For those Navy nurses on board the work was particularly difficult because the ship was originally built as an old-fashioned coal burner of about 5,000 tons. It had been hurriedly converted for its new role as a hospital ship but before the job was finished had been sent down to British Somaliland to evacuate troops. Consequently, unlike other hospital ships, the *Vita* did not have well-designed wards and had no forced draughts of air in them. Moreover the ward floor was often flooded because the sea doors did not have the requisite amount of packing.

Amongst the nurses' duties on the *Vita* when they had no patients on board was training the Goanese cooks in the art of preparing diets for the sick and checking all stores and noting deficiencies in equipment. Thanks to their ingenuity and the ability of the staff to make light of difficulties which resulted from deficiencies in equipment, the *Vita* was nevertheless known as a happy ship. Typical of the camaraderie was an incident involving an Indian needing blood. Agatha remembered him well.

We had picked up some severely wounded soldiers from an Indian division as well as some with a serious medical condition. They had been waiting a long time for a hospital ship to take them home to the east and for weeks they had been existing on iron rations. They were absolutely delighted when they came on board and had real hot curry and rice. We nurses dripped with sweat as we served the walking wounded from the galley hatch either vegetable or meat curry.

There was one young Indian soldier, however, who was dying and urgently needed a blood transfusion. We could never keep fresh blood for long and the medical staff as well as the chaplain and paymaster had already given as much of their own as they could spare, so we had to ask amongst the patients themselves if any of them would give some blood. A Gurkha offered his. You can imagine how we all prayed that it would be the right group. It was. The transfusion was successful and the soldier got safely back to his native land.

What sticks out in my memory too is the way that Moslems and Hindus all got on so well together. True, we had to stop the Moslems putting their clean white bed sheets on the deck as prayer mats but we said they could use the grey army blankets.

Picture the scene if you can as those patients were disembarked at Karachi. The ladies of the local Raj sat on the quayside under large umbrellas and put a gift parcel onto each stretcher as it was carried ashore.

Nurses on another Navy Hospital ship, HMHS *Oxfordshire*, were then working under intense pressure off the beaches of Salerno. By using every inch of space available they sometimes managed to carry to safety as many as 800 casualties on each trip. Once on board the hospital ship, doctors and nurses moved quickly from one casualty to the next, giving appropriate treatment. Today it might seem surprising, but to combat the effects of shock and to make the casualty as comfortable as possible in the ship's ward it was a cigarette which was one of the first things to be given. Surgeon Commander T.N. D'Arcy expressed his belief in the therapeutic value of a cigarette in an article he wrote for *The Journal of the Royal Naval Medical Service*. He said:

Wounded men who have already received temporary treatment are put to bed and made as comfortable as possible and here a cigarette is almost as valuable as the injections given – indeed it is sought before anything else, except in those cases of extreme shock, where all interest, even in life itself, has practically gone. The surgeon takes details. If the patient is in pain, additional morphia to that already given is ordered and the injection repeated as often as is necessary to relieve his suffering. No notice of previous amounts of this drug need be taken into account, for the correct amount required is that for peace of body and mind.[4]

For several weeks the Navy hospital ship *Amarapoora*, like the Army hospital ships and carriers there, worked a shuttle service between the Gulf of Salerno and the base hospitals of the North African ports of Bizerta, Phillipville and Tripoli. In between, there was always the decision to be made as to whether it was safer to anchor offshore amidst the warships and have the advantage of their covering anti-aircraft fire or to cruise out at sea at night with their identification lights blazing.

At all the North African ports, physical activity during the afternoon was difficult. Unloading critically wounded soldiers in the intensely hot conditions, when the sirocco was blowing with its usual accompaniment of dust and sand, and carrying them onto hospital trains left the men, and often the nurses, with their hands padded with blisters, their backs aching and their shirts black with sweat. After the loading of trains was finished there was little opportunity for rest before the return voyage began. Sailing back to the Gulf of Salerno everyone was busy getting cots and wards cleaned and ready for the next load of wounded.

It was all well worth the effort. Surgeon Commander D'Arcy's experience convinced him of the value of having hospital ships as close to the combat zone as possible. He said: 'Practically everyone stresses the great importance of early treatment of wounds from whatever cause. The more likely the wound is to become septic, the greater is the urgency.'

He realized that medical officers and nurses had problems in treating casualties on hospital ships under normal conditions, but when under attack from enemy aircraft he said it became a formidable nightmare of a task.

Anyone who has had to cope with many wounded after action in a small ship will sympathize with the medical officer and nurse placed in a similar position. There's a feeling almost of panic in deciding how and where to begin. Lights are out, wounded are crawling about in dark corners, cries for help come from the bottom of ladders where twisted and torn metal make investigations terribly difficult and urgent cries for the doctor arrive from several parts of the ship at the same time. How can one remain calm in such an atmosphere?'[5]

Mary Johnston remembered all too well how it was in the *Leinster* when they were attacked. On one occasion she had just finished dressing the hand of a lad who had had his thumb shot away when there was a roar and almost simultaneously a crash. The ship rocked, mugs fell off the table, bandages and bowls went in all directions and there was an alarming swish of water in the next ward, where fortunately there were no patients. Casualties who could still stand up automatically flung themselves to the floor. The hard-headed Lancashire sister working with Mary called out, 'It's all right, chaps, it's only a bomb.' To everyone's amazement they found that the ship was still going. People picked themselves up and started gathering up the debris.[6]

Fortunately there were amusing incidents to brighten the day. On one of their shuttle trips to the Salerno South Beach in the *Leinster*, Mary Johnston had just settled the last of the fifty-six stretcher cases into their ward when she spotted a huge basket on the deck. It was full of apples. 'They're bomb falls,' said one of the stretcher-bearers. 'We picked them up when we were on shore.' She looked around again when she heard a strange fluttering noise. There were half a dozen hens fluttering around looking for a perch. It was just the kind of comedy farce needed to relieve the tension, she recalled. 'In between the bombs, gunfire or creaking of the derrick, the rooster would fly onto the bridge and crow with as much vigour and importance as if on a five-barred gate on a Sussex farm.'

On the night of 13 September, all four hospital ships then operating off the Salerno beaches, with all lights blazing, were led out by a minesweeper to a safer anchorage offshore. Soon the hospital ship *Triera* joined them. Patients and nurses settled down to a peaceful night's sleep well clear of the beaches. It was a night none of the nurses would ever forget.

It was exactly 04.55 hours when the first explosion shook the *Leinster*, and dawn was breaking. Mary Johnston got up, dressed and went on deck. Other sisters joined her. A deafening roar came at them from the starboard side, and the hospital carrier lurched drunkenly. The nurses peered towards the other hospital ships in the half-light.

'I can only count three other ships. I'm sure one has been hit,' said a sister. There was only blackness in the place where there had been lights before. Then as Mary gazed through the murky dawn, a glowing eye glittered in the vague outline of one ship. It expanded into a longer array of bright gashes.

The hospital ship *Newfoundland* was flaring up into a great conflagration hurling sparks and long tongues of flame into the grey sky. Boats from the *St Andrew* were picking up casualties, nurses and crew members and bringing them back, overloaded and dangerously low in the water. The survivors brought sad news. The first bomb had fallen directly onto the sleeping quarters of the nurses and medical officers. All five medical officers had been killed, and six nursing sisters were never seen again. Also lost were eight RAMC men and nineteen of the crew.[7] Of the hundred American nursing officers on board who were to set up their own hospital at Salerno, all except one escaped unhurt as they were sleeping in a ward at the opposite end of the ship.

It was crisis time for Salerno and especially for the nurses. Casualty clearing stations on the beaches were under shellfire. A shell which landed on the operating theatre of No.14 British CCS killed the surgeon and his patient. Supported by heavy artillery the Germans counter-attacked, determined to 'Dunkirk' the British once again – as they had in Crete – and run them into the sea.

Plans by US General Mark Clark to withdraw all Americans from their beach-head were countered by Alexander. The battle-experienced Alexander had been at Dunkirk in 1940 and seen how discipline collapsed with a withdrawal. Now he said grimly and firmly, as he had done at the first battle of Alamein in August 1942: 'We stay here and we die here. *We do not retreat.*'

That evening he signalled Malta asking for the battleships, *Warspite* and *Valiant* to come to Salerno and use their 15-inch guns on the German defenders holding up the American attack and silence the heavy artillery shelling the beaches from the hills inland. Royal Marine Corporal Bernard Hallas, in charge of one of the 15-inch gun crews rememberd the day well.

We were only half a mile from the beach and very conspicuous amongst the other shipping. We gave the German gun positions a good pasting and I learnt afterwards that nineteen of the thirty 15-inch rounds fell exactly on target. By the time we had finished firing we were dripping with sweat in our anti-flash and action clothing. We sailed out of the bay but went in again next day. Once more our guns hurled their 1-ton shells into the German defensive positions. But we didn't get away with it. We had just sailed out of the bay when the much-hated radio-guided armour-piercing bomb hit the ship. The first one cut right through the decks into the No.4 boiler room before exploding. Thick clouds of yellow smoke filled every gangway and cabin. Nine men were killed and fourteen wounded. Casualties were nursed by sick-berth attendants until they could be transferred to a hospital ship.

We picked up the bits of bodies; heads we could recognize were put on hammocks and other parts put in with them until they were stitched up and laid out on deck. They were buried at sea when we had time. And that was the thing, really, we had no time to think. None of that post-traumatic stress business for us. We'd grab a bite to eat and get on with what we were doing.

Warspite's boiler rooms were flooded, the engines had given, and she would not steer and she was drifting into a known minefield. To the rescue came two US salvage tugs, *Hopi* and *Moreno*.

All hospital ships now worked at full speed removing wounded casualties from the shell-pocked beaches. In a letter home to her brother, Agatha wrote:

It's so thrilling and I am so proud to be taking part in this phase of the war. I should love to tell you all about it but the censor would not let me. It's all very exciting to be ploughing through the sea with our engines flat out, and the wonderful cheerfulness of our patients. Sometimes they're British Tommies and sometimes American. The GIs don't like our mugs of tea. They want "cawfee" or "tomayto juice".

One night we really packed them in and I was on night duty as we sailed in a storm. I had to go up and down the rows of cots, stumbling over patients lying on mattresses on the floor between the cots, others were asleep on tables and anywhere a stretcher could be wedged. You can imagine how difficult it was trying to find the right patient for the right medicine. The report said there was one patient on the forward hatch who had to have M and B 693 four hourly. When I got there I found ten patients on that hatch and so to find the right one without waking all the others was not easy. We were so rushed that we had to cut out the finer points of nursing and stick to essentials. With hardly any space to put our feet we somehow managed to get round them all, feeding and coaxing the really ill to eat, but in spite of all the difficulties I was happy and we laughed a lot with the patients.

When we came to disembark the patients from the *Vita* on that trip there were only ten walking wounded. We had to lift all the rest. That was really hard work.

And so the evacuation of casualties proceeded. The fuller story of nurses in action at Salerno is told in the companion volume to this, *Front-line Nurse*.

Fortunately for the nurses on the hospital ships, new arrangements were suddenly available for evacuating the wounded. The Eighth Army, which had landed on the toe of Italy a week before the Salerno landings had at last linked up with the Fifth Army and the roads were now open to casualty clearing stations and hospitals in southern Italy.

Four days later General Kesselring decided to withdraw his divisions opposing the Fifth Army on the Salerno beach-head. Salerno was in Allied hands at last. The campaign had, as General Clark said in a message to General Eisenhower, 'been a close-run thing'. The men who had had to fight at Salerno were more forthright in summing up the campaign. 'Salerno was a shambles which only the bravery of the troops and junior commanders coupled with the support of the Navy's heavy guns, together with countless RAF sorties, managed to surmount,' was how infantry officer Brian Harpur saw it.[8]

The ill-starred Operation Avalanche had cost 12,000 casualties.

With the end of fighting in the Salerno beach-head, the hospital ships were no longer needed there. Some of them had a lucky break in the meantime. The *Somersetshire*, with Freda Barnfather aboard, for example, was directed to Alexandria where it took on board patients with injuries which would put them out of action completely, or at least for a very long time.

We had no idea what our destination would be. Medical staff who had been in Alexandria for a long time adopted a supercilious air and assured everyone that we would be going to South Africa. They were wrong. We clapped our hands with delight when we heard where we were in fact going – England. Home. And best of all, home for Christmas.

The remaining casualties from Salerno and new ones from the central front on the road to Rome were evacuated by mules, jeep and motor ambulances to CCS and field hospitals established close behind the Eighth Army front on the east coast directly across the Italian peninsula from Salerno. The hospital ships began pulling in to the small port of Barletta just near Bari. There, in the thick of the mud and bloody casualties of a tented operating theatre, was Sister Lorna Bradey.

13　A Rich Tapestry of Experience

Fifty years ago there was not the variety of drugs to cure
diseases and illnesses, and the recovery of patients
depended largely upon good nursing – tender loving care
or TLC – and of course, good luck.

Sister Betty Halliday (née Lawrence), QARNNS

There it was, at last – Bombay. Betty Lawrence stood at the rail of the
troopship *Strathmore* and marvelled. Never as a girl at school had she
ever thought she would see the country which had intrigued her so
much. India – the very name conjured up the pageantry of mahara-
jahs, tiger shoots, magnificently adorned elephants, polo matches,
princes in shimmering ceremonial dress, brilliant yellow with
diamond necklaces, ruby rings and white trousers and Taj-Mahal-
type monuments.

The voyage had been most enjoyable. A superb ship's concert
party had entertained them and it was after one of those concerts, in
which Betty took part, that she had earned the title of the 'gypsy
princess'. There was also an Army major who had brought with him
a portable wind-up gramophone and a collection of classical records.
He invited Betty to listen to his records and she became hooked on
Richard Wagner.

Perhaps it was the music or maybe the cruise-like atmosphere of
the ship that aroused another passion – a romantic one. She met Bill
Halliday, a Sub-Lieutenant in the Royal Navy, a man who enjoyed
wild escapades, a man she would one day marry.

She had looked forward so much to their arrival in Bombay. For the whole of the long journey from the UK the ship had been 'dry' – no bar, no alcohol of any kind for both officers and other ranks. But it could have been worse, as the purser had been quick to tell the nurses. 'At least we came the short way. We are the first convoy to sail through the Med since 1940 and we fared better than two of our sister ships of the P & O Line, which were torpedoed and sunk just after entering the Mediterranean.'

At last the ship eased its way leisurely into India's best harbour on the Arabian Sea. Now they could enjoy shore leave for a day or two. As they drew near to the quayside the smell hit them first and then the noise. The stench was powerful, as Betty recalled: 'It was a pungent smell you could only describe as a mixture of rotting vegetables, curry spices, charcoal smoke, oil and oriental perfumes. And the noise! A clamorous shouting, barking of stray dogs, clanking of machinery, goods trains blowing their whistles and clattering along the quayside.'

To the newly arrived men and women standing at the rail then, Bombay looked anything but attractive, with paint faded by the pitiless sun and peeling from woodwork. An air of neglect hung over everything, but they were all anxious to get ashore.

First to disembark were the RAF airmen and their officers, after being reminded by the Medical Officer to be careful and avoid the risks of catching venereal disease. They had listened to the MO's fearsome warnings about soft chancres and going blind many times before; now they just wanted to be off that boat and seeing things for themselves.

As soon as breakfast was over the RAF men went ashore.

It was not only the men who were keen to see for themselves.

The nurses had to stay aboard until the next day to sort out their posting orders. It was towards the end of that boring day and evening that some of them passed the time talking to a group of young naval officers on board. They had seen the way the Air Force men had scampered off the boat, hell-bent on finding beer and women, and watched those same men coming back, most of them drunk, arm in arm, helping each other up the gangways with much fraternity and conviviality, many of them talking in loud voices of the prostitutes they had seen in Grant Road. One squadron leader, as drunk as any of the airmen, had been particularly impressed. As far as his slurred speech could convey any sense, he said to the nurses: 'You must go.

Must go to Madame André's brothel. Never seen anything like it. You must go. You'll see!'

'Why don't *we* go and have a look at these brothels, then?' suggested one sub-lieutenant, mainly as a casual remark designed to shock. But it was taken seriously by the fun-loving Betty, who was game for most adventurous activities.

An old sweat with tattooed arms and the lined, leathery cheeks of a heavy smoker, who had come aboard with the Army Transport Section, knew where to go and gave them explicit directions. The Grant Road brothel area, he said, was an essential part of every serviceman's Bombay itinerary.

A few weeks earlier, a young RAF Corporal Physical Training Instructor, James Young, who would later become a top BBC disc jockey and radio celebrity, had already been taken down Grant Road by his mates, who thought his sexual experience needed extending as he frankly related in his autobiography.[1] But it was an experience which was never fully completed for when he had downed a few beers and his pals led him to a house of ill repute in the 'out of bounds' area behind Green's Restaurant and dancehall he thought better of the whole idea and fled. Military Police patrol went in hot pursuit, but they were no match for the former RAF rugby three-quarter, who had dodged his way past many a burly defender.

Betty recalled how she came to see the sights of Grant Road.

Two young naval officers, Bill and his friend, said they'd take my friend and me to see the infamous red-light area. Most of the RAF lads had come back to the ship in the late evening, drunk, regaling their mates with lewd stories which probably owed more to their imagination and secret fantasies than to fact, but they made us all the more determined to go and see for ourselves what went on in that brothel area.

We knew we were taking risks going into the 'out of bounds' area, but when you're young and have been cooped up on a 'dry' boat for six or seven weeks there are some rules which only apply to other people – or so you think.

The next day was fine but it had rained overnight and the water lay around in puddles waiting to be steamed up by the sun. However, the forecast was promising when they set out that evening a cheerful foursome of Betty, her friend Olive and the two young naval officers they had met on the boat.

They hurried along narrow streets, passing legions of underfed, ragged women and children, blind beggars and cripples in various incredible contortions behind their begging bowls. One man had his legs behind his neck, and next to him was a limbless man in a basket. Men squatting with their backs to the shady wall of the buildings were hawking and spitting into the dust.

I thought they were spitting blood, covering the pavement with red blobs, until I was told it was just betel juice from the nuts they were chewing. I was certainly glad to reach the Taj Mahal Restaurant where we had some lovely ham sandwiches with cups of tea.

After this we made the mistake of asking a local Indian for the red-light district and he thought we meant the Red Dock — they had different colours for different docks. So we walked a long way before we realized that we were nowhere near the houses where the prostitutes offered their wares.

A horse-drawn garry stopped by us and the driver, a little man who looked as if the hot sun had shrivelled him into a dry husk, asked if he could take us anywhere. When we told him we wanted to go to Grant Road, he nodded, 'OK, OK, I know', blew his nose on his fingers as he waited for us to get in, patted his hands on the sides of his trousers, and then set the skinny horse off at a steady trot.

At the end of Grant Road the garry driver pulled up and said: 'Here you are. Naughty women. Naughty men. OK?' He held out his hand.

They put rupees in his leathery palm. They looked around and along the length of Grant Road where lights shone from the front rooms of every house they could see. And their eyes widened in amazement. As Betty recalled:

Grant Road was a revelation to us all. The ladies plying the oldest profession set out their stall in their heavily-barred front room windows. It was just as if they were birds in a cage as they sat in provocative poses with their colourful saris tantalizingly lifted to reveal part of a curvaceous breast or thigh. Most of them were heavily made up, with eyebrows plucked and replaced by arched pencilled domes, the eyes themselves lined with black kohl.

It must have seemed odd to those women in the windows and to soldiers walking boisterously down the street to see the four of us, Olive and I in our white uniform dress and the officers in their smart outfits, strolling along Grant Road as if we were just on some ordinary high-street shopping spree.

But what strange sights there were to see in those windows! One glance down the dimly lit street was enough. Women were exhibiting themselves at all the windows, behind the bars.

As they got close to the first of those windows, a girl with little or nothing on grabbed hold of the curtain and dragged it across, blotting out whatever was happening inside. Not so shy was the girl in the next window, sitting and then provocatively prancing on her five-inch heels up and down the narrow confines of the room like a caged leopard. She was wearing a beautiful blue silk sari with a silver border. She smiled timidly at the group when they stopped to admire the view, her beautiful white teeth gleaming in the glow of the street light.

Far from friendly was the older woman in the room next door. She glared at the foursome who stopped to stare at her. She raised her fist and shook it at them. The nurses and their escorts moved off quickly without waiting for one another, for it looked as though the older whore might rush from her den and claw out the eyes of the first woman she might catch.

There was no end to the erotic sights as they hurried on.

There was a pleasant young girl in the next window, standing in a diaphanous sari. We paused. She too was beautifully made up with black kohl pencilling round her eyes. As if to satisfy our curiosity all the more she suddenly stretched out her arms and exposed all of her finely tanned body. Whether it was perspiration or oil it was impossible to tell but it lay on her like a light coat of polish so that her breasts and the dome of her pelvis glistened. She giggled and raised her eyebrows invitingly.

In most of the rooms looking out onto the pavement, the girls – and they all looked like young girls in their teens rather than older women – were trying to please prospective customers viewing from the street, for the foursome from the ship were not the only service people out for an evening's stroll in the forbidden red-light area, though they probably stood out more from the rest in their white nurses' dresses and smart naval officers' uniforms. But no one paid much attention to them. The men were too preoccupied with the scene, living out their own fantasies as they savoured the professionals in their erotic poses.

Betty and her friends thought it prudent to hurry down the road. They could hear music, faint and strange, which became louder as they got nearer to a building which was much bigger than the rest. Recognition dawned on them. It was the place the squadron leader on the ship had recommended – the brothel of Madame André!

Madame André herself was at the doorway taking the evening air and smoking a cigarette. They introduced themselves and for a moment or two she looked at them without moving a muscle of her face. Then she smiled and, turning on her charm, led them inside.

Smoke, sweat and perfume hung over the small hall. Waiters, pallid and perspiring freely under the weight of trays filled with glasses, moved as gracefully as skaters between the tables. Around the large room the usual racial mixture of girls elongated themselves gracefully and lasciviously on wicker couches. There was a remarkable sense of decorum about the whole situation, with the girls showing professional touches of finesse and composure. There was no rushing either to or from the bedrooms. Charm, it seemed, had been instilled into all who worked there. Madame was a White Russian and had her own strict rules and ideas on how a brothel should be run.

The usual procedure, she explained as she sat with a well-filled glass of vodka and lemon in her hands, was for the men to buy a booklet of tickets so that they could give one to each girl they invited to dance. Men, it seemed, usually danced with several girls before making up their minds which of them to take into one of the adjoining bedrooms.

'I recognized the heavy perfume straight away,' recalled Betty.

It was 'Queen of the Night' from the white flower which gives off its heavy scent at night-time. It's supposed to have aphrodisiac powers. Madame André seated us on the red plush armchairs at one side of the room, where we had a good view of everything that was going on. She invited us to take a beer with her and we were all thirsty enough for that.

A waiter brought each of us a foaming glass of warm beer. Madame André could not have been kinder or more helpful. Yet I was frightened. I'd heard all kinds of stories of the white slave trade and there was something about the White Russian Madame André that scared me. However, I came to the conclusion that she ran that brothel with genuine concern for the health of her women, and of the soldiers too. The girls, she said, were not only clean, sensible and reliable but also honest in their dealings with

soldiers who were sometimes so drunk they were careless about putting
their wallets back in their pockets.

For Betty, the visit was an eye-opener. Afterwards she could understand how people could argue that a well-run brothel would cut
down the incidence of the venereal disease which put men out of
action as much as if they had been wounded in battle. Furthermore
it could save the soldiers, their wives and girlfriends a lot of misery
too. As General Montgomery had said in 1940, when he was worried
about the number of men in his division in the British Expeditionary
Force reporting sick with venereal disease, having sex with local
loose women behind a hedge in a convenient field was far more
dangerous than if they went to a supervised brothel.

Betty and her friends did not outstay their welcome. When they
started taking their leave, Madame André, gracious to the last, told
one of her minions to get them a garry back to the boat.

The driver, smelling strongly of the cardomom seeds he was chewing, was eager to please by getting the nurses back to the boat quickly.
Consequently he whipped his emaciated nag into a fast trot which
sent the flea-ridden garry swaying round corners at frightening
angles. It was certainly far too fast for safety in the narrow streets
where locals were still standing about in groups talking.

The adventurous young nurses were lucky to get away with their
jaunt in the 'out of bounds' area. Corporal Bernard Hallas recalled
how such areas were always well patrolled by service police. 'I was in
charge of patrols in the red-light areas such as Grant Road, the Gut
at Malta, the Railway Sidings at Sydney, Sister Street in Alexandria
and so on in every port we docked at. It was an interesting enough
job for us and we got a lot of free beer as we went along.'

On their return to the troopship the nurses were ready for nothing
more exciting than a well brewed, hot cup of tea over which they
planned a more restful programme for the next day, their last in Bombay.

But a surprise awaited them on the noticeboard, which put an end
to their plans. The nurses were to pack and be prepared to disembark
the next afternoon to join a small ship on a nearby jetty, the ss
Matianna, which was sailing for Colombo. From there they were to
join a new hospital at Trincomalee.

On this smaller ship the accommodation was not as we had anticipated. It
was like the days of the old British Raj with even a 'punkah wallah' fanning

the air in the dining room. We each had a lovely cabin and we enjoyed the voyage to Colombo.

When we arrived, we were not at all perturbed to be told that the hospital we were supposed to join had not even been built yet. 'It's going to be over there,' they said, pointing to what was still a coconut grove.

They were taken onto the staff of the combined service hospital, the 54th Indian and British General Hospital. No sooner had they settled into a new routine, however, than volunteers were suddenly called for service in Burma. Betty, always ready for adventure, applied.

Almost immediately she was sent to an army hospital at Kandy, in the middle of Ceylon, midway between Colombo and Trincomalee and close to where Lord Louis Mountbatten had set up the Headquarters of South East Asia Command (SEAC).

There we got a shock. From my pleasant room in the hospital I found my-self quartered in a basha hut made of bamboo and grass! And I wasn't the only inhabitant. There were rats, lizards, and all kinds of revolting creepy-crawly things. What puzzled us all then was the speed at which all the posting and movement orders had been done. It was almost as if something had happened to make everyone move quickly. The nurses originally selected to serve in that hospital had not arrived – and never would. But no one then knew the full sad story.

Something *had* happened – a terrible disaster.

It had all begun with a mounting wave of criticism in Britain about the way the 'forgotten army' and the 'forgotten fleet' fighting the Japanese were being neglected with regard to manpower, medical equipment and nurses. 'It is nothing short of scandalous,' wrote Captain Bellinger MP in a letter to the *Sunday Pictorial*. Letters home from the officers and men of the Fourteenth Army to their own MPs had already prompted some belated remedial action. Part of this was the hasty assembly of forty-four nursing sisters of the QAIMNS, who were issued with tropical kit and posting orders to form the No. 150 BGH in Ceylon.

They embarked on a British India Navigation Company troopship the ss *Khedive Ismail*, as part of a five-ship convoy, and by 11 February 1944, she was approaching Colombo from the south-west. The nurses were getting ready to enjoy taking part in and watching a ship's concert below decks. There was going to be a very appreciative audience. On board were 1,500 troops bound for Burma and 86 young women, many of them barely out of their teens – 42 of them from the WRNS and 44 Army nursing sisters.

On the afternoon of 12 February the concert was going well below decks when there was a terrific crash and then another as two torpedoes hit the middle of the ship under the waterline. The boiler room exploded and the whole of the ship's side was ripped out. It began sinking straight away.

Over a thousand men and women were plunged into shark-infested waters. The horror was compounded when the captain of one of the destroyer escorts was ordered to drop depth charges to force the marauding Japanese submarine to the surface before it could sink any more ships. Meanwhile men and women from the *Khedive Ismail* struggled to survive in the heaving water for several hours. Eventually the submarine did surface and was torpedoed and sunk by the destroyer. In all, only 260 survivors were hauled out of the sea. All 44 of the nursing sisters were lost.

A news blackout of the story was ordered immediately. The records of the Court of Inquiry into the loss, held in Colombo, were immediately sealed and have lain in the Public Record Office for the last fifty years. Those Wrens who did survive were ordered to say nothing of the tragic loss for fear of being court-martialled. It is therefore not surprising that Betty and her colleagues, sent to take the places of their drowned colleagues, did not know why their posting orders had arrived so swiftly.

Hospitals in SEAC were kept very busy during that last year of the war. Every available resource was being concentrated in Europe to defeat Hitler and therefore the combat divisions of the Fourteenth Army were still low on the priority list for assault battalions, aircraft, doctors and auxiliaries.

Amongst the casualties being brought into Betty's hospital at Kandy were Royal Marines suffering from a strange and sometimes fatal malady which puzzled doctors. 'Light began to dawn upon the medical staff,' recalled Bernard Hallas, 'when it was realized that nearly all such patients had spent some time on the Maldive Islands.

Scurrying up and down the trees there were small monkeys which the lads thought very cute, as they responded well to being pets. What wasn't realized was they were suffering from a disease that was quickly transmitted to anyone in close contact with the animal.

The problem was so serious that the naval hospital ship *Maine* was sent out to deal with patients suffering from the disease.

Help was at hand for the heavily burdened nurses. The Commander-in-Chief, Lord Louis Mountbatten, invited his wife Edwina, who had trained as an auxiliary nurse in 1938 and risen to be Superintendent-in-Chief of the St John Ambulance Brigade, to undertake a tour of hospitals and medical units throughout the Indian and SEAC military areas. After inspecting 172 hospitals she submitted a detailed report. It said that during the tour, which took her to the front lines of Burma and up to Chunking, she found that the most urgent need was for more nurses and VADs. Most hospitals were understaffed by a half of their authorized establishment and equipment was lacking, especially in the operating theatres.[3]

When she got back to London she visited one ministry after another, making determined efforts to rectify the situation. There were some very high-pressure sessions, but she achieved her aims. The despatch of many more nurses and 500 VADs was promised. In all the reshuffling of nursing staff, Betty Lawrence was again on the move. She was given a railway warrant and told to make her way to the north of Ceylon and, across the Gulf of Mannar and from there to take a train to Bangalore, 350 miles due north. Today she wonders how it was that young women could be sent travelling on their own in India. Was there so little danger in a woman travelling alone then? Apparently not enough for the authorities to worry about.

I was seeing a lot of the world I would never have seen. Being moved about never put me off volunteering for jobs when they came up on the notice-board.

In Bangalore I was in a huge Fleet Air Arm camp with No. 78 Indian General Hospital. We were busy with wounded coming by hospital ship from Burma to Madras and then nearly 200 miles inland to us. We were also treating many patients with smallpox, typhoid, dysentery and malaria, and conducting a variety of small operations on injuries through accidents. The hospital was insistent upon the technique of 'no-touch' dressings – forceps always instead of fingers. It was there too that we stopped the practice of putting a pillow under the knees of patients recovering from an appendix operation. The surgeon felt a pillow under the knees led to problems of thrombosis.

Although we worked hard there was still time for relaxation and entertainment. I was a member of the camp concert party and performed as an Indian Nautch dancer. I borrowed a flowing dress, had bells round my ankles and used a tan make-up to complete the transformation. I became so keen on the Indian way of life that I used to dress as an Indian and out of devilment went out with my boyfriend, Lieutenant Bill Halliday who dressed up in a dhoti. Together we would then go to the snobbish English Club, where no Indians were allowed.

My Nautch dancing girl act became so good that I was invited to perform on stage with established Indian Nautch dancers and did shows in Durbar Hall, Mysore.

I enjoyed my tour at Bangalore. The food was good, especially on Sundays when we had enormous helpings of Madras curry washed down with Canadian beer. Junior officers were allowed a bottle of spirits and two bottles of wine a month. I did not drink then so I swapped my booze ration for cigarettes. Most nurses smoked then. In the 1940s, before it became linked with lung cancer, smoking was considered glamorous in the style of film stars like Marlene Dietrich. Once they lit up in a film you could see matches striking all over the darkened auditorium as men and women in the audience followed suit.

We worked hard and played hard and now as I look back on those wartime nursing years I realize how fortunate I was to get such a rich variety of nursing experience and travel.

Another Navy nurse who travelled far by herself was Sister J.Barr Beveridge, who had also arrived in Colombo. Her voyage had been in a dirty troopship where the food was not only meagre but repellent. 'The bread rolls walked to your plate at breakfast.'

In Colombo she was handed a railway warrant for Calcutta. It was a five-day journey on a flea- and bug-infested train, but 'thanks to Keatings powder' she arrived at her destination without being absolutely eaten alive. There she joined the Navy hospital ship *Ophir*, crewed by Dutch personnel.

'Don't look over the side!' she was told. But, of course curiosity got the better of her and she did.

It was awful! A constant stream of human and animal bodies floated by. The smells were pungent and the humidity was such that you could hardly breathe properly.

When we sailed it was a relief to get away from the intense humidity. None of us escaped prickly heat and the usual fevers. My ward of eighty swing cots was in the bowels of the ship, with no daylight, one water tap, and 6 heads [lavatories], and the atmosphere was absolutely foetid. The flies were a constant pest. We had no fly papers so we used to hang over each bed bandages dipped in syrup. They were very often quite a success.

Mealtime in the ward was a nightmare with so many different races from India and Africa, with different cultural diets.

The rounds for dressing wounds took such a long time because of the fears and suspicions which native troops had. Such fears had to be allayed every day through an interpreter. Ointments were feared but any liquid that stung seemed to give satisfaction. Pills were welcome but injections were evil spirits entering the body.

I remember a case of a young Sikh who had a head wound and when it was dressed in a field hospital, someone had cut off his top-knot. The Sikh blamed himself for this sin against his religion, and wanted to atone for it by dying. So he stopped eating and drinking. I was determined he was not going to kill himself. The doctor said, 'Do what you can, sister, to get liquids into him as he won't keep in the drips. He keeps pulling them out.' Those were the MO's instructions so I made up six large bottles of water coloured differently and containing traces of Epsom salts and other nasty-tasting medicines, plus some glucose and salt. The sick berth attendants were to administer four ounces every two hours by mouth accompanied by an incantation of his own made-up words. I told the patient that this was 'ju-ju' which was powerful enough to atone for his sin, and before we reached port he would be forgiven and his hair would grow again very quickly. In this way we kept him alive until Calcutta. What the sick berth attendants thought of this treatment I never dared enquire!

Another sad case was that of a Pathan Indian who thought anyone coming near him was going to cut off his hand. He had been sent on a patrol that was ambushed by the Japanese. All the others were killed except for the English officer who had both hands chopped off and was left to die. Somehow my patient got him back to base and then suffered terrible nightmares. The officer without hands was in the officers' ward on the top deck, gravely affected mentally – totally withdrawn and dumb.

There were many other sad cases from Burma. Most were grossly underweight. For example, one six-footer only weighed 6 stones. They had lived and fought in indescribable conditions, always short of food and water, medicines, shelter, ammunition and equipment. Their efforts and suffering have never been adequately recognized or appreciated. Many of them, even when not wounded, would never fully recover.

From the Burma front we took them to hospitals in Calcutta, Madras,

Colombo and once to Egypt. We spent Christmas at Suez. We actually celebrated Christmas twice; as the Dutch do, on 6 December, and then as we
do, on the 25th.

It was not always easy for the two nationalities to get on together. Some
of the salaries on that Dutch ship, those of the crew for example, were paid
by the Dutch government. My Javanese cabin boy earned far more than I
did. But the last straw for our patience came when we discovered that
everybody on board except for the Sisters, was to be paid an extra
allowance when the ship sailed through dangerous waters!

I wrote to Prime Minister Winston Churchill (it remains a secret how I
got the letter past the censor), asking why he and the Lords of the
Admiralty considered my life and services to be worth far less than that of
my Javanese cabin boy. The upshot was that 6d. a day extra was granted for
the nursing staff. We really did have difficulty in managing on the meagre
£120 a year salary we had then, for all personal necessities had to be
bought at exorbitant prices, toothpaste for example cost us between 7 and
10 shillings a tube!

At sea our hours of duty were dictated by necessity – in other words
there was no limit to them. We just kept going. However, now I look back
on my time aboard that hospital ship as a rich tapestry of unique, enriching
and fascinating experiences which I am proud to have shared[4].

She was pleased to have volunteered for hospital-ship duty. In all the
nursing services, appeals for volunteers were always over-subscribed.
When volunteers were called for duty with the newly formed Naval
Medical Air Evacuation Unit, despite the hazardous work involved,
Marjorie Aston and Margaret West were two who applied immedi-
ately.

14   One More River

We left our comrades with a wooden cross
To mark our progress and to show its cost.[1]

H.V.S. Page, 'Prospectus'

The toll of those innumerable river crossings all the way
up could not only be measured in the many thousands of
casualties but in the numbing battle weariness of those
who were left.

Brian Harpur, an infantry officer in Italy.[2]

The Allied advance in Italy was bogged down in the mud of the first
winter, (1943–4) by the heavily fortified Gustav Line and in the
second winter (1944–5) by the almost impregnable Gothic Line.

Nurses working close to the combat areas were appalled by the
casualties which streamed into their care and could not help wondering if it was all necessary. For four long months, Allied divisions
fought battles in and around Cassino. News from the Italian front
appeared as short paragraphs in the national newspapers, and
armchair strategists, huffing and puffing in their clubs, asked, 'Why
don't they push on?' and 'What are they doing?'

Sister Michelle Higgs, tending casualties from those battles, could
have told them. Her memories of those awful days when wounded
soldiers on stretchers crowded every space of her muddy CCS on the
slopes near Monte Cassino remained vivid. 'We were cutting legs off
in a hole in the ground. Nobody can have any idea what it was like
as a young person, to see 19-year-old lads dying in such pain.'

Army surgeons, doctors and nurses moved as close to the front line as possible to cope with the unremitting flow of wounded infantrymen and tank crews. Field Artillery batteries were firing nearby but Michelle found that the patients were so exhausted that the noise seemed to make little difference to them. 'They slept through it,' she said.

Winter had come. Torrential rain fell incessantly, turning mountain streams into raging torrents. The swollen rivers running laterally across the country became sites for bloody battles, many of them named in regimental battle honours, their names forever imprinted on the memories of Eighth Army veterans reminiscing at reunions: the Sangro, Volturno, Garigliano, Trigno, Moro, Liri, Rapido, Melfa, Sacco, Pescara, Chienti, Arno, Cesaro, Metauro and many, many more.

The Allied armies fought in freezing sleet and snow. BBC war correspondent Godfrey Talbot summed up the winter war in Italy of 1943–4 and 1944–5 accurately and vividly in one broadcast: 'I'm so cold I can hardly hold the mike. And the desolation and the scene beggars description. The villages are smashed. The mountains are barren and pitted and hostile, seared by ice as well as shells. Men here are fighting the wind and rain and mud as well as the Germans. Don't forget them . . . .'.[3]

Soldiers were carried into CCS and field hospitals terribly mutilated, as Sister Anne Watt, then in the Cassino area, recalled in *Front-line Nurse*, which deals in greater detail with the nurses' experiences in Italy.

One of the most shocking wounds which nurses had to tend then were the burns inflicted by German flame throwers, burns rarely seen before the war. British surgeon Rock Carling, who specialized in burns, described to a course of Army medical officers and nurses how some of the burns came about.

The flame throwers which the Germans are using – and I dare say we are not very far behind them – are fearsome weapons; they are terrifying and extremely destructive. Standing about 20 yards *to one side* of the line of fire of a medium-sized flame thrower and at least 50 yards from its projection point, a man may have his eyebrows and eyelashes singed off, and a tank has been set on fire at 150 yards distance in a matter of 5 seconds. You can understand, therefore, that the character of the burns inflicted is very serious indeed.[4]

He explained how the worst of the burns which medical officers and nurses had to care for occurred in tanks because it was extremely difficult for men to get out of them and they were easily set on fire because they carried petrol and other inflammable material. The same could be said for burns caused by boiling glycol in aircraft and the terrible burns from high-voltage cables in ships struck by shells or torpedoes.

He reminded his audience that if more than one-third of the body's surface was burned the chances of recovery were exceedingly poor, but with very early treatment in the best of burns units a soldier still had a chance of recovery even if 50 per cent of the body surface was burnt. Nurses had not to give up hope. The main problem with burns was the enormous quantity of fluid lost through exudation from the burnt area. With severe burning this could amount to as much as 6 litres. Therefore the first task in treating burns was to replace the lost fluid as soon as possible. Nurses would have to watch and treat the patient with the greatest possible care for the first 72 hours after burning. He also mentioned a very common cause of serious burns encountered by nurses in the British Army but hardly ever in the Russian – petrol. The Russian Army was short of petrol, and had none to waste. The British had petrol to spare for brewing up tea. Soldiers began to use petrol for cooking in the desert war, and there petrol was responsible for more burns than the enemy. There was no wood for fuel in the desert for boiling water for tea and so soldiers took an old tin, made a mixture of petrol and sand and set light to it. That in itself was not dangerous. But when the flame died down an impatient Tommy would pour on more petrol from his 4-gallon jerry can and immediately the whole lot would flash into an explosion which was often fatal. The practice was carried on in other campaigns, where soil took the place of sand.

Another type of casualty met more frequently by the nurses during that bitterly cold winter in Italy was what fell into the category of 'cold injury'. Soldiers manning the front line in the mountainous ridges south of Monte Cassino 'stood to' in freezingly cold dawns in water-filled slit trenches for days and sometimes weeks at a time. Many suffered from trench-foot. Their feet swelled up like ugly salami sausages, and when they hobbled into CCS the nurses had to cut off their boots; sometimes the surgeons had to amputate their feet.

The infantrymen's ankle-high boots – so good for polishing into a parade-ground sparkle – provided little protection against 'cold injury' which was made worse by other factors such as standing for hours on end in the slit trench – because any movement would be seen by Germans in observation posts overlooking Allied positions.

Sister Pamela Barker was shocked when she saw the feet of some of the men hobbling into her care. 'I don't know how they managed to keep going for so long. Some men with the Battleaxe Division sign on their shoulders said they'd had very little time out of the line during the two months in the Monte Cassino front.'

No wonder trench-foot casualties were seen so often by nurses. In fact medical statistics show how the incidence of trench foot increased with alarming rapidity. During the six-month period ending on 30 April 1944, there were more than 5,700 casualties from this cause in the Fifth Army alone.[5]

Surgeon Edward Churchill, who toured the front lines, saw the condition in which infantrymen were fighting. He noted in his report that a man would become a casualty if he fought under those conditions for longer than five days at a stretch. Some men he had seen as patients had not had their boots off for twelve days in cold, rain and mud. 'The answer lies in more frequent relief,' he wrote in his report.[6]

Angered by this unnecessary injury he took his report to Fifth Army Headquarters at Caserta Palace, Naples, to be sure that General Clark saw it. To his disgust he found commanders there living in luxury, eating in a 'swank private dining room' before going to the opera house to see the San Carlo Company perform *La Bohème*. Clark and his staff were in the Royal Box. For Surgeon Churchill, this was 'a world of contrasts, from mud to opera'.

The irate surgeon, without deference to rank, then told the Chief of Staff that the whole of the palace headquarters was bad for the morale of an army in the field. Commanders, he said, 'should get up in the mud with their men'. Many of the Eighth Army's senior commanders, it must be said, were often well forward, and some were fatally wounded when visiting front-line positions.

Hospital nurses, doctors and their staff also suffered very much from the cold and mud. When visiting medical units, Churchill found that the No.15 Evacuation Hospital, which had crossed the river Volturno on a pontoon bridge 'had become bogged down in one of the worst seas of mud I had ever seen' and that it was impossible to get in or about the hospital 'without wading through thick black custard.'

*

Theatre sister Lorna Bradey was in an Army field hospital at Barletta, in mud so thick that men could hardy walk through it.

Ambulances had to be standing by to carry patients the short distance from the operating theatre to the wards as stretcher-bearers could not carry the wounded through such mud.

It was so cold for us in the operating theatre we had two Valor paraffin stoves going. When casualties began to mount up we worked four operating tables at the same time. Drip pentothal was used and the anaesthetist would walk from one table to the next to keep the patients under. For very severe abdominal surgery and amputations we used a general anaesthetic in addition. Pressure would begin to build up during the day. We'd be operating at eight in the morning and then the dreaded word 'convoy' could be heard shouted along the track. Casualties were brought straight to us. I remember being theatre sister for eighty-eight operations in one day. The agony and suffering shown on those young faces spurred us all on. Sometimes I'd walk quickly along the rows of stretchers, working out who would go next. I could feel their eyes following me. Everyone on a convoy received attention before we stopped.

Gas gangrene was the dreaded condition. I had three other sisters and four orderlies, and there were the surgeons and doctors all working flat out. The impossible became the possible. We ate scratch meals and at night, dead beat, we had to clean up the theatre before leaving. If I managed to get off for a break I'd tell my Number 2 to call me if she got too many casualties to cope with. Often we'd crawl off before dawn only to reappear that same morning at the cry of 'convoy'.

One dark night, when I was coming off duty, literally dragging myself to our hut, I slipped and fell and I was up to my waist in liquid mud – icy cold. An ambulance driver picked me up and my friends cleaned the mud from me after a cup of hot cocoa. Momentarily I was as near to hysteria as I've ever been.

It was always so cold at night. I can remember being called out to the operating theatre and seeing surgeons in their pyjamas with a thick overcoat on top. And it's here I must give praise to our orderlies. Without them none of us could have functioned. They were loyal to a man. There was a Yorkshire steeplejack who did not like taking orders from a woman but once he helped me when I had to resuscitate a soldier who had collapsed. After that he couldn't do enough for me. There was 'Whitie' with the smelly feet too, for whom no job was too big. With him was an odd Roman Catholic character, a conscientious objector who had been a brother in a monastery. He had a pale face with steel-rimmed spectacles and wore sandals on duty. He was an inspiration and an example to us. After the war he somehow traced me and told me that he had trained as a nurse in the operating theatre, became a missionary in Zambia and eventually a prior in a monastery.

I remember that brother for one particular incident in which he was far from calm and saintly. It happened when our senior surgeon, who took a delight in goading me in front of all the team – perhaps because I had once turned down his invitation to dinner – went a bit too far with the crude jokes of which I was so often the butt. He was so insulting one day I walked out of the operating theatre when the job was over, trembling with rage. It was then that our brother, usually so placid, came to me white with anger. He said, 'If that man talks to you again like that I'll tear him apart with my bare hands.'

Fortunately for us nurses, amidst those days in the cold mud and rain, there was the occasional, amazingly happy evening spent with new-found friends in that poor district of Barletta. Though Italians there had little money they were still generous in their hospitality. Their main source of income was from the local vermouth factory and from salt taken to the port in rickety overladen donkey carts.

Sometimes they invited us to eat with their families and we had some really tasty suppers of tagliatelli, garlic, onions and tomatoes. Soldiers said the 'Eyeties' ate roof rabbits – cats – but I'm sure we never did.

Later in the year, when the weather was warmer, we had one never-to-be-forgotten social occasion during a lull in the fighting, when we were invited to the vermouth factory owner's home.

Signor Alves showed us round the factory, explaining how the vermouth was made. Then he took us home to meet his wife, Lilly. We all got on so well together. Language somehow was no problem. Lunch was a positive orgy; enormous platters of *lasagne al forno* with layers of meat sauce, pasta and cheese sauces from mozzarella, bel paese and Parmesan. And this was only the starter! The pork joint came next, roasted on the knuckle and flavoured with rosemary sprigs and garlic. It was so succulent. Wine flowed generously as we moved onto the next course – Lilly's home-made chocolate gateau. Perfection!

Coffee came with small bowls of roasted coffee beans to chew – hot and delicious. Then, just in case we were still thirsty, sparkling spumante was served.

Suddenly music filled the room and men got up inviting us to dance. What energy we all had then despite the hearty lunch we had just eaten. After about an hour's dancing we were shown to beautifully shuttered bedrooms with mosquito nets down. It was siesta time. Kitty and I locked our bedroom door firmly, but no one tried the door. Soon we were fast asleep.

At seven o'clock there was a discreet tap on the door. It was a maid bringing coffee on a tray. We had a shower and then the evening's festivities began. More food and more spumante. By the time we left them that evening, all smiling and happy, we had received invitations to come again any time.

There was no time for further visits. Casualties mounted. Hospital ships eased their way into the tiny harbour of Barletta, where Italian dockhands had made broad gangways suitable for stretchers to be carried onto the ships. Wounded men who were fit enough to travel were taken across to North Africa and sometimes to Port Said and on to Alexandria.

On one of those voyages, naval Nursing Sister Agatha Dampier-Child (later Tinne), was looking after a young woman of the WRNS who had poliomyelitis. Agatha remembers her sense of humour and courage. 'Her arm was in splints as we winched her over the side of the ship into a launch. When we reached the Army hospital, the Reception Sergeant asked for her religion. 'Put down anything. Moslem if you like!' she said.'

During those months, when British newspapers reported 'little activity' on the Italian front other than patrols, 300,000 men of the Eighth Army were constantly in action, probing German defences, so as to tie down the German divisions and prevent their transfer to other battle fronts. Such fighting patrols were costly indeed. Casualties, brought down the mountain by mule and jeep were in a sorry state by the time the nurses removed their field dressings and cleaned them up.

Who was to be treated first? Decisions had to be made quickly and neither doctors nor nurses could ever be sure.

'Some men who had lost a great deal of blood and looked like dying nevertheless recovered because they had great courage and hope. Others who had comparatively little wrong with them, died. I am a great believer in mind over matter and every surgeon of experience knows this,' said Colonel Elliott Cutler talking of his experiences in Italy. With this in mind he urged doctors and nurses not to let their faces show their feelings so that patients retained hope.[7]

Sister Betty Lawrence of the QARNNS often found that patients who faced their injuries with courage and an attitude of 'I'm not going to let the old Devil get me yet', recovered despite their chances of survival appearing almost nil.

Inevitably, though, some casualties were reluctant to go back to their units when they recovered. They talked of their fears to the nurses on night duty, as Pamela Barker recalled:

During the long, lonely hours of night duty we heard all kinds of confidences. The saddest, coldest and loneliest task of all was dealing with a dying soldier. Then we might move to the bedside of a patient in such pain that despite hefty doses of pain killers and sleeping pills, wakefulness was unbearable. Only morphine helped. Then with others on our rounds there would often be a soldier who needed to talk quietly to a sympathetic listener. When one young soldier told me he wasn't going to fight anymore, I didn't have the heart to tell anybody. I felt he'd done more than his bit.

Desertion was a problem in Italy then. In one fortnight 350 men deserted from a veteran division pushed beyond its limits. Some deserters took to the hills and lived as brigands. Reports of British provost marshals and the Special Investigation Branch of the CMP (Corps of Military Police) in southern Italy carried lurid tales of violent crimes committed by them.[8]

Nurses sometimes came into contact with these deserters in a curious way. After being arrested by the Military Police they adopted ingenious means of escaping. According to a report by the provost marshal of No.2 District, they discovered that the easiest way to escape from arrest was to get into hospital for treatment. A way of achieving this was to be diagnosed as suffering from venereal disease, then rife in southern Italy. A deserter would deliberately burn a sore on the end of his penis with a lighted cigarette. This they thought would look like the typical syphilitic chancre when seen hurriedly by doctors and nurses. Hospitals would not accept responsibility for close custody, and in a ward where nurses and orderlies were always busy escape was possible.[9]

A group of deserters known as the 'Free English' enjoyed their freedom for a few weeks, but eventually the bitterly cold winter proved too much for them and they gave themselves up to Colonel Watts of No.31 Field Surgical Unit.

Colonel Watts was good at taking his expertise to the casualties wherever they were. One of his neighbouring surgical units was up in the mountains in 30 feet of snow with a reconnaissance regiment. An officer of the regiment had his leg blown off by a mine and died because he could not be evacuated. Colonel Watts, a good skier, therefore decided to take his unit, complete with nursing orderlies who could ski, up the mountain in order to be ready to give assistance in the snow whenever required.

No sooner had he arrived than he was presented with a soldier needing an appendix operation. In a cottage kitchen with dirty walls reeking of garlic, cheese and olive oil, Watts propped a stretcher on portable trestles, put the instruments into a fish kettle of water boiling on a primus stove, laid the soldier on the stretcher and gave him an injection of pentothol to induce anaesthesia. Watts then washed his hands, poured spirit over them and put on a sterile gown and gloves. He was now ready for the operation to be done under the illumination of a primus-type paraffin Tilley lamp.

In just over ten minutes the acutely inflamed appendix was removed and soon the patient was left recovering on the stretcher in the care of a nursing orderly.[10]

A little to the north of Lorna Bradey's hospital at Barletta, a gang of deserters terrorized the district with their armed hold-ups. Eight men in four jeeps, armed with submachine-guns and Beretta pistols operated from a farmhouse in which their hoard of black-market goods – 2,000 gallons of oil, 176 gallons of petrol and 800,000 lire in cash – was later found. Nurses were warned not to travel far beyond the camp area. They were too busy and too tired to travel far anyway.[11]

But spring was coming. Soon everyone would be on the move with the inevitable spring offensive. The German Gustav Line, centred on the formidable heights of Monte Cassino, had held up the Allies for too long. The Allied landings at Anzio, mounted to cut German supply lines and force a German withdrawal from the Gustav Line, had failed. Three attempts to storm the heights of Monte Cassino had also failed, with horrendous casualties for the New Zealand, British and Indian divisions. Nearly a thousand tons of high-explosive bombs were dropped on the Monte Cassino monastery. Many of them missed their target and killed 96 Allied soldiers and 140 Italian civilians.

The wounded came through Army CCS. Lorna Bradey wondered how it was that civilians stayed so close to the fighting. Sometimes they were cleared away, yet at other times Allied troops were surprised to find an entire family of *contadini* – farm labourers – staying on in their stone cottages. Corporal Jack Stacey, who was in charge of a troop of stretcher-bearing mules, was shocked one day to find three young children outside a cottage singing an Italian version of 'Ring-a-ring-a-roses' at the end of which they all fell down. They taught him the words, which he has never forgotten.

> *Giro, giro tondo,*
> *Gira il mondo,*
> *Gira la terra,*
> *Tutti giu per terra.*

With the coming of spring, General Alexander was about to launch another decisive attack along the 25-mile front from Cassino to the sea. From the Anzio beach-head General Mark Clark prepared for the vital break-out. As usual, hospital wards were cleared and hospital ships stood by. At 11 p.m. on 11 May 1944, 1,660 guns unleashed a barrage along the whole of the Eighth Army front.

This time it was the Poles who had drawn the short straw for the attack on Cassino. Their first assault ended in disaster. Fresh German troops fought tenaciously to hold their positions. At dawn the Polish troops were caught in the open. German machine guns killed hundreds within a few minutes.

Lorna remembered how quickly their wards and corridors were filled with men 'groaning in severe pain and anguish'.

Amongst them was a German officer admitted from the CCS with 'Caution' written on his casualty card. X-rays showed an unexploded missile about 3 inches long lying in his heart muscle, just under the fine pericardium skin covering the heart itself. It seemed impossible, yet there it was. Should we operate or not? By all the rules he should have been dead. If left in he would die. If we tried to take it out he still might die and so might we too if it exploded. It was then I appreciated the skill of my Australian *bête noir*, the surgeon Charles. He knew he was good but this really was a challenge with risk.

The code we lived by dictated what we did then. A man should be given every chance to live. We called for a naval expert from the nearby port, who examined the X-ray of the missile and agreed to be there to handle it once it was removed. My knees were shaking. Then I wanted to giggle as the naval officer tried to fit the surgical mask over his beard. The tension was terrific. The incision was made, slowly the heart was exposed, retractors eased open the wound. There it was, the bulge of the shell or whatever it was, just beneath the pericardium. Meticulously the dissection began with a silver probe easing away the tissue; each stroke could be the fatal one. Finally the probe touched the metal. Calmly the surgeon's fingers took hold of the object and slowly eased it out. He placed it on my outstretched hand holding the pad. I handed it to the naval officer who took it away. The operation was then completed with speed. The German recovered and went off to a POW camp. Sometimes I wonder if anyone ever told him what we did for him that day!

For six weeks the Lancashire Fusiliers of the 78th Division had held onto the slopes of Monte Cassino. Each night, food and ammunition had been brought to them by mule and Indian porters. On 16 May 1944, they received orders to advance from their rocky hollows – the ground was too hard for trench digging. And it was at this precise moment that the Germans began their counter-attack. Two German tanks opened fire. There was no cover for the infantry. Trapped, they died. One man, Francis Jefferson, without any orders, picked up a PIAT anti-tank gun, ran forward and faced the enemy. He had never fired a PIAT gun before. He took aim and fired. The recoil knocked him back 10 yards but his bomb knocked the top off the tank, exploded the ammunition and killed all the crew. The other tank withdrew. The German counter-attack was smashed.

Later in the attack, Jefferson was wounded in the shoulder. When he recovered, King George VI pinned the Victoria Cross onto his chest. Sadly it was to bring him nothing but grief. He went home to a hero's welcome in the small Cumbrian town of Ulverston and a pension of just under £2 a week. He applied for a council house and was placed 10,965th on the list. A burglar broke into his mother's house where he was living and stole his treasured Victoria Cross. Depressed with his loss he came home one night, kissed his mother and told her he had nothing to live for. Later, when she was asleep, he wandered onto the nearby railway line. He was hit by a train and died instantly.

Back in Italy, that spring of 1944, the Poles captured Monte Cassino and opened the way for a rapid Allied advance northwards. On 23 May 1944, the Fifth Army broke out from the Anzio enclave in which they had been trapped, and linked up with the advancing Eighth Army.

General Mark Clark, hungry for glory, headed directly for Rome. The glory of capturing Rome before the Allies invaded France was the prize he wanted, and was determined to have. And two days before the invasion of Normandy, he was able to revel in the hysterical reception given to the American troops entering Rome. But not once during those days of rejoicing did Clark mention the butcher's bill for his triumphal entry into the city. Since landing at Salerno his army had lost 125,000 men, of whom 20,000 were killed. The Eighth Army's rifle companies suffered 30 per cent casualties, dead or wounded. The Polish Corps paid the highest price for that victory: nearly every second Polish rifleman was dead or wounded.

By that time, the wounded had a far better chance of recovering, thanks to the efforts of a modest professor with a name few people then recognized, but one which could be given by anybody in a pub quiz team today – Alexander Fleming. Into Lorna Bradey's hospital came the new wonder drug, penicillin.

We called it *gold dust* then. We could see it was going to alter the whole treatment of the wounded and save millions of lives. I was told that a very senior RAMC brigadier was flying out to demonstrate its use. This first variety of penicillin was in powder form. Injections came later. It was placed in a 'sterile gun' and puffed into the wound. At first it was used sparingly, but later everyone had it. No more gas gangrene – the dread of the wounded. How privileged we felt to be using it. I scrubbed up for that demonstration operation and in walked the VIP. I turned and he rushed towards me.

'You!' he said. 'How wonderful!' and turning to Charles the surgeon he said. 'I hope you realize how lucky you are – one of the best theatre sisters I've ever known.'

I just needed that boost to my ego. We had worked together in a little old schoolhouse outside Dieppe in 1940. He was to go to the Officers' Mess for tea. Before that he said: 'First, though, I'll take a mug of tea with Sister here. We have a lot to catch up on.' Oh James! How I loved you that day.

But that love would not be the love of her life. Another senior officer, at another time and in another place – Germany – was to be that. He was a former patient, and proposed to Lorna after a night at the Hannover Opera House. She accepted and soon began a long and happy married life.

Back in 1944, though, in that Italian hospital, all soon became a hectic bustle as the battle moved northwards and so too did hospitals and nurses. Lorna was posted, on promotion to Deputy Matron of a 2,000-bed tented hospital, to Andrea. A surprise awaited her arrival: 'The bird had flown – that is the Matron – and in disgrace. She and the town major [a military administration officer] had been found *in flagrante delicto*! The scandal rocked the place – a heinous crime.'

The early summer of 1944 was a hectic time for nurses as Casualty Clearing Stations and hospitals packed and joined the migration northwards towards Arezzo and Florence, where hospitals were being set up ready for the casualties expected from new assaults upon the Gothic Line and then the Po.

The battles for the Gothic Line began on 25 August. Facing the Allied armies were over 500 field guns mounted in reinforced concrete pits. They covered all approaches from La Spezia on the east coast to Pesaro on the west. From mountain peaks, 2,500 cleverly hidden machine-guns could decimate any panting infantrymen toiling up the steep slopes.

Hitler ordered Kesselring, with his army re-equipped and regrouped, to hold the Gothic line at all costs. The Allied autumn offensive failed. The infantry dug in for the winter. What little provisions they had came up by mules – 30,000 of them, plodded up tracks often impassable due to mud, snow and landslides. The temperature fell so low that even the fast-flowing mountain streams froze over. And all through that winter Allied infantry were sent out on fighting patrols. Official battalion war diaries tell incredible tales. An Irish brigade on patrol on Monte Spadura ran out of ammunition and although outnumbered 'flung rocks at the advancing Germans, battered them with rifle butts, or grappled with their bare hands. The rocky hillsides were littered with dead from both sides.'[12]

The stretcher-bearers were magnificent. Their job called for great courage of the passive, enduring, unshakeable kind. Often they went out under intense enemy fire and into known minefields to bring back the wounded. At night, they would bring down the wounded in stretchers slung each side of the strong and patient mules. The dead, too, were brought down, lying across the pannier saddles.

Major Denis Healey, who directed the assault forces ashore at Anzio, remembered those last months of the war. 'For the infantry they were the worst months of the whole Italian campaign. The Apennines were bitterly cold and the Germans fought every inch of the way. Men who had come through the desert and Cassino without breaking, collapsed with the strain of the Gothic line.'[13]

Pamela Barker still gets angry today when she thinks of the cost of those final battles in Italy. 'We had been at war for over five years. We kept wondering if the slaughter would ever end. Spring came and we got our wards ready for what we heard was the "final offensive". This time it really was the final one in Italy. It filled our wards.'

That final three weeks of fighting, from 9 April to 2 May 1945 cost the Allied armies in Italy 16,747 casualties.

This is not the place to go into the gallant service of the nurses during the whole of this Italian campaign, for that has already been covered in the companion volume, *Front-Line Nurse*. But what must be mentioned is the high regard in which nurses were held by the young men who came into their care in Italy, all of them part of a team that Winston Churchill called 'as gallant an army as ever marched'.[14]

15   If It's Got Your Name on It . . .

All human things are subject to decay,
And when fate summons, monarchs must obey.

John Dryden, 'MacFlecknoe'

'If only . . .' They must be two of the saddest words in the English language. How often real-life tales of tragedy start with those two words. The true story told by Captain John Macpherson, a British surgeon whose wife was one of the first nursing sisters to land in France in June 1944 is a good example.

We were stationed near Elgin in northern Scotland, with a field dressing station on beach landing training, as part of No.5 Beach Group, getting ready for the D-Day invasion of Normandy. The FDS provided basic support for the two field surgical units, each with a trained surgeon, an anaesthetist and four or five nursing attendants. The idea was to bring high-quality surgery as close to the front line as possible. My own duties were with No.21 Field Transfusion Unit, which was scheduled to land with the FDS on the morning of D-Day. The quartermaster of that FDS was a time-served and retired regimental sergeant major from the First World War, recalled to service. When he heard that we were due to land on the first tide of D-Day, wherever and whenever that might be, he decided that he'd had enough of the sharp-end stuff, reported sick and was downgraded. He was transferred to a general military hospital near Lincoln, which was scheduled to land on D- plus 90. The quartermaster of the Lincoln General Hospital was moved to the FDS; a straight swop.

In due course we hit French soil at Sword Beach on the first tide on 6

June 1944, as planned so many months previously. Strangely enough, though, as expected, numerous casualties were sustained by troops around us, as far as I am aware the FDS with all its nursing attendants and medical staff escaped absolutely scot free. Not a scratch nor even, for my little lot, getting our feet wet! We dropped off a rhino ferry into 2 – 3 feet of water, which our Bedford QL truck took very comfortably.

Ninety days later, again as planned, the British General Hospital, with our erstwhile quartermaster, sailed into Antwerp Harbour. On the way in, the ship struck a mine. There were a few casualties, one of whom was the quartermaster. We could not help thinking, *if only* he'd stayed with us he would have survived the landing.

It was an episode of war that seemed to show the truth of another old maxim – 'If it's got your name on it...' Such is the irony of real life experiences.'

Or looked at in another way, as Appius Caecus did four centuries before the birth of Christ, 'each man is the architect of his own fate.'

Nurses never had time to ponder the philosophy of their own postings. At times they seemed to be drawn from a bag randomly. Freda Barnfather, after coming home on the *Somersetshire* hospital ship and still hoping to meet her penfriend Alex for the first time, got a posting to the Far East, which was changed a few days later for one to Shaftesbury to look after sullen teenage girls on the venereal diseases ward. A month later a new posting came for her to report to the hospital ship *Aba*, which was about to sail from Avonmouth for the United States. Not long after a pleasant trip to New York the *Aba* was ordered to Southampton. There was now a great sense of excitement; the southern counties were packed with troops.

From her rain-battered window at the Royal Naval Hospital Haslar, Sister E.Parslow, QARNNS, could see the grey, wind-swept Solent filling up, day by day, with every type of craft. 'There were cruisers, destroyers and landing craft. The roads as far as the eye could see were lined either side with tanks and trucks of all sizes. Overhead, the activity of aircraft was indescribable as darkness fell. It was the gigantic overture to D-Day.'

In the hospital itself, 80 QARNNS nursing sisters and 140 nursing members of the VAD organized to the smallest detail by Matron Matilda Goodrich (later to become Matron-in-Chief and DBE), had everything ready. Since May 1944 all leave had been stopped, routine work was in abeyance and beds were cleared to receive the casualties expected from the Normandy beaches. Some beds were also stripped of sheets and pillow cases so as to be ready to take the blood- and sand-soaked casualties straight from the battles on the beaches. In addition to the established nursing staff, pharmacists had been called up as sick berth attendants and given instruction in basic nursing techniques by ward sisters.

Everyone, it seemed, was waiting. Nurses waiting for their call to the invasion craft had greased and wrapped in oiled paper every single bit of equipment that needed to be protected against the effects of sea water and rust. They had been stencilled with code numbers so that they could be unpacked without any delay wherever the nurses were sent. Now there was nothing for them to do but wait.

The Supreme Commander was waiting for the moon, the tide and the sunrise to be right. The main invasion force had to cross the Channel by night so that darkness would conceal the strength and direction of the several attacks; a full moon was needed for the airborne assaults; forty minutes of good daylight after sunrise was needed for the completion of the final bombing of the coastal defences; and low tide was needed for the removal of beach obstacles whilst they were uncovered.

But now the success of Operation Overlord depended upon the weather. A wind of almost hurricane violence shook Supreme Commander Eisenhower's camp. Rain battered in horizontal streaks against the shuddering windows of Allied Naval Headquarters. The formidable waves predicted for the Channel would make beach landings a hazardous affair. Air support would be impossible. Naval gunfire would be inefficient. Nevertheless, General Montgomery wanted to go. Air Marshal Tedder disagreed. Tension mounted.

Then the meteorological experts gave the senior commanders hope. The storm would abate for a short period of thirty-six hours. Stormy weather would then churn up the Channel again. The whole invasion was now a gamble. The first assault divisions might be left isolated, easy prey to German counter-attacks, if rough seas prevented further beach landings.

On the other hand, delay could be even more disastrous. Morale would slump with postponement, security would be compromised and the element of surprise would be lost. The inescapable consequences of postponement were almost too bitter to contemplate.

To go or not to go?

At 4.15 a.m. on 5 June 1944, at a final conference, General Eisenhower made the historic decision. No one disagreed. Without another word, all the commanders left to flash out the signals that would set the whole invasion force in motion: To attack as planned on 6 June.

Eisenhower then sat down alone to draft a statement in case everything went wrong. He wrote, 'Our landings . . . have failed to gain a satisfactory foothold and I have withdrawn the troops. If any blame or fault attaches to the attempt it is mine alone . . . .'

He then drove to Newbury airfield to talk to the men of the 101st Airborne getting ready to fly to Normandy, telling them not to worry because the Allied bombers would take out the stone fortifications on the beach. But he had already seen reports estimating that 80 per cent of these men might be killed or wounded.

Nurses moved to the landing craft transit camps to cross the Channel and deal with those casualties.

In one of hundreds of such coastal camps, Sister Ann Reeves and nursing colleagues were wakened before daylight by a big black US soldier. Within minutes they were dressed and queuing up for breakfast. 'Better eat up, Lieutenant. You're going to be mighty hungry afore you're finished today,' another big, friendly black face grinned at her as he ladled breakfast into her mess tin.

Suddenly it was all bustle and clatter, chairs pushed back, equipment gathered, cries of 'Outside now', as a small crowd of battledress-clad nurses, steel helmets clanging against each other, climbed awkwardly onto trucks which, to a barrage of despatching hand slaps on drivers' doors, headed off in slow convoy to the docks. There, still in the twilight before dawn, they walked up the gangway of a grey ship waiting to take them on the greatest adventure of their lives.

From then on, everything seemed to happen in a blur of feverish activity. The sea was choppy. The landing craft which bumped and scraped alongside their ship when they reached the coast of France rose and fell with the waves as one by one the nurses jumped into the arms of sailors waiting to catch them. Engines roared and the craft rushed through the wet breeze towards the shore. A jolt, a rattle and a clang as the ramp clattered down into shallow breakers and then a shout from the landing craft skipper: 'Run for it girls! You're on Gooseberry Beach.'

Another batch of nurses had arrived at Courseulles. It was still dark. 'Welcome ladies! Good to see you.' As if by magic a soldier appeared, carrying steaming mugs of tea. In no time at all trucks drove them through churned-up meadows into a field where four marquees were erected in a cross formation with a central area from which nurses and doctors worked. 'General Montgomery, with his usual insight into the soldier's psychology, decided that the troops needed a little femininity and so whenever it was possible we appeared in the wards in the full glory of our grey and scarlet uniforms and flowing white caps,' recalled Ann.

Vera Bryan, who had recovered from her loss of weight after her eighteen months in West Africa and from her experience when her ship was torpedoed, had at last met George and planned their wedding, but she was suddenly sent to Normandy.

We came ashore in a landing barge and then travelled in filthy 3-ton trucks to our hospital site – tents in a muddy field. At first the wounded were lying on stretchers under the hedges until the tents were erected. There were fifty wounded soldiers in our surgical ward with just two nursing sisters and two orderlies to do everything for them. The men came directly to us from the front line and they were in a terrible mess. I was awfully upset to see them in such a bad state. I found men with severe gashes and wounds getting off their stretchers to get drinks for those more helpless than themselves. There was not one murmur of complaint. As the days went by, what helped to keep me going were the regular, romantic letters I began to receive from George.

Even under terrible wartime conditions the prospect of romance was ever present. One nurse recalled that, when they were at Hermanville, the hospital Colonel, fearing for the virtue of his nurses amongst so many men, had put up an enormous notice saying: 'SISTERS' QUARTERS – KEEP OUT'. The next day, as the nurses passed the lines of the Royal Engineers, they saw another notice which read: 'BROTHERS' QUARTERS – COME IN'.

There was soon no time for such jocularity. Casualties poured into CCSs and hospitals. The nurses could not help being shocked. Nothing in their training could have prepared them completely for all the battlefield horrors. It is easy to see why Vera Bryan found it hard to go back into the ward each day. But go back she did. Worse was in store for her, however.

I was sent with another QA to a field dressing station quite close to the front line. Convoys of wounded would come in and we had to check their dressings, feed them and make them as comfortable as possible for the next part of their journey. Many of them had gangrenous feet. They all looked exhausted and smelt awful. It's a smell that lies in the back of your memory to be conjured up by the mere mention of the words 'gas gangrene'.

They worked non-stop for the next six weeks. Apart from tending to the wounded, there were instruments to scrub, gowns to sterilize, dressing drums to be packed, for they had to make their own dressings and sterilize them. Nevertheless, Sister Ruth Patterson recalled: 'I remember those days as one of the most enjoyable times of my life, quite frankly, because we were so busy but it was so rewarding. We were all very young and we were able to work those long hours.'

By this stage of the war the medical services had learnt how lives could be saved by getting mobile teams as close to the fighting area as possible. To the newly qualified medical officers who, before joining their units overseas, listened to a lecture by Sir James Walton on how to deal with battle casualties, the procedure seemed straightforward enough.[4]

Simple measures of first aid will be given. Wounded men will be laid at rest in a sheltered position and morphia will be given. Its administration is perhaps the most valuable of any simple resuscitation method. Haemorrhage will be controlled wherever possible by direct pressure and the wound will be covered by the emergency dressing [every soldier had a 'first field dressing' sewn into the left thigh pocket of his battle dress] and any fractured limb will be fixed by an improvised splint or by bandaging it to the trunk of the opposite uninjured limb.

At the casualty clearing centre, Walton explained, a routine had evolved whereby the medical officer would examine each casualty, make a list and classify cases in order for the most immediate treatment. He then presented his strongly held views on the use of morphia:

'In the resuscitation treatment, morphia should be given in every case. There is always pain, fear or excitement and whatever the nature of the injury the relief from morphia always outweighs any hypothetical danger; often, however, unnecessarily high doses are given, a quarter of a gram is nearly always sufficient, and it should be administered at once, generally before the wounds are examined. The wounds should be covered with a sterile dressing with or without a dusting of sulphanilamide.'[2]

That was the theory. In practice doctors and nurses learnt to adapt to whatever the situation demanded. 'Adaptation' really was the key word. They had to be ready for anything and be able to mask their feelings – which often could be of horror at the sight of the ghastly wounds. 'One terrible episode haunts me still,' wrote Ann Radloff.

I came to the bed of a Scottish padre who called to me in anguish and terror, 'Sister, Sister, am I going to lose my leg? Please do something.' I turned back the blankets and smelt what was beneath. I laid them back again and went off to drag a blood-spattered surgeon to the bedside. 'Right, Sister, straight to the theatre,' he ordered.

What happened to the Padre I never heard. The surgeons worked non-stop under Tilley lamps sawing off limbs, replacing intestines which had spilled out through dressings, performing miracles of temporary plastic surgery on obscenely mutilated faces.

All the nurses in combat areas have memories of casualties that haunt them still. Freda Reid (née Barnfather) recalled:

The saddest case that I remember was of a young soldier who had been wounded on his shoulder, right over the jugular vein, and the wound was infected by anthrax, and slowly but surely the rotting flesh ate through the wall of the jugular vein and he bled to death. There was nothing that could be done for him, but he was never left alone. A nurse sat by his bedside day and night.

Six days after the invasion of Normandy, the first flying bomb, soon to be known as the 'doodle bug' and later the 'V-1', hit London. It was simply a flying bomb, pilotless and travelling at high speed on a predetermined course and distance. When the engine stopped, the missile plunged to the ground and exploded upon contact. The blast was terrific. London was the main target but southern towns were hit too.

At the Royal Naval Hospital Haslar, whenever air-raid warnings sounded the approach of the flying bombs, nurses who were off duty had orders to put on steel helmets and take cover under their beds. Not many were keen to do that. Instead, still in their night clothes, many of them put on their helmets and stood by the windows to watch the flying bombs approaching like great balls of fire, holding their breath whilst they passed overhead, waiting for the engine to cut and the bomb to crash to the ground.

By day and night and in all kinds of weather, the flying bombs terrorized London and the towns to the south. Now there was an even more desperate need for the Allied troops to succeed in their plans for a breakout of the bridgehead and take the ground from which the flying bombs and rockets were launched.

Already they were behind the planned timetable. Partly this was due to the worst storms in half a century, which struck the beaches on 19 June and for four days stopped all landings of men and weaponry. To mount offensives during such weather was extremely difficult. Meanwhile crack German divisions had rushed to defend key points. The 21st Panzer Division and the pride of the Hitler Youth in the 12th Panzer Division dug themselves into defensive positions around Caen. Consequently that powerful German bastion did not fall to the British 1st Corps on the first day as Montgomery had planned, and fighting dragged on for weeks.

The British Sixth Airborne and Highland Divisions suffered disastrous casualties as German counter-attacks tried to hurl the British back into the sea. Fighting became frenziedly severe after the Scots discovered that the Germans had shot some prisoners. Hand-to-hand fighting of the utmost savagery, in which the Black Watch Regiment was involved, went on non-stop for three days and nights.

One British Army medical officer from Port Talbot, Donald Isaac, remembered carrying out a post-mortem examination with a Canadian pathologist on 25 Canadians in a chateau outside Caen, one of them wearing the red-cross armband of a stretcher-bearer of the Durham Light Infantry, who were shot on the orders of Colonel Kurt Meyer.

Despite relentless Allied attacks, in which the casualties were horrendous, the drive to encircle Caen shuddered to a halt. Thus the Battle of the Beach-head became a draining sore for the Allies as casualties mounted daily. Before the decisive breakout on 25 July, Allied casualties totalled 60,771, of whom 8,975 were killed. The wounded passed through the rows of tented casualty clearing stations and field hospitals at the rate of thousands a day.

Sometimes if a CCS was close to an important military target such as an airstrip, it would automatically attract shelling despite the red-cross flags and signs. No.32 CCS, for example, which was set up near the Jerusalem crossroads in Bayeux, suffered from bombing. Two sisters were wounded and eventually the CCS had to move patients further back, apart from those with abdominal wounds who had to wait eight days before being moved. The sisters took it in turns to stay with three orderlies to look after those patients.

As the battles progressed further inland, there were occasions when badly wounded civilians were brought in with a convoy of casualties. Sister Ann Reeves was on duty when an old man was brought in with a smashed hand.

The surgeon said he could not do anything with it except take it off. I held his arm and watched the saw work its way through the bone, and then stared at the hand thrown carelessly in the bucket below. I had a queer feeling of standing right outside my body and watching myself, saying: 'Is this really me doing this?' I still look back and wonder at what we did as young women with no previous experience of such shocking, bloody cases.

Army and Navy hospital ships sailed back and forth carrying the wounded back to base hospitals. Freda Barnfather was on the hospital ship *Aba* picking up casualties from jetties under the constant clamour of bombardment from naval warships standing offshore to give covering barrages to assault troops inland. She found days and nights merging into one blur of physical activity as stretchers of casualties were packed onto the ship, off-loaded quickly, the ship turned round and wards made ready for the next load.

There was never enough space on the hospital carriers and ships for all the casualties. Many travelled back on stretchers packed side by side in returning tank landing craft. The objective of the evacuation service was to get wounded back to base hospitals such as Haslar, which acted more as casualty clearing stations, where their wounds would be dressed again before they were despatched within 24 hours to hospitals further inland.

For the first three weeks after D-Day, the nurses at Haslar worked with hardly a break for meals or rest. Each wounded man was labelled with details of injury, treatment, and drugs. Penicillin was given to severely wounded men by intramuscular injection every three hours. The stock of penicillin was kept in the pathology laboratory refrigerator, which meant that one of the ward staff had to race up the stairs each time it was needed; the wards had only ice boxes.

'The first casualties to come into Haslar,' recalled Sister Parslow, 'were men of the Royal Marine Commandos and American assault troops.'

They were covered with sand and blood, having been lying on the beach for hours. Stretcher-bearers put their pitiful loads onto beds just covered with a blanket. Many wounds were infected with gas gangrene, which meant wholesale amputations. Fortunately we saved many lives by the injection of large quantities of anti-gas serum and penicillin, which had become available for service use then.

Beatrice French (née Stubbs) a VAD at Haslar on D-Day, remembered some of those first patients from the beaches. One of them, who was brought in unconscious, had to be fed by a nurse spooning pulped food and fluid from a feeding cup with a spout. It amazed her that he was able to swallow without choking. 'He left us, still unconscious, for another hospital inland.'

Another patient that sticks in her memory was one who came in 'suffering from shell shock and was raving mad most of the time'. He was taken to the operating theatre with great difficulty by several burly sick berth attendants, who held him on the trolley. 'It was very distressing. Sadly he died on the operating table,' she recalled.[3]

Helen Long, with two and a half years' exerience as a VAD working in a casualty clearing station in the Western Desert, including the battle of El Alamein, soon got into a routine. To save time they laid out all the instruments in heaps on a long trestle table. They exposed wounds for the surgeon by slicing through uniforms stiff with blood and sand and used razors to cut through the laces and boots of soldiers who had trodden on mines. In the underground theatre extra tables had been provided to allow six operations to be carried out at the same time. In that steamy, underground heat the stench of burns and gas gangrene was almost unbearable.

In the midst of the frenetic activity there came amusing and strange diversions, Helen remembered:

One seaman arrived with the ship's cat accompanying him on the stretcher. 'He never set paw on the beach,' the sailor assured us, 'so he don't need no quarantine.' Someone found time to give his moggie a whiff of anaesthetic before mending its fracture, stitching up the battle wound on its hind quarters and sending it from theatre with a little white stick of plastered leg pointing skywards.

Another strange diversion came when a young Wren was rushed into theatre in labour. The theatre floor was sandy, and heaps of amputated limbs lay outside the doors, awaiting collection by porters who were too busy to take them to be incinerated. In the midst of all this, a baby was born. Helen was surprised to find that some unmarried nurses could not bear to watch a woman in labour, yet they could manage to witness amputations.

One unusual piece of equipment which Helen Long remembers being used was a gigantic magnet which located and retrieved fragments of metal, invisible to the naked eye but fairly close to the surface. The magnet was far less painful and more efficient than probing around under X-ray.[4]

As the British Second Army pressed forward determinedly, the casualty clearing stations and field hospitals moved forward too. The crack Waffen SS divisions fought desperately to keep open the narrow corridor of Falaise through which the bulk of the German beach-head divisions streamed to new defensive positions until, on 27 July 1944, Allied forces broke out of the bridgehead. The retreating Germans left in their wake a picture of carnage difficult to describe or believe. Eisenhower called it 'one of the greatest killing grounds seen in any of the war areas. I was conducted through it on foot, to encounter scenes that could be described only by Dante.'[5]

Ruth Patterson, who had just been sent to help at a casualty clearing station, passed through the area in a 15-hundredweight Bedford truck.

We had an awful job for miles driving round German dead bodies, dead horse gun-teams, trucks and tracked vehicles of all kinds. Never have I seen such a terrifying sight – massacre on a massive scale. The stench of death from all the decomposing bodies lying about was so strong it clung to my uniform for weeks afterwards. I heard later that along that 2-mile stretch RAF rocket-firing Typhoons had caught the Germans in close formation.

Freda Barnfather also remembered with anger a time later in the campaign, when she was serving on the hospital ship *Aba* on a shuttle service bringing back wounded from Normandy.

It was the day we began to carry more and more German wounded soldiers. Most of them were in their early teens from the Hitler Youth battalions, which had been fighting apparently with amazing courage and tenacity. In addition to their gunshot wounds, most of them suffered from frostbite to a greater or lesser degree. This was due to the extremely poor footwear with which they had been issued and the awful conditions under which they had been fighting in the front line. Many of those young boys had feet black and shrivelled and oozing with pus. They were a pitiful sight. Although suffering great pain they did not complain and were so obviously grateful for the care and attention we gave to them. In most cases amputation was going to be necessary, but in others long and patient care and attention would improve their condition considerably. The medical officers took many pictures of the frostbite cases for future reference. I want to make clear – in view of what happened – that these young lads did not display any of the arrogance and superciliousness which we had encountered among their countrymen at the beginning of the war. On the contrary they were just too glad to be out of all the misery they had so recently endured.

It was whilst the stretcher-borne frostbite cases were being unloaded by Allied non-combatants that an awful practice was taking place. Stretcher-bearers were deliberately jolting the German patients up and down causing agonizing and absolutely unnecessary pain. I told our commanding officer who tried to stop the practice.

He was not entirely successful, as he was to write in his Unit War Diary:

The American stretcher-bearers are very rough. They are carrying patients at a run. I drew the attention of the officer in charge of them but all he said was 'to go slower upset his schedule'. One of these days a patient will probably be thrown off a stretcher while being carried down the gangway and fall in the water between the ship and the quay. Still, a warning has been given.[6]

For Freda at that time, though, there was something far more cheerful to think about. She had, at last, met Alex and soon they would be happily married (indeed, for over forty years).

The war in Europe was coming to an end. In the long slog to Berlin from the summer of 1944 through the terrible winter, nearly 600,000 Americans and 200,000 British were killed or wounded.

How was it all going to end? The 30 Corps Commander, General Sir Brian Horrocks, had often wondered how it would be and he found, like so many people, whatever their rank, that it could hardly have been more of an anticlimax.

Heinrich Himmler, Commander-in-Chief of the German Home Army, was dismissed by Hitler. He disguised himself in the uniform of a German soldier with a patch over one eye and was taken by a British control post on the Luneberger Heath. Stripped and covered only by a blanket, he felt the searching fingers of the examining doctor approaching his last precious possession, a cyanide pill. He bit heavily on the poison capsule concealed behind his teeth and in moments he was dead. For a short time he lay on the post-mortem slab. The pathologist cut a lock of thin hair from his head and gave it to Sister Pat Stephens of the neighbouring 74th General Hospital as a souvenir. Before Himmler's thin body, wrapped in camouflage nets, was taken away for secret burial, medical orderlies had sneaked into the post-mortem room and snipped off a few more strands as souvenirs for their folks at home.

Captain John Macpherson, whose story started this chapter, was still with the field transfusion unit attached to No.39 British Military Hospital and there had a bizarre meeting with the infamous traitor William Joyce. Better known to the British public as Lord Haw Haw, Joyce had for six years broadcast venomous 'news' to Britain from Hamburg and Berlin. He was brought into the medical room with a bullet in his buttock. Macpherson described the scene:

During his first few hours in the camp he was almost a circus attraction. He was stuck on a table with his legs in the air and every private in the camp was photographing his bare backside with 'liberated' Leica cameras.

I went in and asked him, without being aggressive or unfriendly, how he was. He was very cool considering how desperate his situation was and he certainly knew there were grave doubts about his future. When I went in he took out his cigarettes and lit one without his hand shaking. He wanted to talk so I just listened. There was a certain formality about it all; no laughing, no smiling.

His main theme was that he had never deserted England or Great Britain. He was born in Dublin and his argument was that he was anti-communist. He was never a Fascist or pro-Hitler. But somebody, he thought, had to take on the Russians and as far as he was concerned the Germans were the best people. He couldn't understand why people in Britain were so against him.[7]

Joyce was taken away soon afterwards, imprisoned in the Tower of London and quickly hanged as a traitor. In reality he was not a traitor. He had, in fact, been born an American citizen and had become a German citizen before America entered the war. He therefore did not betray either Britain or America.

As General Horrocks was to admit, the end of the war in Europe was not only an anticlimax it was fantastically weird. In Berlin, Hitler, cloistered in the Chancellery bunker, went through a freakish form of wartime wedding ceremony with his mistress Eva Braun, pleased that at last she could be called 'Frau Hitler'. He ordered his surgeon to kill his favourite Alsatian, Blondi, and then withdrew to his private apartments for their wedding breakfast and at half past three that afternoon he shot himself through the mouth. By his side on the sofa was Eva Braun, also dead; she had swallowed poison.

In another part of the bunker, Hitler's guards and orderlies held a wild party and danced! The terrible tyrant was dead. Now they could play.[8]

Among the Allies, those with time on their hands enjoyed a period of high jinks, whatever their rank. Nurses took over horses and riding schools on Luneberger Heath and enjoyed themselves. With the German mark valueless, the cigarette became universal currency and a tin of corned beef bought family heirlooms and family honour too.

High-ranking officers were not immune from the temptations. Captain Macpherson was sent by ambulance to recover the Personal Assistant to the Chief of Staff of a well known corps, who had been injured in a car accident whilst on a mission for his boss. He had been to retrieve 'something valuable' his boss had left behind in Vienna – hundreds of pairs of silk stockings which the senior officer then sold at inflated prices to officers going home on leave. As Dr Macpherson wrote to his wife, 'All that just goes to show what a time some people are having.'[9]

But for the nurses left in Germany, some of the worst scenes were yet to come – caring for pitiful inmates of Belsen concentration camp. They left a mark on everyone who entered that camp. One soldier, the future film star Dirk Bogarde, recalled his experience half a century later: 'I entered a hell I should never forget and about which for many years I was unable to speak. Sometimes, perhaps if I'd had a drop too much I might try to explain and usually ended in unmanly tears.[10]

The darkness over Europe had ended by May 1945, but the war against Japan had yet to be won and nurses were already on the way to the Far East.

16 'One Helluva Good Missie'

We took our emaciated comrades
To Colombo, St Joseph's and bed
And not wanting to kill them with kindness
A notice saying 'Not to be fed'.

Bernard Hallas, Corporal, Royal Marines,
HMS *Warspite* 'Betrayal of Singapore'[1]

In the early spring of 1945, when the war in Europe was drawing to its end and the eighteen-year-old reinforcements to the Allied armies there were being killed and wounded at the very moment of victory, a great armada of British and American ships was concentrating in the South Pacific for a decisive assault against the Japanese. In close attendance to that fleet were British and American hospital ships with nurses aboard.

They were all in danger. Japanese troops had no respect for the Red Cross at sea or on land. Sister Winifred Beaumont in Burma recalled how her unit security officer told her to remove the red-cross arm-band as Japanese soldiers made a special target of the emblem. When No.15 CCS, a collection of bamboo huts with 450 beds camouflaged under trees, asked for permission to display a Red Cross flag prominently because they had been bombed by Japanese aircraft, their request was not approved for similar reasons.[2] And in the South Pacific, Japanese *kamikaze* pilots had little time to differentiate between one ship and another as they flew their bomb-laden aircraft straight into any British or American ship targeted.

Fighting in the Far East during those early months of 1945 had never been as ferocious. Heavy casualties were incurred and more were expected as the Japanese fought with suicidal determination, defending one island after another. This, it must be admitted, brought some exceptionally murderous retaliation from Allied assault troops. In the fighting for the Sugar Loaf Island, for example, when eighty-five terrified Japanese student nurses who had taken refuge in a cave with other soldiers refused to come out, the Marines, not recognizing female voices, moved in with flame throwers and killed them all. Today Japanese come to mourn at what is now known as 'The Cave of the Virgins'.[3]

To cope with the increasing number of casualties more and more medical officers, nurses and hospitals were on their way to the Far East from the UK, the USA and Germany. Some were posted, others volunteered.

Sister Diana Wells of the QARNNS was delighted to be on her way there. She had written to the Matron-in-Chief asking for a Far East posting in order to see her brother, John, a wing commander there, whom she had not seen for three years. 'She did not reply to my letter but she did send me to Colombo,' said Diana.

Sister Anne Powis of the QARNNS left RNH Haslar at short notice to board Troopship J8, *Dominion Monarch*, along with 200 nurses. They were to help in setting up Herne Hill Hospital, Sydney, which was to become the largest field hospital in the world, with over 2,000 beds.

Our voyage out was a most enjoyable cruise, with dances almost every evening and a time when I could relax with my tapestry work. After disembarking in Sydney I was driven 11 miles to the north-west to join the hospital at Herne Hill, run by a Matron everyone admired, Miss K. Baker.

I was luckier than most of the new draft of nurses, for I was granted ten days' leave immediately in order to visit my sister whom I hadn't seen since she emigrated to Australia sixteen years earlier.

As each week passed the weather got hotter and hotter. We all changed into tropical uniform, one of the great bonuses of which was no stockings! We were glad of the change for the casualties were pouring in to keep us very busy by day and then we were very busy by night with all the social life. Every known organization in Sydney wanted a female representative of the Royal Navy at their functions. We had to attend in uniform and we envied the Australian ladies in their evening gowns.

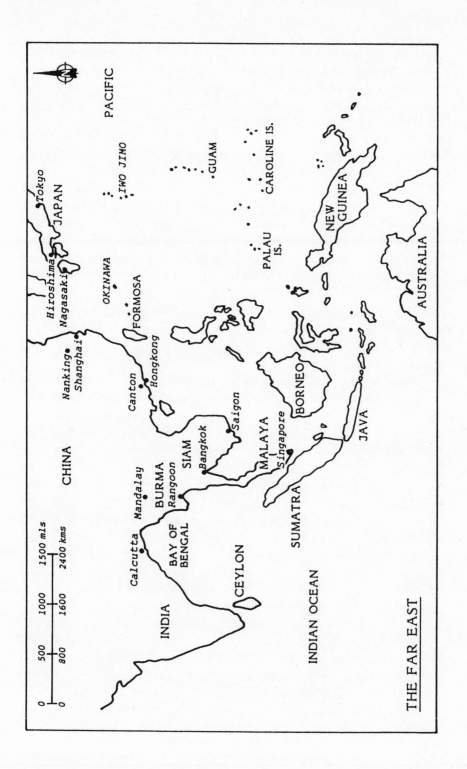

THE FAR EAST

Arriving on Troopship J1, with 4,000 troops on board, were Sisters
Margaret West and Marjorie Aston of the QARNNS. It was a fast
ship and did not travel at the same speed as the rest of the convoy. It
reached Sydney via the Panama Canal in just four weeks. That voyage
remains vivid in Margaret's memory.

There were U-boats about and blackout regulations to be strictly observed.
Even smoking on deck was forbidden. We had to carry lifejackets all the
time, with a small tin of 'iron rations' and a tiny torch with a red light
attached to the life jacket. As we hadn't the luxury of seating on the deck
we were tempted to use the life jackets as cushions but if any of us did
succumb we were soon spotted by the Naval Police, who saluted politely
and reminded us that we should not be sitting on them as that reduced
their efficiency in saving life.

Other nurses drafted in haste to the Far East were posted to the casualty clearing stations, hospitals and hospital ships preparing to
receive the awesome number of casualties expected in the forthcom-
ing battles leading to the invasion of Japan.

In that spring of 1945, the most powerful naval force Britain had
ever sent to war – an armada of 600 ships and 250,000 men of the
British Pacific Fleet – moved into position for the decisive assault.
This fleet was dependent upon another fleet – of supply and repair
ships. Amongst these was the hospital ship *Oxfordshire*, with its full
complement of QARNNS nurses.

The first objective of the final offensive was to be the capture of
Okinawa, an island 60 miles long and 8 miles wide. Lying at the southern tip of the Japanese archipelago, some 350 miles south of Kyushu,
it was perfectly placed and big enough to provide an effective base
from which to launch a massive invasion force onto Japan itself.

But it was going to be a tough nut to crack. The Japanese were
determined to defend the island with all the force they could
command. They were ready with 100,000 soldiers, supported by
2,000 aircraft based in Formosa and Japan. With them was a force of
300 – 400 *kamikaze* pilots willing to give their own lives by flying
their bombed-up aircraft directly onto an American or British
warship. One aeroplane and one pilot was thought to be a small price
to pay for one warship and hundreds of highly trained sailors. This
'suicide corps' had already shown what it could do in the autumn of
1944 during the greatest sea battle in history off Leyte Gulf. They

came roaring in beneath the radar at wave-top height and then zoomed upwards to swoop down almost vertically straight into the deck.

Typical was the Japanese pilot who drove his plane into the flight deck of the magnificent American aircraft carrier, *St Lo*, thereby igniting the battleship's bombs and torpedoes stored below decks. Half an hour later the *St Lo* had sunk. HMHS *Oxfordshire*, with other US and British hospital ships, was stationed near enough to take on casualties, which then had to be moved to hospitals on Allied-held islands.

However, in planning for the reception and recovery of casualties, medical officers and nurses had to consider the latest medical reports, which revealed what many of the nurses already knew: that sick and wounded men recovered more slowly if hospitalized in a tropical climate at sea or on one of the Pacific islands. Everyone knew that the wounds of casualties air-lifted to a cooler hospital in Australia healed more quickly.

Hurriedly, nursing sisters of the QARNNS were posted to Sydney to take over and extend a hospital there staffed at the time by American nurses. Cynthia Cooke, later CBE, RRC, was not at all impressed by her first sight of the place.

It was set in a dry, dusty area burnt brown. The American nurses laughed at our white uniform! They wore light seersucker dresses and caps. We set to work cleaning the wards and pulling chewing gum off everything. We made gardens round the huts and brought colour to the place. Above the main doorway, painters put a large blue and white sign saying 'RN Auxiliary Hospital' and flew a new Union Jack flag alongside it. Inside we wore our uniforms as white as fresh snow.

When we went into town it was wonderful for us, straight from a strictly rationed routine of Britain, to see such an array of fresh fruit and cakes in the shops. That I'm sure is where my weight problem started.[4]

By March 1945 the new hospital at Herne Bay, Sydney, was ready to receive casualties to be flown in from the Pacific Fleet and casualty clearing stations set up on the islands. 'We all worked as hard and as quickly as we could, and it was thanks to the encouragement and ideas of our commander, Surgeon Rear-Admiral Maxwell, and our wonderful Matron that we were ready so quickly,' recalled Margaret Harris (née West).

The next problem to be solved was finding trained nurses to look after the casualties in flight. A few months after Margaret and Marjorie had arrived at Herne Bay, an exciting notice appeared on the Sisters' Mess noticeboard. It called for volunteers for the newly formed Royal Naval Medical Air Evacuation Unit. Cynthia Cooke immediately applied, but she was said to be too heavy – other exciting journeys were in store for her. Marjorie and Margaret, however, were accepted for preliminary tests. Marjorie recalled their excitement.

Many names appeared with ours on the list and enthusiasm ran high, but since only six sisters were required for the first experimental team and six for the second, some were disappointed. I got onto the first six and Margaret was on the second. The risks and hardships involved in the job, such as being shot down by Japanese fighter pilots now absolutely ruthless in their desperation, were explained to us. Our route took us regularly over enemy-held territory but despite the risks involved we were still keen to serve.

Appropriate uniform for the Royal Naval Medical Air Evacuation Unit was not available from RN stores so we were temporarily supplied with Australian Army Sisters' jungle wear. It comprised safari jacket, trousers, jungle boots, gaiters and a 'digger' hat. We then added our own Royal Navy buttons and our QARNNS cap badge. We looked smart enough when we were on the ground but the uniform wasn't warm enough for flying at 8,000 or 10,000 feet. I was lucky enough to borrow a flying jacket from one of the American aircrew at Manus.

The first six volunteer nurses then flew in an RAF DC47 from Mascot Airport to New Guinea for training in the medical care of patients. It was a most uncomfortable flight. There were no seats in the fuselage, which was packed with mail bags for the troops in New Guinea and the Pacific Fleet. For the whole of that journey the nurses squatted on those mailbags which, judging by the sharp corners sticking into their buttocks, were full of tins containing sweets and biscuits. Fortunately they had some relief with a short stop-over for refuelling at Brisbane, where they could stretch their legs and restore circulation into cramped parts before flying on to Townsville as overnight guests in the Officers' Mess of the Women's Royal Australian Naval Service.

It was there that Marjorie Aston had a most unwelcome visitor during the night. There must have been a hole in her mosquito net for a mosquito of the *Stegomyia fasciata* group bit her and caused her to fall victim to dengue fever, sometimes known as breakbone or three-day fever. Although it is not a serious disease, it can cause considerable discomfort, with symptoms of severe pain in the back and limbs. 'I can understand why it's called breakbone fever,' recalled Marjorie.

I felt every bone in my body was being torn asunder. That night, in an Army hospital in New Guinea, I lay in agony, my eyes bulging with high fever. The next morning at six o'clock we took off for Lae. I was not fit for that flight but didn't want to miss my training. When we landed at Lae, much to our amusement, we were asked by canteen staff in their broad Australian accent, how the Pommies at Sydney were getting on.

Our Australian uniform had fooled everybody so much they were shattered when we replied to their question with our pronounced English accents: 'We're doing very well, thank you.'

Hard work started the next day when they were taken by truck to join the Royal Australian Air Evacuation Unit at Nadzab. There the nurses began an intensive two weeks course of practical work and lectures by medical officers and sisters of the RAAF. Margaret explained what the nurses had to learn in those two weeks.

The course covered the preparation of different cases for flying and the reaction of patients to high altitudes; the administration of drugs and sedatives; tropical medicine and hygiene, loading and positioning of patients in the aircraft and many other responsibilities for the escorting nurse. For instance we would have to arrange for the wireless operator to signal ahead to the medical unit on the landing strips with details of the patients, or it might be necessary to request the pilot to reduce altitude or even land if a patient's condition required. We were also instructed in the procedure for crash landings over the sea or in the jungle, and for survival in both circumstances. We learnt about the Geneva Convention and chemical warfare. On the practical side there was dinghy drill in a pool (what to do if the large dinghy inflated upside down, how to right it, how to pull in a helpless patient from the water and how to take cover from hot sun or storm conditions). We experienced simulated flight conditions in a decompression chamber when we were subjected to the equivalent of an altitude of 20,000 feet, at which point most of us found it impossible to write sensibly.

Attending the course in itself was not enough. Each naval nursing sister had to pass a written and a practical test. What came as a surprise to most of us was that there was to be a final passing out parade. So we had to drill and march for the first time! We weren't too clever at that. One girl, finding it impossible to swing her arms alternately with her feet, swung both together and hoped for the best. At the final march past, taken by the RAAF Matron-in-Chief, several girls managed to trip over a peg in the parade ground on the order 'Eyes Right'. Some lost their hats in the blustery wind and the Flight Sergeant collected an armful.

Now that they had all successfully completed the course, the Surgeon Lieutenant-Commander in charge arranged for the dentist to make their aircrew 'wings' – metal badges consisting of one wing inscribed with the letters 'RNMAEU'. The six nurses then flew to the island of Manus to the east of New Guinea. There they met their Medical Officer and Flight Co-ordinator, Surgeon Lieutenant-Commander Alec Mitchell, RNVR, who was going to be responsible for their well-being whilst they were stationed there.

On that island they cheerfully endured the steaming days and suffocating nights, downpours of rain almost every day and humidity which turned boots and clothing green with mildew within forty-eight hours. It was tedious at first waiting for hospital ships or aircraft to arrive with casualties but everyone in authority did all that was possible to make the stay of their 'guests' a happy one. Marjorie remembered it well:

The food was superb! We lived in the nurses' quarters of the US Naval Base Hospital 15, which had 2,000 beds and a very efficient commissariat. Our first mess bill came as a shock. We just couldn't afford such luxury but Captain Robins, our CO arranged with the US Navy Department for the RN Sisters to be messed free of charge – as 'guests' of the US Navy. Our pay was much lower than that of our American nursing colleagues, even though we received 'danger money' because our flight paths crossed enemy-held territory.

Marget also recalled how well they were looked after in Manus:

We were waited upon by native servants. The girls, of mixed island descent, were quite overwhelmed by the sudden blast of civilization that had struck their otherwise peaceful and backward lives. One girl was known as 'Half-leg' because she had sustained a serious injury to her foot when a clam closed on it whilst she was paddling. She dyed her hair bright yellow with mepacrine anti-malarial tablets, while her friend used the gentian violet more often seen on the faces of soldiers with a rash that took so long to heal in that climate.

For the sake of security, white women were not allowed to leave the hospital compound on their own. They had to leave in pairs or in a group, and with at least two armed male escorts. This tended to limit excursions for swimming and picnics, but with a ratio of 46,000 men to 66 nurses there were always plenty of ready, willing and eager escorts.

It takes little imagination to picture the situation at Saturday evening dances! Nurses never had a chance to sit out and rest – they were in great demand for every kind of dance.

Casualties were brought to Manus by air and hospital ships. Marjorie remembered the first of those from the British Pacific Fleet arriving on the hospital ship *Oxfordshire*.

They were mainly sailors wounded in the tremendous sea battles off the island of Okinawa, where the Japanese Navy and Air Force were launching suicide attacks on the British and American ships. Nurses on the Navy hospital ship *Oxfordshire* worked round the clock bringing in casualties to the US Naval hospital, where doctors and nurses decided which of them were fit enough to stand the rigours of a flight of over 2,000 miles in RAF Transport Command to Herne Bay Hospital in Sydney.

The evening before the flight, casualties were taken by ambulance to the sick quarters of Momote airstrip on Los Negros Island and were cared for overnight by sickberth attendants. As I would be travelling with those casualties I visited them at the airfield, assessed their condition and the treatment they might be needing during the flight and we then worked out how best they should be loaded within the aircraft. I also checked the food. The SBA and I had to feed them from insulated boxes prepared by US galleys.

When that job was finished I went back to my quarters and tried to get an early night to be ready for a call at 0300 hours the next day when Dr Mitchell drove me to the airport.

Together they checked the equipment and victuals needed for the journey and by 0530 hours, the patients were then loaded and the aircraft took off at 0600 hours.

Sometimes patients who were in a state of anxiety because of their previous battle experiences were given sedation in the form of Nembutol. It would be four hours from Momote to the refuelling point at Milne Bay or Port Moresby, and in a crowded fuselage a very nervous patient could cause problems.

Margaret felt the drive to the airstrip in the early hours of the morning was particularly eerie. Creepers seemed to grow over the road during the night and land crabs as big as dinner plates scuttled in front of the car by the hundred. The driver could not possibly miss them and they crunched horribly loudly under the wheels.

Even for fit personnel that long flight from Manus to Sydney would have been an uncomfortable one, because at that time aircraft were not pressurized and their comparatively low speed meant long hours at a fairly high altitude.

'Some patients reacted adversely to high altitude flying,' said Marjorie.

They became faint, and felt sick and dizzy. Those with chest wounds suffered more than most. We had to keep a close watch on all patients but it was not easy because of the way that the stretchers were packed on racks in the fuselage as tightly as possible. We just had to totter around the stretchers grabbing hold of anything we could when it was particularly bumpy, and that was fairly often. Turbulence with Pacific weather was to be expected. It was quite hairy at times and we often flew over enemy-occupied territory.

It was a relief for patients and medical staff alike when the aircraft broke the journey for refuelling. The first call was at Milne Bay. There, natives lifted the stretchers out of the fuselage and put them in the shade of the aircraft's wing so that the wounded men could breathe fresher air than that in the crowded aircraft. The walking wounded could stretch their legs. The first time we landed, a native, Billy, offered to bring me something to drink. I asked for cold tomato juice. Every time I landed after that, Billy was waiting with a glassful.

The aircraft then headed for Townsville, Queensland, on Australia's east coast. Patients were taken from the aircraft by ambulance to the RAAF hospital there and given a comfortable bed. The next morning they felt they were on the last lap, away from the war and heading for Brisbane. Each time the aircraft landed, a reception committee took charge and gave everyone a wonderful welcome. Everything was so well organized through signals sent by the wireless operator of the aircraft giving details of patients, the number, condition, how many ambulances would be required and, the expected time of arrival.

The nurses had to keep a constant watch on all patients to make certain their dressings showed no signs of fresh bleeding. Sister Carney, on her round, noticed a dark-skinned patient whose breathing was alarmingly rapid and shallow. She took his pulse, which was also disturbingly fast. Carefully she turned back the blanket covering his body and knew immediately that something must be done. The man was bleeding profusely from severe abdominal wounds. He should never have been put on a plane in that condition. He would soon be dead.

She stumbled hurriedly between the stretchers to the pilot, asked him to contact the nearest American hospital on one of the islands and ask for them to have a medical team and ambulance waiting for an emergency landing. Meanwhile she and the sickberth attendant gave the failing casualty a blood transfusion. The pilot found a small airstrip, made an emergency landing and taxied to a waiting ambulance. Their efforts this time were in vain. Half an hour later the patient died.[5]

From the journey's end at Mascot Airport, there was a long drive for the patients to RNH Herne Bay. Meanwhile, the nursing sisters and sick berth attendants took a rest at Mascot and within forty-eight hours were on the way back to Manus ready to load the next lot of patients.

'In between flights, our American hosts did so much to make those waiting periods a happy and relaxed time,' said Marjorie.

Weekends were usually spent fishing in the lagoon or swimming from the island. A large hut had been erected with showers and a kitchen where any fish caught could be cooked. The main galley of the hospital provided wonderful picnic food but beer and Coke was provided out of our own rations. I recall one very interesting trip across the lagoon to a village built on stilts over the water. On arrival we were greeted by the *lulai* or headman of the village. He was so proud of his peaked cap! He gave me a parting gift – a large carved, wooden alligator which I still treasure. In his presentation speech, in pidgin English, he announced that "Missie from country of Big Massa King", had visited the village and nursed their babies, and he was making this gift to "one helluva good missie".'

For the fighting men everywhere in spring 1945, the end of the war could not be clearly seen. As for the atomic bomb, that was still months away. The Japanese were fighting desperately for every yard of ground on the Pacific islands and in the mangrove swamps of Burma, where lurked poisonous snakes, stinging insects, leeches, mosquitoes and – most dangerous of all – suicidal Japanese soldiers at bay. Whilst in the Pacific the bloody business of 'island hopping' was getting the Allied armies ever closer to Japan, in Burma General Slim's Fourteenth Army had already crossed the river Chindwin and secured firm bridgeheads. Now there remained the broad waterway of the Irrawaddy to cross. As Slim's infantry toiled uphill through ankle-deep and sometimes knee-deep mud, winkling out hidden pockets of fanatical Japanese rearguards, the medical officers and nurses of casualty clearing stations followed close behind – many times too closely for comfort.

Sister E.Leigh Hunt, who had served in horrendous conditions around Kohima and Dimapur, was lucky to escape when attending patients on an ambulance train, which was derailed by special Japanese sabotage forces. For a time she was pinned beneath a carriage, but eventually got away.

Nurses popped up at the most unexpected times and places in Burma. Two RAF nursing sisters, Barbara MacDonald and Patricia Dawson, were flown to Imphal in an old bomber to help save the life of a New Zealand airman who was critically ill with tetanus after a crash. The RAF Medical Officer there, Squadron Leader F.S.A. Doran, formerly of Manchester Royal Infirmary, thought the pilot might live if he got expert nursing. As soon as the nurses arrived he took them straight from the airstrip to the pilot's bedside Gently he touched the sleeping pilot's shoulder and said, 'Look what I've brought you.' The airman, his forehead prickled with large globules of sweat, opened his eyes and said one word: 'Popsies'. Then he closed his eyes again. He recovered.

It was a highly dangerous task for the Fourteenth Army's advancing infantry who had to resort to flame throwers, Bangalore torpedoes and high explosives to make any progress in that gruesome campaign. Casualties came back to casualty clearing stations in a shocking condition. Sister Sheila McDermott (later Bambridge), who was in a forward CCS remembered them well.

They came strapped on litters which swung precariously at each side of a mule's pack saddle. By the time they reached us through the mud and ditches they were often crawling with maggots, and with leeches sucking their blood from legs and arms. We used to put the end of a lighted ciga-rette onto the tails of the leeches to get them off. The medical officers operated on those needing immediate surgery, we dressed the wounds of others and sent them down the line as quickly as possible. For very seri-ous cases there was a small aircraft, something like a Tiger Moth in size, but you could get a stretcher with a patient in the fuselage and it could take off from a small airstrip nearby. Some patients who were dying or in a very poor state were kept with us to give them a chance of recovering strength enough for them to make the rest of the journey. Then they went back by air, or by Jeep ambulance or sometimes by landing craft on the river.

Surprisingly as the front moved on we had one or two visits from show business artistes from ENSA. Vera Lynn arrived and was obviously very tired with travelling, but those troops who could be spared were brought in and she gave a concert that very night and had the soldiers singing with her. Afterwards they crowded around asking for her autograph to send home to their wives and mothers. Unfortunately the only stationery they had was what was known as Army form blank – toilet paper. But Vera Lynn signed for them with a big smile. She really was the forces' sweetheart. Then she went round the bamboo huts and tents chatting to the patients in bed. She was a bit shy at first and I remember she said 'I come from East Ham' and a patient from his bed called out, 'I come from West Ham', then he jumped out of bed and gave her a kiss. Stainless Stephen came and was terrific. Another one who came was that famous comic who sang 'When I'm Cleaning Windows' and played the ukulele, George Formby. He was a real tonic for the troops and especially the wounded ones.

Even in the midst of the tragedy and cruelty of war there were these moments of song and laughter.

· And so, whilst people in Britain celebrated the end of the war in Europe on 8 May, the battles in the Far East went on. Of the US and British fleets, thirty-four warships were sunk with horrendous casu-alties. A crisis point in the campaign came between 6 and 16 April, when mass *kamikaze* attacks on the two fleets reached their fearful climax. Three battleships were damaged, four destroyers sunk and thirty-two ships of the assault fleet severely damaged. In one of the American carriers alone casualties amounted to 800. The Americans bore the brunt of those 1,900 *kamikaze* attacks and suffered terrible casualties. Four of the five British Pacific Fleet carriers suffered hits, which wreaked havoc among personnel and parked planes.

Ready and waiting as usual for the mutilated bodies from those operations were the nurses, taking them into their care in hospital ships and casualty clearing stations, dressing their wounds and passing them back down the line to base hospitals. The nurses on the air evacuation flights sometimes worked with hardly any sleep, snatching a few moments whenever they could.

Statistics of casualties mean little to many people, they are just figures. But those who saw the reality of those statistics were the nurses. Their service in the combat zones speaks for itself – it was always a strenuous and exacting task demanding patience, strength of body and mind. They accepted the dangers and hardships and upheld the traditions of the service.

Suddenly, at twenty minutes past midnight on 6 August 1945, the Allies unleashed on the Japanese city of Hiroshima the most fearful device of war yet produced – the atomic bomb. The war at last had ended.

Even then, though, nurses never knew from one day to the next what they might be called upon to do. But sometimes, the duty thrust upon them at short notice was an unexpected pleasure. Nurses were needed to care for the emaciated prisoners of war released from Japanese camps.

At an hour's notice, Margaret West with other nurses was invited aboard the aircraft carrier HMS *Glory* on her way to Hong Kong to pick up Allied POWs. 'The aircraft hangars had been converted into wards. Nurses slept on camp beds on the quarter deck. The Commander strongly disapproved of women attending the wardroom dinner – unheard of! But he later married the senior sister in charge of the operation.'

Cynthia Cooke took nurses onto HMS *Formidable*, the 40,000-ton aircraft carrier, to look after Indian soldiers released from POW camps on Rabaul.

Though they suffered from most of the deficiency diseases, ulcers, enlarged spleens and liver they were wonderful and never complained. The bulk of the special cooking was done by the fittest of the men in mobile kitchens set up on the flight deck. I used two saucers to scoop up helpings of rice and ladles of yellow curry – usually lamb, fish or eggs. I had to stand on a box to reach the mountain of rice for my eighty patients.

Sister Anne Cockburn (née Powis) remembered receiving those former prisoners at Herne Bay.

Their condition was appalling, really pathetic. Many of them had been working on the Burma Railway, they were walking skeletons and many were blind for want of vitamins. What the Japs did to those young men was dreadfully distressing. Most of them had malaria, and all of them had ulcers of some kind or other – leg ulcers, stomach ulcers – many had dysentery, beri-beri, pellegra, dengue fever and scrub typhus.

When we got them back to Herne Bay Hospital they were sent to special wards where specialist treatment could be given to their needs. Talking was the finest therapy for them, though. And they had plenty of that. One of them gave me a Japanese sword but, having heard some of the stories of the beheading of prisoners with a sword, I thought the gift, though well-meant, was too gruesome for me to keep so I gave it to one of the doctors.

The former prisoners and the fighting men of the Far East forces were on their way home. As one of them, former Lieutenant Frank Palmer, who now proudly wears the Burma Star, said during the celebrations of the fiftieth anniversary of the war's ending:

We could hardly believe we had come through. We were safe. There would be no more bloody attacks. We had struggled to keep fighting against all our instincts for self-preservation during the last few months of the war, fighting more for the sake of our mates in the platoon than for any other reason. But we had come through. And then when we saw those nurses it was just like a taste of home. A home that was after all worth fighting for.

You can't help thinking of the pals you've left behind in the jungles of Burma or on the beaches of those Pacific islands. You can't forget the sight of all those men lying dead, fly-blown, maggotty and swollen grotesquely.

And when we got home, what could we say to the wives, sweethearts and mothers of those pals we left behind? I tried my best. But my lips always quivered. I gave them a hug and cried.

And the nurses in those combat zones throughout the world? What indelible memories remain for them of the young men they tended with such care, men maimed beyond belief who could still whisper to their nurse those two words, 'Thank you'?

One of those nurses, Sister Ann Reeves, in her memoirs, echoed the thoughts of so many of her colleagues with the words: 'Never again would I work in such terrible conditions, but never again would I be part of such camaraderie. I feel privileged to have been there.'

References

1. *Where Do We Go from Here?*

1. Joyce Drury *We Were There*, (Jupiter Press, 1995)
2. E. Rock Carling, 'Burns' in *War Surgery*, BMA, London, 1943
3. Quoted in Drury *op cit*.
4. Helen Long, Change Into Uniform (*Terence Dalton*, 1978)

2. *A Funny Kind of War*

1. Sam Lombard-Hobson, *A Sailor's War* (Orbis Publishing, 1983)
2. *Ibid*.
3. *Ibid*.
4. Winston Churchill, *The Second World War* (Vol 2, Cassell, 1948)

3. *The Spectre of Defeat*

1. PRO File WO-177–633
2. Joint Services Staff College, 18th Lecture, Script 10, 'Narvik, Opening Phase'.
3. PRO File WO 177–633
4. PRO File ADM 199–485
5. See Francois Kersaudy, *Norway 1940* (Collins, 1990), also PRO File ADM 186–798.
6. PRO File WO 177–633
7. See Raoul Solar, *Souvenir* (Raoul Solar, 1947)
8. PRO File WO 177–633
9. PRO File WO 177–633
10. *The Abyssinian Campaigns, The Official Story of the Conquest of Italian East Africa* (HMSO, 1942)

4. *In the Thick of It*

1. In *Merchantmen at War* (HMSO, 1944)
2. *Ibid.*
3. Brigadier John Durnford-Slater, *Commando* (William Kimber, 1953)
4. QARNNS Archives, Gosport
5. Surgeon Lieutenant-Commander A. Ian L. Maitland, 'Survey of Treatment of Burns' in the *Journal of the Royal Naval Medical Service*, volume 28, 1942
6. PRO File ADM 199–921
7. PRO File WO 177–1443
8. Mary Kent Hughes (Major Thornton, RAMC), *Matilda Waltzes with the Tommies* (Oxford University Press, 1943)
9. Theoretically fraternization between German prisoners and British women was not allowed. Military courts could award sentences for 'establishing relationships of an amorous nature'. Eventually, with a quarter of a million fit young German POWs working close to British women on farms and on forestry work, romance inevitably developed. See Eric Taylor, *Forces Sweethearts* (Robert Hale, 1990)
10. PRO File WO 177–1443
11. PRO File WO 177–1432

5. *A Nurse for All Seasons*

1. George Aris, *The Fifth British Division 1939–45* (The Fifth British Division Benevolent Fund, Rainham, Gillingham, 1943)

6. *In Peril on The Sea*

1. In *Merchantmen at War* (HMSO, 1944)
2. QARNNS Archives, Gosport
3. Additional details of the sinking of the *Britannia* are from Captain David Parsons, MNI of the Merchant Navy Welfare Board.
4. A pre-war report of the London School of Hygiene and Tropical Medicine stated that the mortality rate below the age of fifty-five was twice as high for seamen as for the rest of the male population.

5. I am indebted to Captain David Parsons, MNI of the Merchant Navy Welfare Board for information on what happened to seamen whose ship was lost through enemy action. These were the remarkable conditions under which those brave men of the Merchant Service then lived – and 32,000 died.

7. *Humanity in the Midst of War*

1. Doris M. Hawkins SRN, SCM, *Atlantic Torpedo* (Victor Gollancz, 1943). In her account of the sinking of the ss *Laconia*, Doris Hawkins never revealed why she had been entrusted with taking baby Sally back to England.
2. Details of Hartenstein's efforts to rescue the survivors and of the Liberator's attack on the U-boat are given in his evidence at the Nuremberg International Military Tribunal, *Trials of War Criminals*, English edition published 1948, documents D650 and V13, pages 338, 368 and 375.
3. Captain David Parsons, MNI, provided further details of losses through the sinking of the *Laconia*, published in J. Young's *Britain's Sea War* (Patrick Stephens)
4. This account reported in *Nursing Times*, 2 August 1941.

8. *Third Time Unlucky*

1. In *Soldiers of the Sea* (Haxby, York, 1997)
2. Report of First Radio Officer on *Stentor*. PRO File 1–15 421
3. *Ibid.*
4. *Ibid.*

9. *Armada to Africa*

1. Quoted in Kathleen Harland, *A History of Queen Alexandra's Royal Naval Nursing Service* (Royal Naval Medical Service). See also PRO File ADM 1–15 421
2. Howard Marshall, *Over to Tunis* (Eyre & Spottiswoode, 1943)
3. PRO File WO 177–1360
4. Geraldine Edge and Mary Johnston *The Ships of Youth* (Hodder & Stoughton, 1945)

10. Choices and Decisions

1. In *Collected Poems* 1909–1956 (André Deutsch, 1949)
2. PRO File WO 177–1734
3. Fiona Glass and Philip Marsden-Smedley (eds), *The Spectator Book of World War Two* (Grafton Books, 1989)
4. Lord Moran, *Anatomy of Courage* (Constable, 1966)
5. QARNNS Archives, Gosport
6. PRO File WO 177–1437
7. PRO File WO 177–1447

11. A Soft Under-belly

1. PRO File WO 177–1437
2. In conversations with the writer. See also Geraldine Edge and Mary Johnston, *The Ships of Youth* (Hodder & Stoughton, 1945), and PRO File WO 177–1431
3. Edward D. Churchill Md, *Surgeon to Soldiers* (Lippincott Company, 1972)
4. PRO File WO 177–633
5. PRO File WO 177–1431
6. See Edge and Johnston, *op. cit.* and PRO File WO 177–1431
7. Churchill, *op. cit.*
8. Donald G. Taggart (ed.), *History of the Third Infantry Division in World War Two* (Gale & Polden, 1950)
9. Field Marshal Viscount Montgomery, *The Memoirs of Field Marshal the Viscount Montgomery of Alamein KG* (Collins, 1958)

12. The Avalanche that Never Was

1. Hamish Hamilton, 1945
2. Denis Healey, *The Time of My Life* (Michael Joseph, 1989)
3. Geraldine Edge and Mary Johnston, *The Ships of Youth* (Hodder & Stoughton, 1945)
4. Surgeon Commander T.N. D'Arcy, 'Casualties of War', *Royal Naval Medical Services*, Volume XXVI, 1940
5. *Ibid.*
6. Geraldine Edge and Mary Johnston, *op. cit.* Also in conversation with the writer.
7. PRO File WO 177–1431
8. Brian Harpur, *The Impossible Victory* (William Kimber, 1980)

13. A Rich Tapestry of Experience

1. Jimmy Young, *J.Y. the Autobiography of Jimmy Young* (W.H. Allen, 1973)
2. Captain F.V. Bellinger, MP, in the *Sunday Pictorial*, August 1944
3. Edwina Masson, *The Biography of Countess Mountbatten of Burma* (Robert Hale, 1958)
4. QARNNS Archives, Gosport

14. One More River

1. 'Prospectus', from the collection *'Poems from Italy'* by H.V.S. Page
2. In *The Impossible Victory*, (William Kimber, 1980)
3. Godfrey Talbot, *Ten Seconds From Now* (Hutchinson, 1973)
4. E. Rock Carling, 'Burns' in *War Surgery*, BMA, 1943
5. Charles M. Weltse, *The Surgeon General's History of World War Two*, from Office of the Chief of Military History, Department of the Army, Washington D.C. 1965
6. Edward D. Churchill MD *Surgeon to Soldiers* (Lippincott, 1972)
7. Colonel Elliot C. Cutler, 'American Views', in *War Surgery*, BMA, 1943
8. PRO File WO 216–168. After July 1943 the British suffered an alarming increase in recorded desertions. Of these 80 per cent were infantrymen from battalions which had suffered heavy losses.
9. PRO File WO 170–677 and 272
10. See Lieutenant-Colonel J.C. Watts, MC, FRCS, RAMC, *Surgeon at War*, (George Allen & Unwin, 1955)
11. PRO File WO 170–677 and 672
12. Cyril Ray, *History of the 78th Division, Algiers to Austria*, (Eyre & Spottiswoode, 1952). See also PRO File WO 216–168–180559
13. Denis Healey, *The Time of My Life* (Michael Joseph, 1989)
14. Winston Churchill in the House of Commons, 2 May 1945

15. If Your Name's on It . . .

1. I am grateful for this account to Dr John Macpherson, consultant gynaecologist at Torbay Hospital for 29 years, who wrote to

me in June 1997. Sadly, he was only halfway through this second letter to me when he died suddenly. His son, David was kind enough to send me this account.

2. Sir James Walton, KCVO, MS, FRCS 'Recent Advances in the Treatment of War Wounds' in *War Surgery*, BMA, 1944

3. Joyce Drury, *We Were There*, (Jupiter Press, 1997)

4. Helen Long, *Change into Uniform* (Terence Dalton, 1978)

5. Dwight D. Eisenhower, *Crusade in Europe* (William Heinemann, 1948)

6. PRO File WO 177–1414

7. Letter to the writer and interview with the *Mid Devon Advertiser*, 27 May 1994

8. Hugh Trevor-Roper, *The Last Days of Hitler* (Macmillan Press, 1947)

9. Letter to his wife, which was sent to the writer by his son after his sudden death.

10. *Daily Telegraph*, 26 November 1988

16. 'One Helluva Good Missie'

1. In *Soldiers of the Sea*, (Haxby, York, 1997)

2. PRO File WO 177–2084. Also Winifred Beaumont in conversation with the writer and in her book *A Detail on the Burma Front* (BBC, 1977)

3. Martin Gilbert, *Second World War* (Collins, 1989)

4. QARNNS Archives, Gosport

5. QARNNS Archives, Gosport

Index